Acclaim for

While the City ...

"An arresting narrative . . . Certainly a stor~~y~~ . . . ~~something Simpsons well~~ worth learning . . . It's heartbreaking all the way around." —*The Seattle Times*

"Gripping . . . Moving and unsettling . . . Told with incredible sensitivity."
—*Minneapolis Star Tribune*

"[A] disturbing, sometimes-horrifying story of true crime and justice only partially served."   —*The Huffington Post* (11 Books That Grab You from Page One)

"Compassionate . . . A meticulous indictment of the way America reckons with mental illness."
—*Mother Jones*

"Engrossing, elegantly written . . . A story that we need to hear."
—*Seattle Post-Intelligencer*

"A gripping and sensitive account."
—*St. Louis Post-Dispatch*

"Riveting . . . Absorbing and meticulous."
—*BookPage*

"Told with care, compassion, and the kind of details that will force you to catch your breath."
—*The Stranger*

"An exceptional story of compelling interest in a time of school shootings, ethnic and class strife, and other unbound expressions of madness and illness . . . The author's opening pages are among the most immediate and breathtaking in modern true-crime literature, as evocative as any moment of *In Cold Blood* or *Helter Skelter*."
—*Kirkus Reviews* (starred review)

"Astonishing . . . Pair with Jill Leovy's *Ghettoside* for powerful . . . analysis of the failures of our criminal justice system."   —*Library Journal* (starred review)

"A page-turning indictment of a perfect storm of preventable events . . . delivered with a powerful sense of both dismay and compassion."
—*Booklist* (starred review)

"Gripping . . . Moving . . . Sanders's meticulous narrative [is] a disturbing indictment of society's neglect of the mentally ill."
—*Publishers Weekly*

"This book is important.... Sanders writes with an uncommon empathy.... On both a human level and a policy level, *While the City Slept* makes a vital contribution and deserves a wide and receptive readership."   —*NWLawyer*

"Superb, pulse-pounding ... Moving and mesmerizing ... Grimly fascinating ... Hair-raising ... Every public official in a position to effect change in the mental health system ought to read this book and reflect deeply on its lessons. The rest of us can simply be moved to the tears summoned by the enduring love, tentative hope, and inconsolable pain of this searing human tragedy."   —*BookBrowse*

"The book is wholly remarkable.... Sanders has given us the tools for a needed conversation, and it is high time that we started it."

—*The Seattle Review of Books*

"Inspiring . . . a book I'll be recommending for years for the way it appeals to both the conscience and the heart ... From a harrowing crime, it draws powerful lessons for our mental health and criminal justice systems that can't be ignored."

—Sister Helen Prejean, #1 *New York Times* bestselling
author of *Dead Man Walking*

"The great achievement of this book is that it shows how any crime is ultimately a failure of systems and of citizens, and that to some degree we are all complicit when a person who needs help is cast aside. To show empathy for a criminal, especially a criminal who has committed such a violent act, ennobles the process and purpose of journalism."   —Dan Zak, author of *Almighty*

"Written with great sensitivity and even greater beauty, it is about so many things: a city, childhood, family, failure, loss, horror, forgiveness. It is, very nearly, about everything."   —Jeff Hobbs, *New York Times* bestselling author of
The Short and Tragic Life of Robert Peace

"*While the City Slept* reveals the American landscape of a horrific crime. Eli Sanders, with a rare quality of attention, does this clearly and judiciously. Because of his outstanding reporting, we see not only the complex workings of one's environment on the course of one's life, but also how what we consider a tragedy is almost an inevitability—and how, of course, it doesn't have to be."

—Adrian Nicole LeBlanc, *New York Times* bestselling
author of *Random Family*

PENGUIN BOOKS

WHILE THE CITY SLEPT

Eli Sanders is the associate editor of Seattle's weekly newspaper *The Stranger*. He won the Pulitzer Prize for feature writing in 2012 for his reporting on the murder of Teresa Butz. His work has appeared in *The New York Times*, *The Seattle Times*, *The American Prospect*, and *Salon*, among other publications. Sanders lives in Seattle.

www.elisanders.net

@elijsanders

While the City Slept

A Love Lost to Violence and

a Wake-Up Call for Mental Health Care in America

Eli Sanders

PENGUIN BOOKS

PENGUIN BOOKS
An imprint of Penguin Random House LLC
375 Hudson Street
New York, New York 10014
penguin.com

First published in the United States of America by Viking Penguin,
an imprint of Penguin Random House LLC, 2016
Published in Penguin Books 2017

Portions of this book appeared in different form as "While South Park Slept," "The Mind of
Kalebu," "The Bravest Woman in Seattle," "Behind the Guilty Verdict," and other works by Eli
Sanders published in *The Stranger*.

Excerpt from "It's a Hard Life Wherever You Go," words and music by Nanci Griffith. Copyright
© 1989 Irving Music, Inc., and Ponder Heart Music. All rights controlled and administered by
Irving Music, Inc. All rights reserved. Reprinted by permission of Hal Leonard Corporation.

ISBN 9780670015719 (hc.)
ISBN 9780143109518 (pbk.)

Printed in the United States of America
1   3   5   7   9   10   8   6   4   2

Set in Warnock Pro
Designed by Alissa Rose Theodor

For survivors, living and in memory

CONTENTS

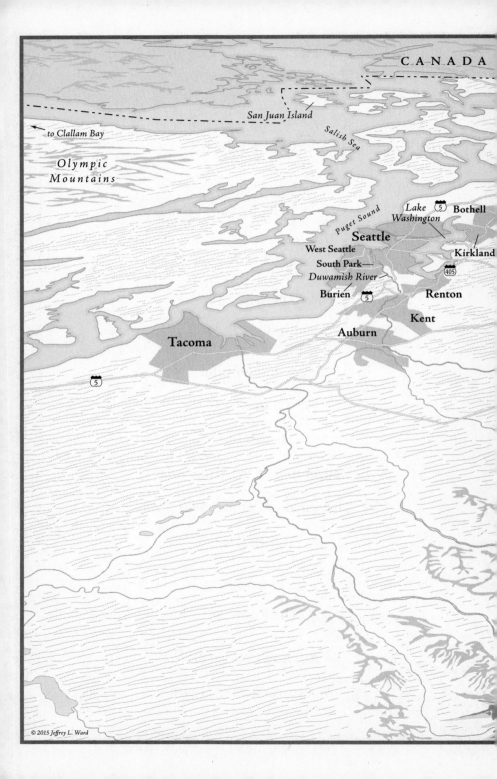

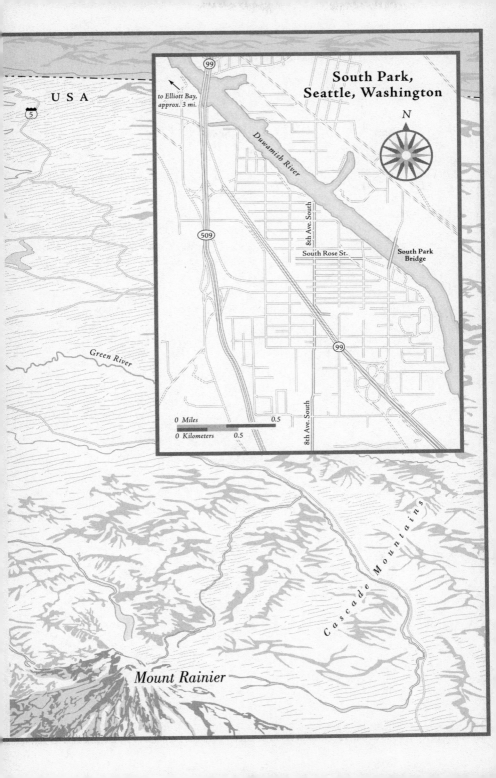

While the City Slept

South Rose Street

1

On old maps, the Duwamish River bends like discarded ribbon as it passes through a valley on the southern end of this city, winding across land that was once marshes and tribal fishing villages and then emptying into the salt water of Elliott Bay. Melt from nearby mountains carved this path, rich with salmon that fed the Duwamish Indians in the years before their last unfettered chief, Si'ahl, learned his name would be hammered by white settlers into the name of a new American city: Seattle. Not long afterward, the U.S. Army Corps of Engineers showed up and spent a few years straightening and deepening the Duwamish for the purposes of large-scale commerce. Now the river looks more like a ribbon pulled taut.

Heavy industry lines its sides, dingy barges fill its moorings, and its last five miles have been declared a federal Superfund mega-site, so thick with PCBs, mercury, and arsenic that eating anything that lingers here is inadvisable. This is Seattle's only river. At what's been called its dirty mouth sits a mammoth artificial island built from dredged Duwamish silt: flat, paved over, and planted with tall orange cranes for unloading shipping containers at the international port. Upriver, toward the other end of the Superfund stretch, is a shallow bend that seems an homage to an earlier time, and tucked in the crook of this bend, across from a former Boeing plant where World War II bomber production helped begin the river's fouling, is the neighborhood of South Park.

In the summer of 2009, the best way to reach South Park's main strip of taquerías and tire shops was by crossing an ailing drawbridge over this bend in the Duwamish. The decks of the bridge swelled in summer heat so that opening and closing became impossible. Its two halves, and their identical brick watchmen's houses, were drifting in opposite directions. Its support pilings failed to find solid purchase beneath the toxic river-bottom muck. As a consequence, the South Park Bridge ranked as one of the least safe spans in the state.

Near the riverbank where one of the bridge decks descended into the neighborhood, on the wall of a bar called the County Line, a hand-lettered sign urging downtown politicians to do something other than the stated plan, which was to close the bridge and let residents find other ways into the neighborhood. The back route, for example, along a highway that, like the Duwamish, faintly bends as it passes by.

The land between the damaged river and the rushing highway is equal to about one square mile, a confined space steeped from its first platting in cycles of need and neglect. In the years after the Duwamish people were dispossessed, and around the time the river was being straightened, this land was farmed by Italian and Japanese immigrants who cleared the camas plants and seeded its soil with radishes, spinach, peas, and mustard greens. In search of a venue for selling their produce, these farmers helped build the Pike Place Market in downtown Seattle. In need of a bridge across the Duwamish to help get their vegetables to town, and in need of electricity and fresh drinking water, too, they petitioned to be annexed by the young city and in 1907 got their wish. South Park became part of Seattle's southern edge, and a rotting trolley bridge linking it to the other side of the river was torn down, replaced by a new bridge built from timber trestles and a plank deck. It didn't hold up long.

In 1931, another attempt at connection: the steel-beamed South Park drawbridge. Owing to time, inattention to upkeep on the part of downtown power brokers, and an earthquake that rattled its crumbling concrete at the start of the new century, this bridge presented by 2009 a dangerously decayed visage, demoralizing and perfectly aligned with the economic moment, all busted potential and uneven openings.

Closure without remedy was not acceptable to South Park's four thousand residents, by now mostly Hispanic and mostly not speaking English at home. But their demand for a new bridge was a hard one to meet the year after a financial crash, the city budget tapped out, more people than usual showing up at the river with fishing rods, hungry, casting next to warning signs posted in Spanish, Laotian, Chinese, Korean, Vietnamese, Russian. Complicating matters, a new bridge was not the residents' only demand.

The people of South Park lived, for the most part, on a core of tree-shaded streets, many of them dead-ending at the river, or the highway, or the circumference of fenced lots that otherwise hemmed in the neighborhood, lots holding businesses like Cain Bolt & Gasket or Sound Propeller Services, lots that, when they didn't contain elemental companies in low industrial buildings, tended to hold giant spools of marine-grade rope, ship winches, metal buoys, all of it detritus washed up from the nearby port. On one inland corner of the neighborhood was something referred to by city signage as a "transfer station," a delicate way of saying city dump. No one was asking for extravagant changes to this environment. The odors from the dump, the scents of creosote drifting in off the water, the taste of ammonia blowing through cement factory fences, the howl of jets on descent toward the airport, so close that conversations below had to pause—such things came with the territory. But people who made their homes here did feel that in addition to a new bridge they deserved more police to patrol their roads, some of which appeared to be crumbling back into dirt, and better lighting so that fewer night shadows would be on offer along the main avenues, inviting unpredictable characters who trudged up from the ragged vegetation along the riverbank or wandered in from the budget motels and homeless encampments of the surrounding industrial netherland. It was hoped as well that better sewage and drainage pipes might someday stem the flooding that swamped many South Park basements when rains came down heavy, sending rats and spiders scurrying for higher ground.

All of this would likely have to wait and, if history was any guide, might well be forgotten amid demands from other neighborhoods that were not majority Hispanic, and working class, and from a trammeled river delta. It had always gone this way. So people in South Park had learned to counter inevitable disappointment with reeled-in expectations. With patience, too, when possible, sometimes helped along by a measured pleasure at the way South Park's neglect, in a familiar paradox, made the neighborhood. Made it one of Seattle's most diverse communities. Made its homes a bargain during the boom years. Made its food affordable and filling. Made it clear to those living along the botanically named residential streets—Thistle, Elmgrove, Rose—that they should not expect outsiders rushing in to make things better, that instead the mix of languages and ethnicities within this one square mile would have to get by on their own. Which meant together.

Meant, in practice, that an English-speaking white woman in South Park would mow her Chinese neighbor's parking strip and he would give her green beans from his garden, neither able to speak a language understood by the other, both frequenting the Hispanic grocer, all doing what was needed to get by, and to work on time. For the most part, on most days, this was how it went, a majority of residents abiding by an unspoken rule that to live in this place was to be implicitly drafted into doing what one could to make sure everyone made it through. In exchange, one probably wouldn't be bothered for petty things that might cause trouble in other neighborhoods, such as placing wet laundry to dry on a chain-link fence or hanging it in the trees across from the Cesar Chavez Village housing projects, damp socks joining the leaves in obscuring a view of the distant downtown high-rises.

That summer of 2009 it was unusually warm. Kids played late into the evening on the field outside the South Park Community Center, where dirt from the baseball diamond kicks into dust filtering last light. Men in white undershirts leaned against the wall outside Juan Colorado restaurant. Brisk business was done at Loretta's, a bar with a Ping-Pong table and a refurbished Airstream trailer for patrons to sit in out back.

In the middle of July, on one particularly hot night, well after the ball field had cleared and not long after Loretta's and Juan Colorado had served last call, Jennifer Dawson-Lutz could be found standing silently in the bathroom of her narrow, one-story house. It was a house wrapped in white siding that evoked wooden slats, and it was set on a block of similarly compact homes, a block where South Rose Street dead-ends near the ball field, a custom metal fabrication factory, and a stretch of freeway that bisects the neighborhood. She had just put her newborn daughter back down to sleep after a 3:00 a.m. feeding and then, before going back to bed herself, had tiptoed into the bathroom, keeping the light off so as not to wake her daughter. Outside, she heard the sound of breaking glass.

Her daughter was seventeen days old, and she herself was still recovering from a cesarean section. But she climbed onto the edge of her bathtub so she could peer out her bathroom window. Across the street and down the block was a small red house that happened to be well lit by a streetlamp. Jennifer Dawson-Lutz heard a scream. She saw a person who appeared to be falling out the window. She noticed a white curtain billowing through the window. Her mind, trying to make sense of this, suggested that someone was trying to break into the home, which she knew was shared by two women. One of them had purchased it a few years earlier; the other had moved in more recently. Both were attractive and outgoing, in their thirties, with smiles that stuck in memories, and they could regularly be seen gardening together in the front yard, or walking to Loretta's, or chatting with people they bumped into along the sidewalk.

Jennifer Dawson-Lutz went to wake her husband. She dialed 911, some-thing she'd never done before. She got a recorded message and was on hold for what felt like a long time.

Up the block, where South Rose Street intersects with Eighth Avenue South, Israel Rodriguez was watching his eighteenth birthday party wind down. His actual birthday had come three days earlier, but the celebra-tion was postponed in order to take advantage of a fast-arriving Saturday night. Now it was 3:00 a.m. on the Sunday after that Saturday night. Israel stood on the sidewalk outside his family's home, lit a cigarette, and smoked it near the spot where roots of a large maple tree had cracked and raised the concrete on a scale not normally seen in a city accustomed to sidewalks rearranged by tree roots. Here, the whorled roots had created a small mountain of vaulting cement whose peak passersby were forced to ascend and then descend. As Israel pulled on the cigarette, he, too, heard glass breaking. The sound seemed to come from the direction of the dead end on South Rose Street, and his mind identified it as a window being smashed. Israel found this odd for the neighborhood. He decided to head over to see what was happening.

About halfway down the block, he spotted a woman in the middle of the street. "She was white and wasn't wearing nothing," Israel would later tell a courtroom. The woman was screaming for help.

Israel ran back to his house. In the basement, Sara Miranda-Nino, his twenty-one-year-old cousin, was on her cell phone arguing with an ex-boyfriend. Israel told her to call 911, and then he and Sara ran down South Rose Street together.

Israel's eleven-year-old sister, Mariah, followed. So did a young neigh-borhood friend named Diana Ramirez, whose father was once Israel's boxing coach. Diana was fourteen and lived on South Rose Street just across from the red house.

Jennifer Dawson-Lutz, watching out her front window, saw them all run past. She told her husband, "Go outside, go outside, help." Then she heard one of the kids saying, "Get back, somebody's been stabbed." "And that's when I told my husband, 'Stay inside.'"

By this time, Israel and his cousin Sara could see there were two women in the street. One screaming for help. The other on the pavement. This woman, too, was without clothes, and Israel could see wounds on her.

He told Mariah and Diana to get out of there. Diana didn't listen. She knew the women who lived in the red house. Didn't know their names, but knew them by sight. They would wave to her as they were going about their days or as they were heading to and from work at their downtown jobs, and Diana would smile and wave back, say hi. Now one of the women was running in and out of the cone of streetlamp light, pounding on a neighbor's door to no avail, coming right up to Diana, looking at her, saying, "Help me." She was holding her neck. It was bleeding.

"I took off my sweatshirt," Diana would later testify. "I wrapped it around her neck to stop the bleeding. Then I ran inside my house to get towels and paper towels."

Sara recognized the women, too. "I seen them," she said on the witness stand, "but never conversated with them. They were just two women that always got involved with the community. I remember seeing them around when South Park had its festivals."

Now Sara was with the woman who was lying in the street. Her name was Teresa Butz, and the red house belonged to her. The woman calling for help, Diana's sweatshirt to her neck, was Teresa's fiancée, Jennifer Hopper.

Sara knelt. She held Teresa's head in her lap. She spoke to a 911 operator through tears, terrified, and she spoke to Teresa, too, telling her, "Please wake up, ma'am. Ma'am, wake up! Please wake up, ma'am!"

She took off her shirt and tried to wipe the blood away. She wanted to see where Teresa's major wounds were, apply pressure. It was difficult. "The bleeding wouldn't stop," she said.

There were no police officers in South Park when the calls began coming in from South Rose Street, but the neighborhood did have a fire station. It had been there for more than a hundred years and after a few relocations was now situated near the red house. "Listen to me," a 911 operator told Sara, trying to calm her. "There's a fire station less than two blocks away from you. They're going to come and help her right away. They're like two blocks away, okay?"

Sara heard this and told Teresa, "Keep breathing. The ambulance is coming. Please keep breathing."

The first officer to respond was Thomas Berg. He was driving up a steep hill that leads out of the valley that holds South Park when his patrol car radio advised him, "Stabbing on South Rose." He made a U-turn, headlights sweeping across high grass on the side of the road, and, with his siren off so as not to tip the perpetrator, sped down the hill. It was 3:09 a.m.

As Berg descended the hill, the view out his windshield tightened, from a panorama of lights in the industrial valley below to a tunnel of amber-lit arterial with darkness beyond its edges. He braked for a stoplight and cross traffic at the bottom of the hill, pulled around a pickup truck that was in his way, turned on his flashers, then raced across a stretch of flatland and under a highway overpass. He passed lots holding stacked metal drums and lengths of construction cranes lying on their sides. The dump was now on his right in the darkness.

He turned left at an intersection where a city sign for Holden Street was bolted to the corrugated-metal wall of a warehouse. His cruiser rattled over potholes, past moss-covered Greyhound buses long retired from service, past Fire King of Seattle and its pile of old extinguishers rusting in an adjacent lot, past Custom Crating and Wood Box Company.

The road Berg was on would soon dead-end at the Duwamish, but before this happened, he pulled right onto Fifth Avenue South. Past Swift Tool Company, past Rogers Machinery, and then, six blocks from the scene, Berg stopped his patrol car and waited, headlights shining on an overgrown lot. He'd often trained new officers, so he knew protocol dictated he arrive at South Rose Street with backup.

The fire truck, too, was stopped and waiting, now parked near Israel's house, several hundred yards from where the shouts were coming from, a standard procedure designed to protect unarmed firemen and medics. Still the truck's lights flashed, and its headlights beamed down the block toward the red house, as if in promise to the women and in warning to their attacker.

Berg knew the guy who was coming to watch his back while he focused on the victims, Officer Ernest DeBella. As soon as the radio told him DeBella was close, Berg headed for South Rose Street, alternately gunning and slowing his engine to try to synchronize his arrival with his fellow officer's. He passed a stack of wood pallets on a sidewalk, turned onto Eighth Avenue South, accelerated, turned his flashers back on. He passed under a canopy of maples, including the one that had buckled the sidewalk in front of Israel's house.

At the intersection with South Rose, he drove up on the curb to get around the fire truck and then stopped at a collapsible basketball hoop set up for playing in the street. It had been five and a half minutes since the call came in.

What Berg now saw stood out from "hundreds, maybe a thousand" violent crime scenes he'd walked into during his twenty-five years as a police officer. He saw Teresa Butz lying in the street, her head no longer in Sara's lap. He saw Jennifer Hopper standing above her, partly shrouded in a white towel Diana had given her. He saw blood.

The waiting medics came in behind Berg and DeBella, and then additional police cars behind them. Officer Melissa Wengard was driving one. She'd just checked in for first watch—3:00 a.m. to noon—and during roll call, she later testified, she was told to get to South Park "as quickly as possible." With Officer Nilo Dela Cruz, who likewise was sent directly from roll call to South Rose, she proceeded to "clear" the red house.

"It was a very brief clearing," Wengard said. "It's a fairly small house."

They shouted "Seattle Police!" as they entered the front door, noted blood on the floor and in the main bedroom. They looked in closets, under the bed, accidentally knocked over an ironing board, saw a large knife on the floor, checked the low-ceilinged basement. They stayed on the perimeter of the rooms as they did this so as not to disturb evidence. "We actually walk the walls," Dela Cruz explained later, on the stand. "That's what we call it, walking the walls." They found no one.

Officer Brian Downing, part of the canine unit, arrived with his German shepherd, Jack. They found a scent of interest outside the red house, just under its bathroom window, which was open, and Jack followed the scent across an alley behind the home. He pulled Officer Downing along hard—"I call it dog skiing," he said—onto the community center ball field, toward an edge of the field where a scrim of trees bumps up against the stretch of freeway bisecting the neighborhood. There, Jack lost the scent.

Someone called over the radio for the police helicopter. It wasn't available. Someone else called over the radio for a blood run. Officer Curtis Daniel Woo offered himself. He'd come to the scene without being told. "Wasn't so much dispatched," he said, "as I volunteered for the call. This is probably one of the most serious calls a police officer will go to. When something like this comes out, everybody that's working goes. You drop what you're doing and you just go, because you know the other people there are going to need help."

In the back of an ambulance, paramedic Les Davis tended to the woman with the towel draped around her and, as he worked, noticed the look on her face. It was unique to him in thirty-five years as a paramedic. "Absolute terror," he said. "I've never seen that. I've seen a lot of people."

This was Jennifer Hopper, Teresa's fiancée. Before being taken to the ambulance, she'd been heard to say, "He told us if we did what he asked us to do, he wouldn't hurt us. He lied."

Jennifer kept asking about Teresa. A second paramedic, Carlos Valdivia, told her, "Other people are taking care of your partner right now. We're here to take care of you." She screamed out for Teresa from the back of the ambulance, telling her she loved her.

Valdivia and Davis then drew a small vial of Jennifer's blood and handed it to Woo, who raced "lights and sirens" to the Puget Sound Blood Center as the ambulance itself headed for Harborview, the region's Level 1 trauma center, perched on a downtown hill distant from the Duwamish River valley.

Later, when the doctors were done, Woo walked in and asked Jennifer the required questions as gently as he could. "Name, date of birth, address," he recalled on the stand. "Asked her for the name of her partner."

Jennifer still wanted someone to tell her about Teresa.

"I lied to her," Woo said. "I told her I didn't know if her partner was alive or not."

Jennifer didn't believe him.

She held a thought she'd had standing there on South Rose Street: "I have to be able to tell people what happened."

———

Somewhere in the night was the man who'd done this. In the grip of what, no witness to his violence knew, though a small number of people, on hearing what occurred on South Rose Street, would get an uneasy feeling and think to themselves: Isaiah. They knew him to be a young man reeling, raging. They had feared him, and it was fear of a certain kind. Not the primal, salable fear of violence, not fright of the unexpected arriving with sudden brutality from an unknowable beyond. Theirs was fear of a known man and an outcome not yet known but likely to be grim. Fear of a person who, regrettably, had lived and delivered pain already, a man intelligent enough to impress yet with seemingly no handle on where his disjointed thoughts, speech, and actions might be headed. Or, if he did have some premonition, no firm brake, internal or external.

To the police, the most easily deduced thing was that the man who'd done this was brazen. He'd left bloody footprints and fingerprints at the red house, as if he lacked any thought of capture or consequence, and this now added to fears about his next thoughts, to the urgency of the gathering manhunt. In a basement apartment near the center of the city, a cell phone rang.

Detective Dana Duffy was asleep on a mattress on the floor, her service weapon, a .40-caliber Glock, stuffed under her pillow. She didn't feel safe in this place. It kept getting robbed, which was strange because Detective Duffy didn't have much of interest. When she left her husband of twenty-three years and found this cheap one-bedroom, she'd brought with her just the mattress, a used couch, an old TV, and a $40 microwave, the sparseness of the furnishings in direct proportion to the urgency of her need to get away.

He hadn't wanted her to be a cop, thought she should keep working as an emergency room nurse. Her father wouldn't have liked her career change, either. He was a drunk and a bank robber and, for a time, an out-of-state fugitive. Detective Dana Duffy is not one to appreciate being told what to do. Six years as a cop, first on night patrol, then in the gang unit. After that, homicide, a perch it usually takes officers twenty years to climb into. Seven years as the only female detective in homicide, left her husband along the way, and when her cell phone rang in her basement apartment that night in the summer of 2009, Detective Duffy picked it up, forty-five years old, fit and compact, adrenaline rising, ready to work. "A lot of people get up, and they'll shower," she said. "For me, I like to get there." She listened to the brief synopsis of what first responders were seeing. She put her light brown hair in a ponytail. She threw on some clothes. She grabbed a Diet Coke out of the fridge, to throw some caffeine behind the adrenaline. She got into her take-home car, an Impala, a car that, being speed oriented, she was happy to have, because the other choice for Seattle detectives was a hybrid Toyota.

Onto the empty freeway, into the Duwamish valley, onto South Rose Street, out of the Impala, into the warm morning, past the yellow tape and the top brass. "It was summer," she said. "It was a beautiful day."

At her desk at police headquarters in downtown Seattle, Detective Duffy keeps pictures of all the people whose deaths she's investigated, tacks them to the walls of her cubicle. She's lost track of how many yellow-taped murder scenes she's arrived at, all told. This one stood out. "I remember seeing the house, and seeing the curtain flying from the bedroom window, drifting through the air, with blood all down the bottom," she said. "And looking across at the neighbor's house, and seeing blood all over the neighbor's door, thinking, 'What in the hell happened?'" Teresa's body was still in the street, now covered by a yellow emergency blanket. Detective Duffy took this in and was still knocking the cobwebs out of her head when she walked through the red house. "A dynamic scene," she said. "This wasn't just a shooting where somebody's dead, and that's it. Something happened. There was a story."

The interior was a grotesque hieroglyph hinting at strong emotion and violent struggle. Investigators began bagging evidence, and Detective Duffy's mind turned to another unusual aspect. "I've never had a murder case where there's two victims," she said, "and one survives."

She got back in the Impala. She drove to the hospital. She walked into Jennifer's room, put her hand on Jennifer's wrist. She said, "Hey, Jen. I'm Detective Duffy. I'm Dana, and I'm gonna be one of the detectives working on your case."

"And I remember," Jennifer said, "the first thing I asked her was, 'Did she make it?' And without hesitation—and I was so grateful for this—she just said, 'No, she didn't.'"

Jennifer screamed.

Some time passed.

Detective Duffy pulled out an audio recorder. She turned it on.

"Okay," she said to Jennifer. "Let's start at the very beginning."

Back in South Park, the Duwamish moving through another warm day. In the city beyond, people awakening to work. On television, the launch of a familiar narrative: a neighborhood in shock, a manhunt, vows to make an arrest.

But the story of a crime like the one that occurred on South Rose Street does not begin with the news. Look down into any stretch of the Duwamish, on any day, and offer a variation on Detective Duffy's request: Where is the very beginning?

The tributaries that feed a moment are vast. At the riverside, countless water molecules in motion and the din of the surrounding city. It could be concluded, standing there, that a very beginning for what occurred on South Rose Street will never be located. That one might as well ask how three drops of rain, each cast from different skies, came to float in one fouled bend in the Duwamish at the height of summer.

Even so, some stories are worth assembling. Some crimes cry out for an accounting. Some offenses indict so much, and reflect so much, that they demand attention—to what was taken, to the taker, to the trials that preceded and followed.

There were two women in that red house who, searching for love, had found each other. There was one man who, needing a halt to his psychological descent, had found nothing but an open window. All of them human with human limits, their routes winding backward through St. Louis, where Teresa grew up stubborn and tough in a large family; through the mountains north of Santa Fe, where the newborn Jennifer was cradled by two adventurous spirits; through Uganda, the country Isaiah's father fled for Seattle; and through the neighborhoods of the father's new city, where he met Isaiah's mother, where their son was raised amid difficult circumstances, and where, nearly twenty-four years later, Isaiah's disintegrating life collided with the life Teresa and Jennifer had made.

That collision, and the histories that precede it, have something to offer the present. All three lives have something to teach. Upstream then, eyes wide, against the current.

Teresa and Jennifer

A brick house on Holly Hills Boulevard in St. Louis, and a large sweet gum tree towering above it. Towering above the stone porch, above the green Spanish-style tiles that cover the home's roof. The limbs of this tree bustle about during the high winds that signal tornado season, and on still days in summer a boy and his younger sister play inside a ring of bushes surrounding the tree's base. This is their spaceship. The ring of bushes is their cockpit, and secured inside this cockpit, they fly their craft, using some branches as switches and other branches as control sticks by which to navigate. He is Tim. She is Teresa. But on these voyages into outer space, they travel under assumed names. He is Bob. She is Pete.

She prefers her brown hair short and a little ragged, demands scissors from her parents so she can do it herself. Later, she keeps the style but adds a few blond highlights, an effect that echoes her eyes, which are hazel with brown flecks. People will mention a sense of sparkle, and it may trace to the flecks or to the smile, contagious, confident, a smile consonant with the air of invincibility carried on her short, solid frame, a smile that easily, and often, cracks into a body-shaking laugh.

It is a laugh to be imitated, and many of her closest people try. The women on her softball team who come to call her T-Buzz. The friends who come to call her T. The family members who, out of love and exasperation, come up with all manner of name shortenings, dropping letters and syllables to more easily race back into the thick of conversation with her, saying, "Hey, Reese . . . ," "But, Treese . . . ," "Come on, Reesy . . ." The laugh begins as a kind of chipmunk giggle, and then her head starts nodding up and down, and then the clapping, loud cracks that can be identified from way off as hers. If the laughter becomes more intense, a sort of convulsion follows, head thrown back, shoulders thrown back, everything quaking. "Like she's trying to exorcise the giggle," a friend will say. Then she reaches out, grabs the booth if there's a booth—and with Teresa there is often a booth—or she starts pummeling the people next to her, hard. Everyone gets a turn. Longtime friends, wise to what's coming, place newbies next to her for buffer. Toward the end of the laughing fits, tears. Then more clapping.

Her full name, Teresa Ann Butz, is given to her October 19, 1969, when she arrives the ninth of eleven children in a loud Irish-German-Catholic family in south St. Louis. Her mother, Elaine "Dolly" Butz, traces roots back many generations in "Missoura," which is how Dolly learned to say it from her grandparents, who were farmers. Dolly grew up down near the St. Louis rail yard, not far from the Mississippi River, close to the Anheuser-Busch brewery and a burlap bag factory, and hers was a musical household, with Dolly's mother playing the upright piano, her father playing banjo, guitar, and piano, too, everyone singing all the time. The family of the man she married, Dolly will say frankly, "is not musical at all."

Dolly's husband, Norbert Butz Sr., would agree. He grew up a few blocks from Dolly, the two of them first dating when he was sixteen and she was fourteen, Norbert senior drawn to the songs pouring out of the living room in Dolly's house on South Tenth Street. The opposite of songs pouring out of a living room—that was his home. Norbert senior's father was an immigrant baker with only one good eye, the other damaged by a branch while he was climbing a pine tree in his youth. He'd left Germany as a teenager fleeing his own father, who refused to get him medical care for the scratched eye, who once horsewhipped one of his daughters for talking to a boy in the middle of town in the middle of the afternoon.

Having fled home, Norbert senior's father, in America, fled father-hood. As a consequence, Norbert senior's mother raised him and his older sister on $15-a-week child support, which it was Norbert senior's job to collect at the bar his father frequented, plus earnings from her work in sweatshops along Washington Avenue, plus a little money from newspapers the whole family sold on weekends.

In college in St. Louis, Norbert senior walks up to a military recruiter and says, "You get me out of this town in two weeks and I'm yours for life." The marines take him to postwar Korea, then onward to jobs guarding military brigs in Japan and San Diego. In 1957, he returns home and asks Dolly to marry him. "I was in my dress blues looking good," Norbert senior says, "so she could hardly say no." He comes to run a small insurance company in south St. Louis. Dolly runs the household.

Every Sunday, no negotiation allowed, the Butz children and their parents, along with just about all the other families in their neighborhood, head for the nearby St. Stephen Protomartyr Catholic Church. Norbert and Dolly are adherents to the church's ban on contraception, and have had nine of their eleven children between the years of 1959 and 1969. "Bang, bang, bang, bang, bang" is how Tim Butz, their eighth, describes it. Teresa comes right after Tim, and she surprises and pleases Dolly, who's just had six boys in a row.

After Teresa, a seven-year hiatus in Butz offspring. It means she's the baby of the family for some time, and it proves retrospectively mystifying to Tim, who never hears a reason for the hiatus.

Sometimes, out front of the brick house, when they are under the sweet gum tree and playing spaceship, dangerous aliens threaten in the minds of Teresa and Tim. If this happens, they gather up red berries from the bushes and toss them outside the circle, bombs for blowing up the bogeymen. Or they pick up a racquetball and move around to the side of the corner lot, where four cement steps lead to the backyard. Pitch the racquetball at the steps, and depending on how it bounces, it's a single or maybe a grounder. Hit the steps in the right spot, and the ball arcs high overhead, across the street, beyond the fence surrounding a neighbor's yard. Teresa tends to win and prefers to play in the character of Keith Hernandez, her favorite St. Louis Cardinal.

She is naturally athletic. "Built like a bulldog," Tim says. Which means, built like her father. She's tenacious on the baseball diamonds and soccer fields at Carondelet Park, a few blocks away from their house, and she can beat boys her age in a sprint. It's her body that gets her there but also her will, and this is another way she's like her father. Determined, to a degree that determines outcomes.

The Mississippi River is a ten-minute drive away, and Teresa's parents take her and other Butz children down there to watch the water, or look at the arch, or eat at the floating McDonald's. They shoot a homemade movie to remember it all, catch the river-cruising paddleboats moored at the water's edge and the old Busch Stadium, its rim lined with rows of arches reflecting the larger waterfront arch. A few hours' drive away is "the Farm," a neglected property that Norbert senior purchased at a cut rate. Teresa loves it out there. "The sky could just thrill her," Dolly says. It's a place for the wider Butz clan to gather for playing touch football in the fields, or catching minnows and crawdads along the banks of the Meramec River, or jumping off a railroad bridge thirty feet above the river's surface and then, at the end of the day, walking back to the red farmhouse with its wraparound front porch to eat barbecue cooked on grills laid over huge metal drums cut in half, and corn on the cob, and watermelon. These meals have to be huge. Dolly has two sisters, and between these three Catholic women there are twenty-seven offspring.

At home in St. Louis, on summer evenings when it's too hot to do much else, the Butz kids pile into the bedroom Teresa shares with her older sister, Kathy. It has air-conditioning, and in the cool they sing along to records by John Denver and Amy Grant, music cleared in their parents' vetting process. Other times, they go to the living room, where Dolly, like her parents, keeps a piano, a baby grand. With Steve, the first Butz child, on guitar, and Mike, the third Butz child, on accordion, and Norbert junior, the seventh child, on piano, they do the Billy Joel songbook, or gospel tunes, or pieces they're practicing for choir. Below, a basement room where Steve and Mike keep a private, un-vetted record collection: the Beatles, the Rolling Stones, the Eagles, Fleetwood Mac's *Rumours*. "This very hip, clandestine, smelly lair," says Norbert junior.

Teresa, at a certain point, gets her hands on Michael Jackson's *Thriller,* listens to it incessantly, puts posters of him up all over her room. Never the best singer in the family, she dances to everything she hears. "From a very young age," Dolly says.

At Christmas, when the eight boys in the Butz family receive boy things and the three girls in the Butz family receive girl things, Teresa is noticed to prefer the boy things. There is not much time to reflect on this in a family with eleven children, and in any case Teresa doesn't run entirely against expectations for a young Catholic girl growing up in the middle of the country in the mid-1970s and early 1980s. She thrills at wearing pretty dresses for Communions and weddings, puts on a blue dress with a butterfly embroidered on its neckline for a family photograph, and beneath this dress wears a yellow collared shirt with yellow ribbons trailing from each collar point. Directly behind Teresa in the photograph is Norbert junior, wearing a gray suit and a similar smile, both of them looking markedly more mischievous than the rest of their siblings.

As she grows, Teresa amasses a large trove of Precious Moments figurines, small religious-themed, cherubic-faced ceramic statues that are taking off in the Midwest. Her friends never quite square this side of her with the rest of her, but that's Teresa. "As tough as she was on the exterior," says Rachel Ebeling, her lifelong friend, "inside she was the mushiest person you would ever know." Teresa and Rachel meet in kindergarten at St. Stephen Protomartyr elementary school, a small tan-brick building attached to the large tan-brick church they both attend on Sundays. Jean Fox, another lifelong friend of Teresa's, is also in this kindergarten, where the girls all wear uniforms of red plaid jumpers and white blouses and where the classrooms are tiny, up on the second floor and tucked beneath the eaves of a slanting roof, the floor covered in old carpet samples, the teacher in various psychedelic print dresses, and throughout the room the smell of old crayons and warm radiators.

Rachel doesn't have any sisters. Teresa has too many brothers. Jean has only brothers. So the girls become each other's sisters, the ones who tell the truth to each other, laugh at each other, protect each other as they rise through the grade levels at St. Stephen and beyond. There are some tougher students at St. Stephen, girls Rachel is afraid of, and she marvels at how Teresa simultaneously resists and disarms them, how she manages to locate their good side. This despite, or maybe because of, the way that Teresa, with her aggressive sturdiness, with her jeans and flannels in the cold seasons, sticks right out as a tomboy. If there is any instinct to marginalize Teresa over this difference, Rachel and Jean—Ray and Ween, if it's Teresa talking—never see it.

At school, Teresa becomes a protector for her older brother Tim, who's shy and timid. She plays this role at home, too, where their father's punishment philosophy is, as Tim describes it, "kick ass first, ask questions later." Norbert senior's work is draining, and he sometimes returns to Dolly's crying from the stress of managing the huge brood all day long. Seeking to bring order to mayhem, "I'd walk in like a drill instructor," Norbert senior says. "I'd take my belt off. And I never had to once hit 'em. But I tell you, they'd scurry like roaches, and within fifteen minutes, twenty minutes, they had all their jobs done." In Tim's memory, there is, in fact, some hitting, for not keeping books off the stairs or failing to keep hair out of the sink, and when the hitting happens, Teresa comforts him and makes her displeasure known.

On the soccer field, her preferred position is defender. She inhabits this role with full intensity, too. Once, during a play-off game at Carondelet Park, Norbert senior watches Teresa tackle three girls on the opposing team with such force they leave the field in pain. He thinks it's overkill. So at halftime, when her team is huddled around the coach, he steps onto the field. "Just walked right into the middle of the group," Norbert senior says, "and I said to the coach, 'I want my daughter.' I said, 'Get over here, Teresa.' And I talked to her. I asked her what the hell she was doing. She's hurting people. Now, there was some bad blood between these two girls' teams, I guess with verbiage or whatever, and I remember she cleared her throat, and she spit on the ground right in front of me, and she said, 'They got everything they got coming.' You know, so."

Her strident side comes out at school as well, along with a serious altruism. With Jean and Rachel, she joins the Bellarmine Speech League, and at its meetings the three friends practice elocution while reading famous speeches and dramatic monologues. Teresa always picks from the "serious" category. "Tear-jerking, heart-wrenching stories filled with human empathy," Jean says. "People in nursing homes. People dying. Stories set in the Holocaust. A guy who volunteers to be shot so a father doesn't have to be shot in front of his family."

One year, for an all-school talent show, Teresa and Rachel sign up to perform a song from the 1972 Marlo Thomas album *Free to Be . . . You and Me,* which has been on heavy rotation in the Butz household ever since Dolly spotted the album while out shopping and remembered liking Marlo

Thomas on the television series *That Girl*. "There were little secular influences that kind of made their way through in subversive ways," Norbert junior says. "And that record is the perfect example." It plays in the opening shots of the Butz family home movie, its earnest lyrics cheering self-discovery as the camera pans across views of the downtown St. Louis waterfront, the old stadium, the Mississippi. In another home movie clip, Teresa, intent but far from on key, practices the song from the album that she and Rachel are going to sing in the talent show. It's "When We Grow Up," a duet for a male and a female—Michael Jackson and Roberta Flack in one popular instance. In the living room of her family's brick home on Holly Hills Boulevard, Teresa sings the song wearing a white dress with a lacy collar, which is not what she wears to the talent show.

When they walk onstage, Rachel is in a long dress with her hair in curls, playing the girl who asks in the song's opening line whether she'll grow up to be pretty. Teresa, always short and destined never to get above five two, is dressed in brown corduroys and a brown plaid shirt, the little boy who asks in the next line whether he'll grow up to be tall and strong. It continues like this, two kids aware they are expected to become something in particular and also aware they might disappoint, alternating lines and arriving together at the chorus, and a declaration: "I like what you look like, and you're nice small. We don't have to change at all."

Somehow, Teresa never triggers the word "lesbian" at school. "We didn't even contemplate it," Jean says. "It was outside our world." Perhaps, as well, an unseen force in their world. Teresa expresses herself as a seeker, eager for experience beyond the existing confines. The first time Jean cracks open a beer, it's with Teresa. Her first drag off a cigarette is with Teresa, too. The first time she hitchhikes, it's Teresa's thumb in the air, and when they grab Mom or Dad's keys to the station wagon, long before any of them have their licenses, it's Teresa grabbing her parents' keys, Teresa getting behind the wheel. "We were going to, like, the Taco Bell drive-through," Jean says. "You would have thought we were orbiting Mars, the charge we got out of it." The first time Jean and Rachel stay up all night is also with Teresa, during some sleepover or other at the house on Holly Hills Boulevard. The three of them climb out a window and, at Teresa's urging, sit on the roof to watch the sun come up. She hands around some Kents, probably stolen from her dad. "I just remember feeling kind of wild, sitting up there and watching the sun come up and smoking a cigarette," Jean says. "I felt, 'Wow. I'm getting old.'" They were about thirteen.

When Teresa is a little older, her parents decide to move from the house on Holly Hills Boulevard to a new home only a short drive away. It's a nice place, but Teresa never forgives them, the change triggering her stubborn sense of nostalgia, plus a special umbrage she reserves for people who transform something that's working just fine into yet another thing she'll have to be nostalgic for. With Tim, she walks the empty brick house one last time, drinking cans of Busch they probably swiped when their father wasn't looking, and, before she leaves, climbs the porch's stone railing, reaches up, steals the sign holding the address numbers, takes it with her. It is like this, too—her nostalgia primed and ready, her special umbrage rising—when Anheuser-Busch sells to a foreign company, and when the Cardinals' old, arch-rimmed stadium is torn down for a new stadium that has no rim lined with arches.

If there is mystery about whom the teenage Teresa is meant to love, she doesn't help with the untangling. When Jean and Rachel head for an all-girls Catholic high school, Teresa chooses a different route, following her siblings to the coed Bishop DuBourg, a parochial school that by now is giving Norbert senior a bulk discount on tuition. She does keep in touch, and her friends notice that while they're finding boyfriends, Teresa never has a boyfriend, ever. Her two older brothers at DuBourg, Tim and Norbert junior, notice this as well, although everyone hears Teresa talking a lot about an extended crush she's developed on a neighbor boy named Dan Kolath. He rejects her, gently, yet Teresa continues to nurture this crush in a way that gets attention, writing letters to Ray and Ween about Dan Kolath, thinking and talking about Dan Kolath long after it has become apparent there is no chance.

When it's near time for Norbert junior to graduate from DuBourg, he applies to study theater at Webster University across town but does it in secret, fearing his father's reaction. When the reaction is as feared, Norbert junior plays a trump card, an offer of financial assistance. His father relents.

Teresa watches all this, watches Norbert junior's new world forming, watches their parents make peace with it, watches her older brother bring home friends who are lesbian and gay. Soon, Norbert junior lands a role in a production of Larry Kramer's *Normal Heart*, cast as Felix, the open-hearted, HIV-positive boyfriend of a fiery gay rights activist. He's going to have to kiss a man onstage.

This information is not well received by Norbert senior, who, in the marines, saw a man beaten and then kicked out because Norbert senior himself reported the man making advances. Later, when he was guarding the brig in San Diego, Norbert senior noticed how many of the inmates were soldiers about to be discharged for homosexuality. They seemed to him the saddest people he'd ever seen, forced to shower alone under watch, not allowed belts or shoestrings as a precaution against suicide. "My experience in the brig was, I didn't know what I was gonna do in life, but I was gonna follow the rules," Norbert senior says.

Though the subject matter of his son's play concerns him, he comes to the performance anyway and afterward shows a mix of pride and upset. Teresa absorbs all this, too, Norbert junior believes.

Next to graduate from Bishop DuBourg is Tim, and once he's gone, it's just Teresa at the school, her two younger siblings still back at St. Stephen because of the seven-year gap. She's popular enough to be elected class president, but then her senior prom comes around, and no one asks her to go. "Well, Teresa, you can't not go to your senior prom," Tim says. They go together. They dance, drink, attend the after party at a nearby hotel, and then the actual couples begin heading off to their hotel rooms and Teresa begins to cry, telling Tim she's never going to have anybody, that she's always going to be alone.

Around this time, she decides to run away. "She was dealing us a fit," Norbert senior says. "And one night, we got into an argument and she packed a bag and she started walking across right where I'm standing, walking toward the door." Norbert senior tells her it isn't going to happen, that she'll have to go through him first. "And so we had words. I says, 'Put your bag down.' I said, 'You've given your mother and I a bunch of bullshit all year. If anybody should be leaving, it should be Mom and I. And we're staying. We're committed. You're committed to staying until you get done with high school.' And so, she walked towards me, and I'm not proud of this, but I took my two hands and I pushed her on her shoulder. But I pushed her so hard she fell backwards on the floor, right where I'm standing now. And she's laying there on the carpet. She wasn't hurt. But I come over, I felt so bad that I knocked her down—not with my fists, I just pushed her and she fell backwards—but I felt so bad I went over to help her up, and she starts swinging at me. She says, 'Go ahead, I don't care if you knock the shit out of me.' You know, you couldn't scare her. She was tough. A tough young girl."

4

In a small adobe house in the mountains, a couple hours north of Santa Fe, Jennifer Hopper. It's the winter of 1972, and she's just over a week old. The town holding the small adobe house is Vallecitos, which means Little Valleys, and this is where Jennifer will spend her first years, raised by parents in hiding.

Her last name, Hopper, is a fiction. It was invented by her father, Sam, who is absent without leave from the military. Years earlier, Sam shipped out to help in Korea after the armistice, but at his next assignment, a recruiting center in San Francisco, became disenchanted. Unwilling to send more young men off to Vietnam, he disappeared, with like-minded friends, to this spot along a river through the Carson National Forest. Jennifer's mother, Marcia, is twenty-five years old and also in Vallecitos to disappear. She dropped out of the University of Washington to sell beaded necklaces on "the Ave," something like Haight-Ashbury at Seattle latitude, and then at a certain point decided to ditch that scene. A few people she knew were into rock climbing. Vallecitos had good rock climbing.

Sam is about twenty-six, walks around in a snap-brim hat, gray vest over white T-shirt, weathered jeans. Marcia finds it a handsome look. He works summers fighting fires for the forest service, and it pays enough that the entire young family can make it through the fall and winter on his earnings. He takes odd jobs as well, and when not at those jobs helps tend corn and sweet peas in the family's garden. Marcia begins using his last name, makes it semiofficial by having it typed on a flimsy local

Democratic Party registration card. Later, she makes it a bit more official when she uses it on a hard-laminated New Mexico driver's license.

In his free time, Sam sketches in ink on paper. Marcia nurses Jennifer and, in her free time, works on beaded necklaces. She appreciates the way the hard days in their valley are wrenching her out of her "spoiled" upbringing in Seattle, making her grateful for basics like indoor plumbing and hot water, especially in winter as she walks across snow to the outhouse. Her hair is wavy, black, long, washed once a week in a big metal tub. Her glasses are horn-rimmed. On balance, she prefers this life. But she finds herself wanting more for her daughter, feels pained that Jennifer's grandparents haven't yet been able to hold her. Gnawing at Marcia on a more regular basis: Sam's drinking. Eventually, she says, "he stayed, and I left."

Around 1974—"could have been earlier, that's kind of foggy"—Marcia returns to Seattle, to her parents' brown split-level home in a middle-class neighborhood in the northern part of the city. The place has a two-car garage, a den on the lower level with shag carpeting and wood-paneled walls, plenty of room for her and her two-year-old.

Jennifer's grandfather Sidney Leavitt works for a jeweler in downtown Seattle. Her grandmother Ida Leavitt works at the American Discount Corporation as a bookkeeper. It's good that Jennifer now has three people taking care of her, and Marcia also notices that her daughter has a strong tendency toward entertaining herself. "Which I appreciated," she says. It all gives Marcia more time for figuring out her next step.

As Jennifer grows, she shows an ability to entertain others as well. Spends a lot of time in the basement den with her grandfather, who sits in his recliner watching Lawrence Welk as Jennifer watches with him, then reenacts. "Loved to sing," Marcia says. "Loved to dance." Ida Leavitt, seeing this, buys her granddaughter a dress that twirls, pea green with little yellow dots, a design Marcia finds atrocious. Jennifer thrills at spinning in the dress, long black hair in a bun, the overture to *Gypsy* playing or Lawrence Welk singing in the background, her grandfather amused, and when she can draw more people to the performance, more people amused.

They move, mother and daughter, to a small yellow house about a mile away. Marcia's parents own it and offer it to her for minimal rent. It's laid out economically, one story and not a hallway in sight, "almost like a circle," Jennifer says. "You could go from the living room to one bedroom, to the bathroom, to the other bedroom, to the living room." Marcia is still looking for steady work, but the search halts when she wakes up one Mother's Day with a disk ruptured in her lower back. The rupture requires surgery. The surgery doesn't work. A second disk ruptures. She has another surgery. That surgery doesn't work, either.

It is in this way that Marcia comes to stand as she does now, bent at the waist in a perpetual bow. She and Jennifer end up on welfare and food stamps, and Marcia tries to get help for her back through a state-funded program for people without health insurance. The program pays for Marcia to have two spinal fusions, and after the fusions the program also pays for a cheap pain medication to help Marcia through recovery. "And I didn't know what it was, but I felt fantastic," Marcia says. "It came in a big jug, and you could see there was white stuff at the bottom, and you'd have to shake it, and I found out later that it was methadone. And a bunch of other meds. And that was what they called their pain cocktail. And I became addicted to it."

In response, Jennifer becomes a fixture at her grandparents' house. Her father is out of the picture now, but his parents, who live in rural Washington, are not, and in the summers they take Jennifer fishing on Hood Canal, teach her how to ride a bicycle, show her how to garden. Jennifer also becomes a regular at the methadone clinic, tagging along with her mother, sitting in a waiting room filled with people who have taken many routes to the same addiction, most by way of heroin but a number of them, like Marcia, by way of addiction to prescription painkillers. A few of her fellow addicts later show up at the small yellow house, dating Marcia. "So I was essentially an only child and had a single mom," Jennifer says. "But a single mom with lots of boyfriends." Jennifer isn't too fond of any of them. Anyway, they come and go.

"I wasn't a great role model," Marcia says. "I didn't go to work. I didn't do much. I mean, between my back and the methadone and trying to, I guess, find my way about things, it wasn't a very great life."

Jennifer is too young to do much more than react, and when she isn't upset, she feels for her mother, thinks, "What a pain to have to go to this place every day, get your little cocktail." They divvy out her mother's cocktail, and Jennifer watches as they do this, watches them lower the dose, visit after visit, and then, when there is no more lowering to be done, hears her mother say, "I'm not ready." This happens many times, and whenever it happens, Jennifer is devastated. She goes to the store near their house carrying food stamps, sees eyes roll or hears a comment made, wonders, "Why are they doing that?" She goes to her grandparents' house, watches Lawrence Welk, plays her grandfather's show-tune records, twirls, sings.

First Jennifer's family, then people on the outside begin to notice her singing voice, unusually strong and clear. They ask Jennifer's mother and grandparents where it comes from. They don't know. Marcia guesses it comes from Jennifer's father, Sam. He was adopted, so the deeper origins remain a mystery, but Sam has rhythm, and a love of music, and Marcia is sure of this: "I don't have it."

At public school, teachers notice and encourage Jennifer to join the choir. At temple, a cantor notices and offers her a solo. She feels a little guilty. Everyone seems impressed, but to her this is easy, natural. When she's eleven or so, she tries out for a youth production of *The Sound of Music*, hoping to be one of the kids singing in the background, but she's deemed too tall for the background of a youth production. A year later, she tries again and gets cast in *The Music Man* as part of the ensemble. She feels an instant fit. She can memorize, she can take direction, and being one part of an appreciated whole is bliss, as well as helpful contrast.

At home, her mother, deep in the methadone distance, sleeping a lot. Also, her mother's boyfriends, some of them "quite abusive," Jennifer says, to both Marcia and herself. Some try to be father figures for Jennifer, which she resists, hoping they'll just disappear. "The pattern I recognized," Jennifer says, "was in between relationships, my mom kind of showed up more." So she hopes for the in-between times, though they sometimes involve grown-up tasks.

Marcia develops epilepsy, from the stress of her situation, she believes. She has two seizures, one of which requires Jennifer to call for help, and then one Sunday Jennifer's grandmother is driving her back to her mom's place, and when they arrive, Marcia waves them off. "Saw us pull up," Jennifer says, "and just said, 'Hey, guys, I'm really, really, really tired. I'm just, I feel like I need some rest. Do you mind going back to Grandma's until later?'" Her grandmother doesn't mind, but Jennifer feels something's wrong. Feels it all the way back to her grandmother's.

When they get there, she tells her grandmother to take her back home. Her grandmother won't, so Jennifer sets out walking, Ida Leavitt following along behind in her car. Eventually, she picks Jennifer up four blocks away from the yellow house and drives her the rest of the distance, and when the two of them walk in, they find Jennifer's mom lying down, as if for a nap. "House was perfectly clean," Jennifer says. "She was in bed. Perfectly neat. Just kind of laying with her hands like this"—and here Jennifer places her hands on her stomach, one gently over the other—"but I immediately saw the empty pill bottle, and I got her out of bed." She carries her mother to the bathroom, hits her to try to startle her back to consciousness, asks her grandma to call 911. She remembers her mom coming to and begging them to let her die. She remembers not knowing how to respond, feeling a cutting of a cord between herself and her mother. "I don't know that there was any other way I could deal," Jennifer says. Marcia's next memory is waking up in the hospital with her stomach pumped.

So, whenever possible, to the theater. "And, you know, I'm sorry, when you do theater or any kind of performance, at the very end people clap," Jennifer says. "And then people come see you, and they say, 'Good job,' and they smile, and they're happy, and it brings them together." The adults in the theater become surrogate parents to her, the other young actors a kind of sibling group. The problem is that it ends. "Boom, you're all alone again," she says.

The first gay people Jennifer meets are through the theater, all of them men. There is no issue with homosexuality among this crowd, and so it all enters Jennifer's mind as unremarkable, just something that exists. It doesn't occur to her that it might be her way. She has crushes on boys in elementary school, a new one almost every year, and no crushes on girls, though she will later look back and see how certain friendships with females really upset her when they ended. How, in grade school, one especially close female friend would come over to her grandparents' house to spend the night and, down in her grandfather's den, she and Jennifer would share the hide-a-bed. With lights out, they would touch their lips through the sheet, practice for when the real thing came along.

In the spring of 1981, Jennifer's grandfather dies. Around the same time, her grandmother retires from bookkeeping at the American Discount Corporation at the age of sixty-five. Now, when Jennifer comes over, it's just her and her grandmother in the house with the wood-paneled den. They become very close.

Jennifer's mom is dating a new man, Vance, who drives a tow truck and does maintenance at the Nites Inn Motel. Vance has a daughter, and the two of them move into the yellow house, Jennifer now sharing a small room with someone who might, or might not, become her sister. Marcia is now several years into her methadone addiction, maybe two, maybe five. She doesn't remember how long it all lasted. What she does remember is how Vance helped her get off the drug cold turkey by checking her into the Nites Inn for about a week. "Holed up," Marcia says, "and just went through the whole stuff. It was tough. I remember sleeping a lot."

Jennifer is grateful, but the relationship between herself and Vance is difficult, and Marcia's recovery is gradual. One day, a small argument between Jennifer and Vance explodes into a loud standoff, things get said that are hard to back away from, and Jennifer leaves home to go live with her grandmother. Around the same time, Marcia and Vance move out of the rented yellow house and call off a wedding they've been planning. Where they go, Jennifer doesn't know. She doesn't speak to her mother for about two years. "When she left, I felt horrible," Marcia says. But she also felt grateful. Jennifer's grandmother would be able to give her opportunities Marcia couldn't.

High school is a slippery place, so while Jennifer makes plenty of friends, she doesn't tell any of them what's been going on at home. She has her first boyfriend, tall, handsome, too cute for her in her mind, though she is aware of a certain amount of attention she receives from young men, sees heads turn to take in her olive skin, deep brown eyes, shiny jet-black hair. She just doesn't put it all together. There's a lot going on.

She does share a few things with the woman who teaches the school's vocal jazz class, Susan Bardsley, who notices that outwardly none of it seems to be dragging Jennifer down. "She always had this innate goodness and strength in her," Susan says. And then there was the voice. "It would be hard to miss what Jen had," Susan says. "She possesses one of the most naturally beautiful voices I have ever experienced in my life, and I'm a professional musician now. I do nothing but musical theater. A voice like hers is very rare." It's not just the voice, Susan says, but her ear—her control of pitch, her innate sense of musicality and rhythm, her ability to inhabit a song. "It's as if her cup is very full of the music gift," Susan says.

The public school Jennifer is attending, Roosevelt High School, is known for its musical theater program, and the director of that program, Ruben Van Kempen, notices Jennifer's voice, too. Is stunned by it, actually. "A very clear, legitimate soprano voice," he says. "It was pure. A really great vocal instrument." In a setting that brings him mostly belters and character voices, Jennifer's voice remains one of the top voices he's ever heard.

She is in the ensemble for *Oklahoma!* as a freshman, then in the ensemble for *42nd Street* as a sophomore. In her junior year, she plays Fiona in *Briga-doon,* a leading role and one her soprano seems perfect for, the role of an ingenue. The performance is exceptional, but Ruben and Susan see something that concerns them. While Jennifer's voice is Broadway caliber, her body is not what Broadway will want. "Her voice is an ingenue voice," Susan says, "and her body is not an ingenue voice. Her body is a character voice. She does not fit—and unfortunately this is the case—in terms of visually, looking at her, her body does not fit the sound of her voice." In the cookie-cutter world of professional musical theater, her body will likely get cast as an older matron, and Susan worries that on Broadway Jennifer will be "chewed up and spit out," if it doesn't happen on the way there. "I always worry for girls, because girls are judged so harshly," Susan says. "Just like the quirk of the genetic gift of the voice, you're given a body, and there's only so much arguing you can do with the body you've been given."

Jennifer is aware she's larger than other girls at school, but this is not the difference on which she's most focused. What strikes her is how, even though she's seen as talented, she feels invisible, alone, older than other students because of what she's been through at home and, at the same time, younger than them because of what she's lacked. Food soothes and also contributes to her being "a little chubbier than the average girl," she says. "But I wasn't huge by any means."

In class, she has a hard time keeping anxiety at bay, but in the school's theater she can focus, or helpfully lose focus, morphing pain into propellant. Susan has seen this before and since: "Those who have hard times at home early on are deeper, stronger. If they're not smashed to smithereens or completely drugged out, which is often what happens, they are strong. There is a grounding and a strength and a depth that you can see onstage. They understand more the pain that they're supposed to be acting out. And you don't wish that on any kid, but you see the benefits."

Classes remain a different matter, and Jennifer begins cutting them. She knows she's smart enough, just hates the anxiety, the feeling of failure. Eventually, her grandmother catches wind, gets school counselors involved, explains Jennifer's home situation. "It was amazing," Jennifer says, "how every teacher sort of rose up to the occasion to try to get me through." She's already been accepted to the Boston Conservatory, known for training Broadway actors. She just needs to finish senior year.

In that year's production of *Fiddler on the Roof*, Jennifer stars as the mother, Golde. In the spring, she skips the senior prom after a friend she's going with backs out to go with someone he's actually interested in romantically. She wonders why other guys aren't asking her, is hurt, but doesn't dwell. She's headed elsewhere.

Susan and Ruben, seeing Jennifer closing in on graduation, hope that she'll find her place in Boston. "One never knows," Ruben says. "You have a person that's great, but there are thousands and thousands of high schools, and they all have a person that's great in their school as well, so."

5

College is a time of uneasy fits for Teresa. At first, she heads to Truman State University, set in rural northeastern Missouri, once described as "the Harvard of the Midwest" by an East Coast magazine. She doesn't want to be there, but her father likes the in-state tuition and thinks the academic rigor suits her, and he's the one paying.

She arrives in the fall of 1988 and, looking to make friends, decides she should join a sorority. "Butz, you're not sorority material," says Rachel, who's attending the University of Missouri at Columbia, also known as Mizzou. Jean, who's at the University of Kansas, agrees. They're correct. Teresa doesn't do well with a bunch of other young women sitting in judgment of her. At the same time, she's crushed when they don't let her in. Determined to get into the Greek life somehow, because it's the heart of the school's social scene, she discovers it's possible to become a "little sister" to certain fraternities. It doesn't go well. One night, Teresa, in her role as a fraternity's little sister, is invited to a keg party. Plastic cups filled with beer, the whole classic thing. At some point, someone throws a cup of beer at someone else, and then suddenly everyone is throwing beer at everyone. Teresa is standing in the corner of the room when the drink-tossing crowd, as if with one mind, notices an opportunity to direct its energy outward. "She said, 'It just became focused on me,'" Jean says. "She said, 'All I could do was crouch down.' Every time I think of this story, it makes me upset. She just crouched down in a corner next to a wall, and they just pelted her with beers. That was kind of her experience at this place. Very soon after that, she transferred out of there."

In the fall of 1990, Teresa arrives at Mizzou, where she'd wanted to go in the first place. Plays a lot of softball, parties a lot, tries to figure out what her major should be. Her dad thinks it should be business. She's interested in psychology and criminal justice. She keeps trying to make it work with men, but her friends speak of an encounter around this time that sounded to them like a sexual assault. Soon, Teresa transfers out of Mizzou, too, and by the winter of 1991 she's at the University of Missouri in St. Louis, closer to home. She stays, graduating three years later with a degree in business, as her father wanted. She finds work at an Olive Garden and does some housecleaning. It's enough to pay rent on a small apartment where, on the mantel, she keeps her old Precious Moments collection. Jean laughs at this, threatening to smash the sentimental tchotchkes with a baseball bat.

She hears, through cousins, about work on the Clipper Cruise Line. It sounds like a great way to disappear. "Didn't care what she was going to do for Clipper," Tim says. "She just went." The company is sailing boats out of Seattle up to Alaska, smaller vessels that look more like luxury yachts than cruise ships, and this becomes Teresa's route, the family-like closeness of the crew drawing her right in. For a while, she keeps in touch with the outside world, sending Jean and Rachel ten-page letters about her escapades. She's at a casino onshore, losing all her money. She's trying out a new cruise route, headed for the Caribbean, or Peru, or Jamaica. Then, over time, she loses contact. Jean sends her a series of increasingly exasperated postcards, trying to get her attention. Nothing. Teresa is somewhere else. She'll be back in touch when she's ready.

6

Seattle is a new city by American standards, founded as states along the Eastern Seaboard were headed toward civil war, and so when Jennifer arrives at the conservatory in Boston, one of her dominant senses is that the city seems old. Another sense is claustrophobia, brownstones that rise well above the height of Seattle's single-family houses, a downtown more densely packed with tall buildings than the downtown she knows. In Seattle, she can see the sky. In Boston, she's surrounded by brick, by large buildings and monuments, by a humidity she's unfamiliar with, by smells of urine and dirty sidewalks. It's exciting to her, step one on the way to Broadway. Even when winter comes, colder than anything she's known, she tells herself, "This is where I'm supposed to be."

She meets a conservatory student named Kerri Sanford, who's drawn to Jennifer by her striking beauty, by the way she puts her heart right out there, and by her voice. "Amazing," Kerri says. "One of the best voices I've heard in my life. As a singer, I was so taken with her." But the conservatory, by design, is tough on everyone. There are classes in which students share their private fears, their family histories, their personal challenges. "You go around the room and talk about whatever abuse you had in your life," Kerri says. "It was like an AA meeting or something, where we all had this code of silence. And then, I mean, they tear you down. Literally. When you're performing, they say that you suck, that you're not good enough, that you're never going to be good enough. And then they tear you down mentally regarding your own childhood, all of it, and then they sort of build you back up. That was my experience at least." In one of these classes, Kerri talks about her own Mormon upbringing, then does a movement piece in which she tears pages from the Book of Mormon and stomps them. She's never in a class like this with Jennifer, but when Jennifer privately shares stories of her own upbringing, they're on a different level. "What happened to Jen," Kerri says, "was far more traumatic than many of the stories that I heard."

The self-exploration is all in the pursuit of better performances, the theory being that acting is the study of human behavior, and to understand human behavior, one must begin by better understanding oneself. In a movement class focused on authentic physical expression, Jennifer begins to see how much she's holding inside out of habit. One day, during an exercise, she just screams. An angry scream, something she hasn't accessed before. She's surprised by the intensity. In acting classes, when she tries to connect to characters going through difficulty, she begins to notice she has easy routes to connection with them, realizes, as well, how much control she's been exercising over her interior relationship to her own difficulties, walling off pain, developing an ability to talk "stone cold" or "clinical" to classmates about her life before the conservatory, in a way that sometimes surprises them. It takes her entire time at the conservatory, but she begins to become better at what her movement teacher is encouraging, better at having an authentic relationship with her own pain. "Actually letting it be you," Jennifer says, "versus shoving it away. To have control over it, but actually allow it to get in."

At the same time, she struggles with the competitiveness of the environment, doesn't feel as if she plays the game very well. And then there's the weight issue. "A lot of those girls are skinny-tiny," Jennifer says. She's not. There is a particular acting class she has to take, and the teacher seems to either ignore her completely or assign her sad, matronly roles. Anything the opposite of young, spirited, or sexy. She finds this odd but finds the characters interesting. Over time, though, the pattern becomes something she wants to challenge. "I did a scene with a partner," Jennifer says, "and I don't remember the details, but the teacher just went on and on and gave so much feedback to the scene partner and got to me and just didn't say anything. And to me, lack of feedback—you don't necessarily want good feedback, you want bad feedback, too, because that's how you get better." It made her start to tear up in frustration, a reaction she's long wished she could avoid so as not to appear weak. She told the teacher she was just hoping for feedback, and his reply made her go from tearing up to crying. "Then he threw a quarter at me," she says, "and was like, 'Oh, here's a quarter, go call your mom.'"

She misses Seattle and her grandmother. She feels defeated. A number of people she's met at the conservatory that first year are planning to work the *Spirit of Boston* cruises over the summer, singing for tourists taking a spin around the harbor, and Jennifer notices there's a *Spirit of Seattle* cruise line. She heads home, where it's cheaper, and becomes a singing waitress there.

It's summer. She's out on Elliott Bay all the time, cruising waters that are more familiar, more Pacific, cradled between the two mountain ranges she grew up with, peaks so high they poked up above the last glaciation, the Cascades to the east, Olympics to the west. At night, the sun sets behind the Olympics, and lights blink red atop the downtown skyscrapers, atop the football stadium to the south, and, farther south, atop the tall orange cranes at the dirty mouth of the Duwamish.

It's a fun gig, a revue with a ridiculous mix of show tunes and Americana, songs from *The Phantom of the Opera* and *South Pacific* merging into "God Bless the U.S.A." She's earning more money than she's ever seen, minimum wage plus a couple hundred bucks a night in tips, and there's a familial connection among the crew. To Jennifer, it's the heartening opposite of the conservatory, where everything felt tenuous and shallow.

7

In June of 1994, in Alaska, Teresa finds herself needing old friends. A gangway collapses while passengers are disembarking her boat in Juneau, and shortly afterward she writes to Jean, saying she's just tried calling her in St. Louis "but to no avail." She's tried calling other friends, too. "Can't reach a single soul." A woman is dead, the mother of Teresa's cabinmate. It's on CNN.

During dinner service, Teresa fights tears. She feels anger rising when she tries to act as if nothing's happened, "wearing this fake fucking smile trying to please all these damn passengers." This is her regular route now, and the boat will be back in Juneau every Saturday. She can't escape the memory.

One evening, after receiving a large tip from a passenger, Teresa decides to share it by buying all the crew members in sight drinks, which is not the way tips are supposed to be shared. When management finds out, she's fired. She heads back to St. Louis and, at a dark Irish bar named McGurk's, gets drinks with a friend who has an in at a different kind of cruise company. "You gotta hire me," she says.

By the next year, Teresa, now twenty-six, is out on the Mississippi River, a maid aboard a steel-hulled paddleboat called the *American Queen*. One morning, she knocks on a cabin door to introduce herself to a new employee, and John Schuler, twenty-two, opens up. Like Teresa, he's from a river town, in his case Aurora, Indiana. Like Teresa, he's from a strict Catholic family. He's never had a girlfriend, or a boyfriend, ever.

They become fast friends, John training to be a purser, Teresa on her way to becoming head maid, two escapees floating together through the bayous and prairies and high plains. "It was a very isolated life," John says. "Which was kind of nice." They sit evenings on the top deck, unspooling their stories.

When the boat gets north of St. Louis, around the town of Hannibal, where Mark Twain lived, the river transitions from the dark colors of its more industrial southern stretches into an inviting green surrounded by cliffs and bluffs. During staff parties, crew members leap from the side of the boat, swim around the back, touch the stopped red paddle wheel.

This is a much larger vessel than those on Clipper's Alaska run, close to five hundred feet long and carrying 180 crew—"I mean, the boat is huge," John says—with 222 cabins to tend and, when the ship is full, more than four hundred passengers. Most of the crew are like John and Teresa, under thirty, in search of the next step, not in any particular hurry, earning around $10 a day and padding that with tips from the well-off clientele. "You have no bills, you have no car, you own no apartment, you owe nothing to nobody," John says. "And the company's buying all your food; they're buying all your clothes." Everything is covered, easily, "except for the damage we could do on our two weeks off," John says. "Which—we could do some substantial damage."

When they work the outer decks, they hear the sound of water rushing around the hull as the boat pushes onward. Inside, a different sound, piston-powered steam engines reverberating through the vessel's walls, a melodic *kathunk-kathunk-kathunk* that becomes background to the workday and lullaby at night, so much so that John wakes from sleep if it stops. Then there are the sounds of the *American Queen*'s steam-powered calliope, which plays when they go through a lock in the river or pull into or out of a port. It does old ragtime songs and, once, "Like a Virgin." "God-awful," John says.

As they pass days together, he notices some things about Teresa. She's inquisitive, hardworking, hard partying, happy to be on the boat, but also helped along by a huge amount of coffee. "No one has brought up how much coffee Teresa Butz drank?" John says. "Oh. Ohhhhhhh. Teresa drank twelve to fourteen cups of coffee a day. And that's a conservative estimate. The way she would walk, it was like her coffee was leading her. One of her bosses told her, 'You need to stop following your coffee cup around; you need to start leading the way.'"

On a break from her new job, Teresa visits Jean, now living in London. Keeps going on about this big thing she has to tell her, so of course Jean wants to know immediately. "Not the kind of thing I'm going to handle on public transportation," Teresa says. They get back to where Jean is staying, Teresa pulls out some whiskey she's bought in Ireland, they have a drink, and then Teresa tells her. "It was like, 'Oh,'" Jean says. "I hadn't expected her to tell me that. It wasn't any of the stuff I was guessing. But it was like, 'Oh, of course.' I'm not sure why it never occurred to me, because when she said it, it made total sense."

Not long after Teresa came to the realization, the riverboat had docked in New Orleans. She'd gone to the St. Louis Cathedral in the French Quarter, walked inside, knelt, and prayed that her homosexuality, which she knew her church considered a sin, would be taken away. Hearing this, Jean says, "I felt my heart rip."

8

When her summer on the *Spirit of Seattle* is over, Jennifer returns to the conservatory. Then, after one more semester, she leaves. Her teachers in Boston ask if it's money. It's not money, she tells them. She just wants out. Back in Seattle, she enrolls in a community college and reconnects with Ruben, the musical theater director from her high school. She tells him she's thinking of giving up on theater and becoming an accountant, and he listens but puts her back onstage in a community production he's directing, sees in her eyes how much she loves it, says, "You know, I really think you should just go back to the conservatory."

She asks a dean if it's possible, and the answer is yes. They'll continue a scholarship she'd been on, too. In the fall of 1993, Jennifer returns to the conservatory and this time finds friendships easier. The teacher who'd been cruel to her ends up leaving soon after she gets back, and she's rooming with a supportive man from Cincinnati named Michael Grayman. He watches, impressed, as Jennifer performs in a new kind of role, playing one half of a lesbian couple in *Falsettoland*. "Just owned it," Michael says. Jennifer feels herself connecting, too, but doesn't make any link between herself and the sexuality of her character. "Didn't really think anything about it," she says. "Again."

Most of the men Jennifer meets at the conservatory are gay, like Michael, and most of the women are straight, like Kerri, but with one of the few lesbians she encounters, a musician rooming with a friend of hers, Jennifer notices something. "I remember being like, 'Ooh. Hmm, that's interesting energy,'" Jennifer says. "Because it's just different energy."

Jennifer is an acute measurer of human energy. When she likes someone, it's because she picks up on a good energy, or powerful energy, or irresistible energy. An empath is how she describes herself, someone who noticed early her ability to read the emotional weather, a skill she thinks developed as a protective measure amid the chaos and quick mood changes of her home life. It has become like one of her senses. She will look at someone, and listen to someone, and hug someone, but all the while she is also measuring energy. Perhaps it is this ability, working beyond its usual parameters, that around this time begins delivering a kind of electric shock in response to certain women.

She is by now very familiar with the coming-out process, has watched it over and over with her gay male friends in the theater, sees how the pain only intensifies the longer one waits, has said to herself, "Man, if I ever wake up one random morning and I'm suddenly attracted to a woman, I'm gonna deal with it." The summer of 1995—the same summer Teresa, who's almost three years older than Jennifer, is floating the Mississippi aboard the *American Queen*—Jennifer decides to stay in Boston. In the evenings, she waitresses, and during the day she works for the conservatory at a job that involves setting up a Boston Harbor cruise for incoming freshmen. She works with the school's bursar on this project, and when the cruise is over, the bursar approaches to offer congratulations. Jennifer is now twenty-two and about to become a senior. The bursar is thirty-five.

"She put her hand on my shoulder," Jennifer says, "just completely appropriately, too. And I was like, 'Oh.' Like, here's that moment that I never expected to happen." The moment keeps repeating. Being in the woman's presence makes Jennifer nervous; routine work conversations make her sweat. She writes the woman a card. She receives a card in return.

The woman thanks Jennifer, reminds Jennifer that she works for the

school, and then writes something like, "Whether I wanted to or not—
and we're not gonna go into that—nothing could ever happen. So, I want
you to know, because of that you actually can completely trust me. My
heart belongs to someone else right now, but what you're going through
is normal. It doesn't necessarily have to mean anything. It could just be
me. But, if you want to talk about it, I'm here for you. I always will be here
for you. I think the world of you."

Jennifer doesn't do much in her exterior world with the experience.
Thinks it might be just this one woman, although one of her friends,
when she tells him about it, says something like, "We've all seen that
coming." Jennifer hasn't. At the same time, she's becoming distracted by
graduation, is preoccupied with what to do next in pursuit of landing on
Broadway. She gets several callbacks for roles in *Les Misérables,* which is
encouraging, but again her size is an issue. It still doesn't fit, in Broadway's eyes, her voice. She sings in a workshop that year and a respected
agent is there, and this agent passes word to a friend of hers, Craig, that
she has potential—if.

"Craig was the kindest," Jennifer says. He tells Jennifer he's passing
on the agent's words because he believes in her, then tells her something
like, "The agent says you are so beautiful, so talented, but he can't do anything with you. He says your face, and your beauty, and your voice sound
like leading lady ingenue. But your body is, like, the best friend. If you
took care of that"—and here Jennifer snaps her fingers, mimicking the
way Craig snapped his fingers, mimicking the way the agent snapped his
fingers—"he would sign you in a second."

Jennifer absorbs this, is grateful for the feedback. "It's amazing how
you can have that carrot and still not be able to do anything about it," she
says. She heads home to Seattle, planning to get a job, save money, and
then move to New York.

9

Teresa has been dating a fellow crew member aboard the *American Queen*, a woman from California named Carolyn. She won't speak about their relationship, but she's had the day she first saw Teresa tattooed on her: May 25, 1995. "They did not hide," John says. "Once Teresa went somewhere, she went all the way."

On another break from the boat, Teresa heads for Montgomery, Alabama, where Norbert junior is living with his first wife and earning an MFA in theater. After a performance, she tells him. "That was a great, great night," Norbert junior says. "We sat in my little Datsun B210 station wagon. We were probably smoking cigarettes and drinking at this big park in Montgomery, Alabama. It was late. It was late, late. And there was no one around. We had the whole park to ourselves." He encourages her, tells her he isn't surprised. "I was like, 'My God, I've known for years.'"

Next, Teresa writes to her mom. "A wonderful letter," Dolly says, but also "heartbreaking." It's not what she's wished for her daughter. "If I could have changed anything," Dolly says, "I would have done whatever." At the same time, "I loved her dearly, and telling me she was gay was certainly not going to change that." She lets Teresa know this, in person, and after she does, Teresa begs her not to tell Norbert senior.

The relationship with Carolyn doesn't last, and Teresa's work takes her onward to another boat in the fleet, the older *Delta Queen*. She becomes executive housekeeper for a time. Then in the fall of 1997, at Seattle's only lesbian bar, Wildrose, two women, Carley Zepeda and Carmen Hernandez, notice a woman sitting alone, sipping a beer, watching a football game. They stop their pool game and ask if she wants to come sit with them. "And she's like, 'Sure!'" Carley says. "You know Teresa, she wasn't gonna be shy. I think she was very happy to be invited. She was drinking a Bud Light in a bottle, of course. Cold as they come. There was no other beer." (By now, Teresa had gotten over the worst of her anger at Anheuser-Busch.)

Teresa tells Carley and Carmen she's from St. Louis and has just moved to town. Knows the place from her time on the Clipper Cruise Line and is now working for one of her older brothers, Tony, who's started a small catering business in the city. Tells them about life on the Mississippi steamboats, tells them she's still thinking about Carolyn. It's a great night, the first of many for the three of them, a new triumvirate. "We were young," Carley says. "We had easy jobs. We weren't doing anything but working to play."

A year passes like this, and then Teresa decides it's time to relocate again. "Her brother fired her three times," Norbert senior says. It's likely her departure from Seattle is connected with one of those times, perhaps with a story Norbert senior tells, with certain pride, of Teresa's helping her brother at a catering gig for Microsoft and a man in a suit saying to Teresa, "Hey, babe, come over and give me another cup of coffee."

"Well," Norbert senior says, "if you call Teresa 'babe' and give her directions, you know she's not going to do it."

On October 20, 1998, the day after her twenty-ninth birthday, Teresa sets out on a drive to New York City, where Norbert junior is now living and working on Broadway, making a name for himself as Norbert Leo Butz.

The journey inspires a four-page letter to her friend Carley, in which Teresa recounts "many miles, ten days, and many stories and incidences— as I'm sure you can imagine, even traveling I'm the same old Butz." As the letter tells it, in Yellowstone National Park she almost walked into a bison. In Custer State Park, she stopped for a picnic and ended up in a standoff with a wild mule.

In La Crosse, Wisconsin, she paid a visit to one of her old boats and, as she was waiting along the Mississippi for it to pull in, ran into a local television news reporter doing a human-interest piece. The segment still sits in the News Channel 8 archives in La Crosse, and it shows the *Delta Queen* pulling in to town, decked out in patriotic bunting, red paddle wheel spinning, steam whistle blowing, and Teresa there to greet it in gray shorts and a white sweatshirt, eyes bright with excitement, brown hair short, earrings shaking as she shouts, whoops, runs up to two African American crew members and bear-hugs them, then sneaks up behind a white guy in an officer's uniform and hugs him, too, from behind, startling him.

REPORTER: Teresa Butz was visiting La Crosse today for the first time, but in many aspects she returned home . . .

TERESA: There's no escaping it. You know, your whole life is on that boat . . . You eat there, and you sleep there. I miss it, because life slows down on the water.

She speaks of the "old, mystical feel" of the riverboat, and the encounter makes her think about going back to the *Delta Queen*. "Then again," she writes to Carley, "I may ditch all of the above and go to Australia." She promises to let Carley know "as soon as I know myself."

She doesn't end up in Australia.

Instead, after arriving in New York, she becomes a nanny for Norbert, who's just landed a role headlining the national tour of *Cabaret,* playing the show's master of ceremonies. "Sexually deviant, androgynous, bisexual," Norbert says. "A great character."

10

Jennifer lives with her grandmother upon her return to Seattle, working days at a photo-processing business as a receptionist. It's a job where no one makes much money and the employees all tend to eat lunches together, brought from home. During these lunches, Jennifer begins to develop a crush on a co-worker, and to her surprise it's reciprocated. When they kiss, Jennifer thinks about the smoothness of women, how much she prefers it to stubble. She performs in local musicals and goes to local auditions, and after one a theater director chases her outside, tells her she's beautiful, her voice is incredible, she's a great actress, but he just wants to be honest with her: it's hard to know where to place her because of her size. "You know," she says. "I've heard that before. Thank you."

There's another call from *Les Misérables* in this year. They want her to audition again, will fly her down to Los Angeles, and the opportunity feels huge, defining. She stays with a friend in L.A., ends up awake all night with stomach pain from nerves, barely has a voice the next day. "Didn't have the greatest audition," she says. When she doesn't get the part, she tells herself she's ruined her chance.

The woman from the photo shop is thirty-seven, and she's worried her relationship with Jennifer won't last—that Jennifer will want to date other women soon, that Jennifer's theater ambitions mean she's not long for

Seattle, anyway. She's right. But while they're still together, Jennifer tries to come out to her grandmother. It doesn't go well. Her grandmother says she must have been manipulated, doesn't want to hear it when Jennifer says she's actually the one who initiated things. "So, what do you wanna do?" Jennifer says. "You want to run three thousand miles away and live your life where you don't have to explain anything to anybody."

She arrives in New York in the fall of 1997, about a year before Teresa does. She knows people who temp at Manhattan law and financial firms, has heard it's decent money, so she gets right into that. She meets a woman in a basketball league—"Crazy attracted to her," Jennifer says— but they don't have a lot of kissing chemistry. She meets a woman who lives in Boston, and it's better kissing chemistry, but that woman cheats on her. She goes to auditions. Nothing comes of them.

Something isn't feeling right, singing is harder than it used to be, and it turns out she needs surgery for a condition akin to calluses on her vocal cords. After the surgery, her voice is slow to return.

At a workshop, someone tells her she doesn't seem to have much vocal control. The stress of auditioning begins to outweigh the joy, and outside her theater pursuits she isn't feeling a part of anything. So she gets on PlanetOut, an early gay dating site, and just after the turn of the millennium meets a preacher's daughter who lives near her in Brooklyn. Their first date is at a lesbian bar called the Rising Café. Jennifer, who doesn't drink much, has a beer, and the woman, Ann Kansfield, notices they click easily. Ann makes plans to go see Jennifer perform a show she's been working on with Kerri, her conservatory friend, a cabaret act at a Manhattan club. As the show approaches, Ann finds herself getting more nervous than Jennifer. The night of the performance, Ann's blown away. Soon they're living together in Park Slope.

11

Norbert junior and Teresa are quickly taken out of New York by the tour for *Cabaret*, which goes to Minneapolis, Toronto, San Francisco. Along the way, Teresa becomes close with her brother's wife and two daughters, but when she isn't busy nannying, she's pensive. Nearing thirty, she talks about time slipping away, spends a lot of hours in hotel bedrooms writing in her journal. "She drank heavily when she was depressed," Norbert says. "But she was always on a journey of self-improvement, too. So I think she mustered up. She kept on going."

She continues toggling between worlds that are hard to reconcile. "Always spoke about her struggle with religion," her friend Carmen says. "Always." She returns to St. Louis for a time, prays about it with her younger sister, Annie, and with one of her sisters-in-law, Jenni Butz.

On a churchwomen's retreat, Jenni and Annie share some Bible verses with Teresa. "Some difficult verses," Jenni says, "about her need to turn her entire life over to God and make some really tough changes. And we all were crying, and I remember Ann saying to Teresa, 'Are you sure you're going to heaven?' And with tears streaming down her face, Teresa saying, 'No.' And Ann said, 'Do you want to, right now?' And she said, 'Yes.' And so we prayed with her, and we showed her scriptures that talked about how much God loved her, and had such great things in store for her life and wanted to bless her, but that that sin was getting in the way and she needed to put it down, and get the forgiveness and the healing that only Jesus can give. And so she did. We prayed, and she gave her whole heart to Jesus that day, and committed to follow him for her life, and she was assured of her place in heaven, because of what Jesus did on the cross. And the following months, we sat and we studied the Bible together, and we learned, and she was baptized, and she grew, and she struggled, and she raged. She did all of those things. But it was real. Her love for Jesus was real. And she was changed."

After this, after the *Cabaret* tour is over, Teresa heads for Seattle again but doesn't let her lesbian friends know. She tries dating men, creates an account on eHarmony. Later, when they reconnect, Carley tells Teresa, "Even if you weren't gay anymore, you could have called."

She is still gay. She gets into a relationship with another former boat worker, a woman named Amy. It's 2002, and they live together in a small condo Teresa buys using money she's been socking away since her time on the boats, even amid all the instability in her life. It's yet another way she's like her father, a serious saver. "Did not want to owe anybody anything," Carmen says. It also helps that Teresa has steady income from work she's begun doing at Seattle-area hotels, essentially a stationary version of her boat life. All of it adds up to Teresa's having great credit at a time of exceptionally easy credit, which allows her to get an affordable mortgage on the $145,000 condo. It's located in Renton, a working-class suburb south of Seattle that the Green River runs by on its way to becoming the Duwamish.

Like Carolyn, Amy won't talk about their time together, but by all other accounts her relationship with Teresa is intense and rocky. Teresa, Carley says, "put her whole heart into all of her relationships," and this one ends hard. So do some of the hotel jobs. Teresa tells friends she's lost one because she disappeared from work to fly back to St. Louis to see her Cardinals in the World Series and lost another because she was told by management to fire maids who were undocumented immigrants, but refused. These endings bother her less than might be expected. "You get fired from one job, you get another one," is how a friend describes her attitude.

Girlfriends are a different matter. Teresa has a difficult time getting over people, Amy included.

On the night of Saint Patrick's Day 2005, a Washington State Patrol officer notices a car drifting across lanes on Interstate 5 where it passes through downtown Seattle. It's Teresa's black Saab convertible, the car she bought so that when the sun was out in Seattle, there would be nothing between its warmth and her skin. The officer pulls the car over, smells alcohol on Teresa's breath, notices her bloodshot eyes. She can't find her registration, keeps handing him, according to the officer's report, "papers that looked nothing like a registration." Her speech is slurred, her coordination poor. Perhaps relevant to the standard field sobriety test, she's noted to be wearing boots with round toes and "two-inch, chunky" heels. Teresa tells him she's had "a few" beers. Given a Breathalyzer, she blows a .151, which means she's had more than a few. She's arrested and later specifies it was four to five Bud Lights, consumed earlier that evening with friends at a gay dance club in Seattle called R Place. She was trying to get back to her condo in Renton. Her occupation: "Currently unemployed." Paperwork processed, convertible impounded, she's dropped off at a Denny's where a friend picks her up.

The arrest shakes Teresa. This is not how she thinks of herself. She gets a large fine, does forty hours of community service at a local chapter of the National Federation of the Blind and with a program called Books to Prisoners. By the time she's done, her relationship with Amy is over.

12

Sundays, Ann and Jennifer attend a progressive service in lower Manhattan. "She dragged me to Broadway shows," Ann says. "And I dragged her to church." Jennifer joins the church gospel choir, her Jewishness no obstacle because she's fundamentally ecumenical, eager to accept community and connection wherever they present. Ann appreciates this, likes that Jennifer is open and spiritual. "Which is kind of a low bar to set," Ann says, "but when you're a lesbian, you think that nobody's ever going to want to come to church with you."

What Jennifer likes about Ann is that she's a good writer, smart, well educated, and even-keeled, and "she had that heart quality." This is what Jennifer says about people she deeply connects with. They have a heart quality.

It's the first serious relationship either of them has been in. "It was like the butt of every lesbian joke, actually," Ann says. "You know, like, three hundred fifty square feet, and two lesbians and four cats." They'd each brought two. Ann is working at the World Trade Center for PricewaterhouseCoopers, and Jennifer is working at Update Graphics, where she helps place creative temp workers at advertising firms, fashion houses, financial behemoths, all swollen with excess cash from the tech bubble. When people ask Jennifer why she isn't doing theater anymore, she tells them, "I just need a break." Privately, she feels her voice hasn't fully returned, worries about her weight, begins realizing she can't deal with the financial insecurity of auditioning full-time. It's too much like those early years at the yellow house, the hand-to-mouth existence, the food stamps, the beginning of a downward spiral always close. Plus, desk work is fine. One day, she tosses her musical theater song sheets in the trash.

Ann wonders what's going on. "Here she had these dreams, and she didn't audition," Ann says. "It was hard for me, because she clearly had the talent and the ability."

One morning, Norbert Leo Butz is on the stoop of their Park Slope building. He lives there, too, one of those New York coincidences. Looks familiar to Jennifer, so she strikes up a conversation, and when Norbert tells her he's an actor, she asks what he's working on. "He was like, 'Oh, I'm in *Rent*,'" she says. Jennifer has a friend from the conservatory who's in *Rent*, too, playing his love interest. So they talk quickly about their mutual acquaintance, and then Norbert heads off into the day. She never sees him at the building again, because he moves out shortly afterward.

On September 11, 2001, Ann has just quit her job at the World Trade Center and has begun a new job as a financial planner. With the towers where she used to work in a smoldering heap, she quits her new job, too, and enrolls in seminary. Her relationship with Jennifer hasn't been working for some time, both of them know it, and with a reminder not to waste time still being picked through across the East River, they split.

13

Teresa, needing work, takes a job as a barista at a Starbucks in Seattle. One day, John asks how she remembers all the different drinks. She tells him she's just making the same thing for everyone. It's 2006, a time when better-paying jobs are easy to find if she can just get herself together. Eventually, she does, landing work at a company that manages office buildings all over the world, including some in downtown Seattle.

Her new co-workers adore her, the confident Teresa returns, and she decides to make another change. She sells her condo in Renton, takes the $80,000 in equity she's amassed during the hot housing market, and buys a small red house in South Park, a much shorter drive to work. The house isn't her first choice, but this is 2007, the height of a real estate bubble that's been inflating for years now, fueled by unsustainable calculations made in rarefied neighborhoods on the other side of the country, neighborhoods about as unlike South Park as one can find. She's already been outbid about a dozen times on homes in other parts of the city, and if she wants a house with a yard, which she does, and if she wants to hold to her beliefs about not incurring unreasonable debt, which she does, then this is what she can afford: a $286,000 home with two bedrooms, a yard, a ball field nearby, and a river a few blocks away.

The yard is tiny, the ball field is no Carondelet Park, and the river is a Superfund site. Still, Teresa feels intense pride. She walks people through the place, saying, "I know it's not much, but it's mine." She sticks a George

Bush magnet to her fridge, a totem of the small-business Republican politics she's inherited from her father. She thrills at meeting her new neighbors and having old friends over for dinner. She sets to work on the yard, which her father comes out to help clear. "It was nasty," he says.

Because secrets do not keep long in families with eleven children, Norbert senior now knows Teresa is having relationships with women. He keeps his mouth shut and gets to clearing weeds. "We just never really got into it," he says.

14

Jennifer stays in the gospel choir even after the split with Ann, and Ann laughs at how Jennifer is now becoming more popular at her former church than she ever was. Jennifer thinks, "I'm singing a lot. It's on my terms. It may not be my career, but this feels pretty good." She gets a new apartment and a new desk job and then, after a time, ends up moving back into the Park Slope building she and Ann used to share, buying a studio there with help from Ann and from her grandmother in Seattle.

She gets into another relationship, of a sort, this one surprising to her and disappointingly one-sided, an extended crush she's developed on a handsome Orthodox Jewish guy. Still open to all kinds with the right qualities, Jennifer has found herself drawn to him after "incredible conversations about God, and light—and straight in the eyes." Conversations about mind, body, spirit. "Things that I'm a sucker for," she says.

By 2006, the housing bubble that followed the dot-com crash that followed the tech bubble is well inflated—close to bursting, though few people are focused on the possibility. With her relationship with the Orthodox Jew going nowhere, Jennifer isn't sure what's left for her in New York except the studio apartment in Brooklyn. When she purchased it, monthly payments for the $120,000 mortgage were cheaper than if she'd been paying rent, and now the place sells for $265,000, more than double the purchase cost. She repays Ann and moves back to Seattle in the summer of 2006, thinking, "Maybe I'll meet a nice Jewish guy there."

She meets a Catholic lesbian instead.

Not at first, though. First, she gets on JDate and goes out with a few nice guys. Nothing much happens. She lives again with her grandmother, who's in her nineties now and getting sick. It feels good to be able to help the woman who helped her when she needed it in childhood, and it feels good to be near her mother, Marcia, too. On one of Jennifer's visits home from New York, she'd gone to Marcia, now years into marriage with Vance, and in tears confessed she'd been dating women. In this moment, the open, vulnerable, beaded-necklace-selling side of Marcia offered something Jennifer's grandmother had been unable to give, something Jennifer needed: support, acceptance, relationship advice. A cord between them began to reconnect.

The money from the sale of Jennifer's Brooklyn studio allows her a year of relative freedom in Seattle. She does some long-distance freelancing for her old company in New York, temps for a local nonprofit, volunteers with the Juvenile Diabetes Research Foundation. After a while, though, she needs a full-time job and finds one at a company called Creative Circle, doing placement for temp workers again. The company trains her in Los Angeles, which is where she is when she places a call to an office building manager in Seattle, a woman named Teresa.

15

When Jennifer begins her job in Seattle, that same Teresa is the one who takes her to get an ID badge. "That's kind of when I was first drawn to her," Jennifer says. "Not necessarily in a romantic way. More like, 'Who is she? She's got great energy. I like to be around her.'" Teresa walks with Jennifer down a few floors to get the ID photograph, then walks Jennifer back up to her office. "I remember she was just crisply dressed," Jennifer says. "She wore a suit every day. She was just happy and positive, wanted to ask questions of our business, how could she help us." It turns out their offices are across from each other, on the twenty-second floor of the City Centre building, right in the middle of downtown. As a consequence, Jennifer and Teresa see each other often. "And then it really developed in that very, almost childlike crush fashion," Jennifer says.

She likes watching the way Teresa interacts with people, her smile, her vibrancy, her focus. One day early in this watching, there's a birthday celebration for a receptionist who works on their floor, a celebration to which they're both invited. Now, work hours over, she sees a different Teresa. "Outside of work," Jennifer says, "she was really funny and goofy. Toootally let loose."

They end up talking music, realize they both love Patty Griffin, both end up saying at the same time, "Ugh! 'Heavenly Day' was the best Patty Griffin song." That weekend, Teresa flies off to Norbert's second wedding, in Florida, and is gone ten days. Jennifer notices she's missing her. When

Teresa returns, they pass each other in the hallway, and Teresa mentions she's headed that evening to the Tractor Tavern, an old bar in the former fishing community of Ballard. A singer-songwriter from Brooklyn is playing. "I know you lived in Brooklyn," Teresa says. "You should come." During the concert, making small talk, Teresa says to Jennifer, "My ex, Amy . . ." Later, Jennifer says to Teresa, "My ex, Ann . . ."

As she says this, she notices surprise in Teresa's eyes.

The concert ends, they say good night, and then a weekend intervenes. Jennifer thinks about her the whole time. The next Tuesday is July 31, 2007, the day they'll come to consider their anniversary. Walking by Teresa's office at the end of the day, Jennifer notices Teresa looks upset. She asks her if she's okay, and Teresa replies, "Do you want to get a drink or something?"

They head across the street to a hotel with an outdoor bar on the third floor, a kind of tree-house platform amid skyscrapers, and sit there for about three hours, Teresa talking about the difficulties she's been having with her ex, whom she's still untangling from after their breakup, Jennifer listening. After a time, Jennifer tells Teresa, "I feel like you have a choice now. You can keep wanting something from her that you'll never get, or you can release her. And release yourself."

Teresa has a gift certificate with her for a coffee shop on Capitol Hill, once auto row and now Seattle's gay neighborhood. "I'll drive," Jennifer says. It's evening, but Teresa isn't one to stop drinking coffee just because it's evening. They walk around, talking for what seems like hours more, commonalities pulling, silent cautions nagging, "and then I drive her back to her car," Jennifer says. "One of the very last things she told me as we're driving into the parking lot was 'Oh yeah, I'm a Republican, and I voted for George Bush in the last two elections.'" She tells Jennifer about the DUI she got a couple years back, too, which is typical Teresa, getting everything on the table at once. Jennifer takes it all as a sign that Teresa feels safe with her. She pulls up next to Teresa's car. She parks. They keep talking. And then Teresa says, "I really want to kiss you."

Jennifer wants to kiss her, too. "Probably did the entire night," Jennifer says. "I mean, I found her to be stunning in every way. In this crazy way." She's already picked up on a dichotomy in Teresa, and she likes it: the core firmness, the strong sense of right and wrong and family and how, at the same time, "she was kind of a mess." But the firmness, the rootedness, was clear. "The rest of her could be a mess because of that," Jennifer says. "And I think that's what I found to be so beautiful, is that she could laugh, and cry, and clap, and giggle, and be crazy, or be sweet, in all of these ways, yet there was this, like, line, this really clean, firm— almost like a tree trunk. Of course we kissed. And it was awesome. And we sat in the car, in the parking lot, for probably like an hour and a half. I remember, it was different than anything I had ever felt. I felt at home."

16

A t the end of the next workday, Teresa finds Jennifer, says, "Where do we have to go so that I can kiss you again?"

They go to South Park, to Teresa's house, which she shows off with that line, "I know it's not much, but it's mine." Jennifer has never been to the neighborhood before, even though she's spent most of her life in Seattle. Didn't even know it existed, which is not uncommon in this city, where the major thruways have been constructed in a manner that reinforces the idea of South Park as a place to drive past, not through. She notices the rows of small, single-family houses and assumes from their 1930s architecture that early Boeing workers once lived in them. This is true. She thinks of her father's father, the one she saw occasionally in summers growing up, the one who'd taught her to fish. He was a career pattern maker for Boeing, outlining, for mass production, the parts that made the planes. She imagines South Park back then as "this very middle-class, American-dream neighborhood, where people owned their homes, and drove to work, and took care of each other." This is also true. People back then drove across the steel-beamed South Park Bridge to Boeing Plant 2, where the B-17s were made, past checkpoints when fears were high, to a workplace protected from possible enemy bomber strikes by an entire fake neighborhood constructed atop the plant's roof as camouflage. In a fake pasture in this fake neighborhood, a fake cow was said to roam.

The South Park that Teresa lives in is still the same in many respects, except Plant 2 is soon to be razed for environmental remediation, the racial makeup of the neighborhood is now less monochrome, and due to stagnant wages and rising home prices the middle class is now insecure and in decline. Jennifer meets Teresa's two cats, Carter and Nixon. ("She wanted a well-balanced household," Jennifer says.) She hears how much Teresa loves her neighbors, and meets them, too. She passes Teresa's tests. "Does it bother you when I chew gum?" "Do you hate these pants?" Teresa is conducting an extended experiment, and what she appears to want to know, bottom line, is whether Jennifer will accept her for who she is, or whether she'll demand a lot of changes. "I took it lightly," Jennifer says. "I remember saying to her, 'It's kind of an as-is sale, Teresa.'"

Teresa doesn't want to be physical right away, tells Jennifer it's because she did that in previous relationships that didn't work out. This is fine with Jennifer. "So we waited," she says. Each weekend they spend together, they become closer, and during the week, when Jennifer stays with her grandmother to help keep an eye on her, excitement builds for the next Friday night, when she'll be back in the red house with Teresa. Feeling safer and bolder, Jennifer comes out to her grandmother again, this time with less concern about the reaction. Again, her grandmother is upset. "That's really sad," Jennifer tells her. "If we're not going to have a very close relationship, it makes me sad. But I still love you." She isn't negotiating on this one.

The new couple learn each other's rhythms. The way Teresa can be a little short with Jennifer in the morning. The way Jennifer, an only child, is accustomed to moving through home life in a more self-contained manner. When she gets up from the couch to grab a glass of water, for example, she doesn't automatically ask if anyone else wants one, while Teresa, one of eleven kids, retains the reflexes of a member of a pack. She also retains her strident and confrontational side, which has its problems and also its highs, as when, one day at work, Teresa notices her purse has been stolen from her desk and figures out the thieves are probably a couple of strangers who've just been wandering through the hallways on the twenty-second floor of the City Centre building. Teresa calls her credit card company to see where the most recent transaction was, races over to the nearby mall where it occurred, finds the thieves, and with a security guard chases them through the mall shouting "Citizen's arrest!"

The two of them sit on the couch and watch movies and eat kettle corn with Milk Duds melted into it by the microwave, Teresa's favorite. They head to Teresa's church on many Sundays. It's important to Teresa, and Jennifer comes to enjoy the services. She has been to church before, with Ann, and is still eclectic and ecumenical when it comes to spirituality. They begin doing service work together, volunteering for the Juvenile Diabetes Research Foundation, joining the board of a homeless advocacy organization.

They break up, for a brief moment at the seven-month mark, over the question of whether Teresa loves Jennifer. "Love" is a word Teresa doesn't use lightly in her most serious relationships. She ends phone calls with friends saying, "Love ya, mean it," but with someone like Jennifer she wants to be deliberate. Paradoxically, she also wants to be spontaneous. What she means, it seems, is that it should feel exactly right, never forced, never casual.

Jennifer already knows she's in love with Teresa, is ready to use the word heavily, regularly, and finds it too painful to think the same might not become true for Teresa. There's a concert they've long been planning to attend, and after the breakup they still go but don't sit together. Instead, Jennifer spends the concert watching Teresa from a distance, and as Teresa does her thing—the clapping, the laughing—Jennifer feels herself crying.

Later that night, Teresa gets in touch. "Just come over," she says. Jennifer doesn't think it a good idea. She asks if Teresa can ever love her. Teresa's response: "I already do." After that, it's like a whole new relationship.

Things begin moving fast. Three months later, the two of them are at Wildrose on Gay Pride weekend. It's now coming up on a year since that first kiss in the parking lot, and in an outdoor beer garden set up to handle the crush of Pride weekend visitors, in front of Teresa, another woman tells Jennifer she looks adorable. When the woman leaves, Teresa says, "I'm gonna have to get you off the market, aren't I?"

"Well, yeah!" Jennifer says.

"Okay. When?"

"And we just kind of dealt with it that night," Jennifer says. "I don't think we talked to anyone about it. We just had a good night." Same-sex marriage is still illegal in Washington State, so technically what they're planning will be a commitment ceremony, but to Teresa and Jennifer it's a wedding. They tell their friends. A date is set for just over a year out: September 12, 2009.

Not all the Butzes are willing to attend, Norbert senior chief among the resisters. "In my heart of souls, I would not have attended that wedding," he says. "I believe that God put male and female together. It goes back to the beginning of time." He has internal negotiations about it, though. He thinks he might come to Seattle to support Teresa and Jennifer but skip the ceremony. He wonders whether, once in Seattle, he might take one more step and show up. He recalls the character Tevye in *Fiddler on the Roof*, who, upon seeing his daughters heading toward marriages he doesn't support, says, in Norbert senior's paraphrasing, "If I give you the blessing, I have to bend, and if I bend anymore, I'll break." Dolly, after her own internal negotiations, decides she will come to Seattle that weekend. "I thought, 'This is a big occasion for her,'" Dolly says. "There is no way I could not be there with her." Whether or not Dolly will be at the ceremony, she doesn't know.

One Butz certain to attend is Norbert Leo Butz. Conveniently, as the date nears, he's already in Seattle, playing a leading role as an obsessed, determined FBI agent in the out-of-town preview of *Catch Me If You Can*, a show that is eventually headed to Broadway. That summer of 2009, Norbert says, "I spent a lot of time with Terese." Which means spending a lot of time fending off her many suggestions for fun to be had.

"It would be like a Tuesday night," Norbert says, "I would have been rehearsing all day, it'd be ten o' clock, she'd be like, 'Yo. There's a band you gotta go check out with me.'

"I'm like, 'Teresa, I'm exhausted.'

"'Screw that. What time you gotta be up tomorrow?'

"'I gotta be up at 8:00.'

"'I gotta be up at 6:30. I'm coming to get you in fifteen minutes.'

"'Do not come get me in fifteen minutes. I have to sleep.'

"'Okay.'

"The next night: 'There is a softball game that you have to come to, and after that there is a karaoke session at this bar. You have to come. You have to come. I can't—you have to come. I'm coming to pick you up.'

"I saw her more in the four weeks before she died than I'd seen her in ten years."

She tells Norbert about Jennifer. He talks to her about his struggles raising his daughters. She listens, reassures him. One night, Teresa tells Norbert he has to come see Jennifer sing in a small competition at a club, and Norbert, who has been listening to Teresa go on about her girlfriend's voice all summer, thinks to himself, "Yeah, I'll go humor you, I'll go humor you. Show up and see this little amateur competition." He stands in the back of the club, near the bar, watching. "She takes the stage," Norbert says, "and she busts into a version of 'Feel Like a Natural Woman,' and I went, 'Holy shit.' Teresa actually—she underplayed how Jen can sing." Jennifer remembers Norbert walking slowly from the back of the room to the front and, when she was finished singing, his clapping, his beaming.

———

On Sunday, July 19, 2009, Teresa is supposed to meet Norbert at his place near the 5th Avenue Theatre so they can go to church together. She doesn't show. "Then the phone started ringing a lot," Norbert says.

His brother Tony reaches him. "He said, 'Meet me downstairs.' And then he told me on the street there, in front of the hotel."

The preview is suspended for two weeks. "We got her home to St. Louis," Norbert says. "And we buried her."

Capture

17

Nine o'clock on a Friday morning, summer of 2009, a police manhunt under way, and in the suburbs south of Seattle a public bus rolling past a strip mall, through a neighborhood of low houses, up a steep hill. On one side of this hill, the rocky banks of Puget Sound. On the other, the muddy banks of the Green River, tributary of the Duwamish. At one time, almost everything that can be seen from this bus route sat beneath thousands of feet of ice: the suburbs, the city, the sound, the river valleys draining the Cascade Mountains. The ice advanced, weighing on the land, sinking it hundreds of feet, wrapping itself around surface rocks of all compositions. Created in obscurity, the rocks now faced an altering in obscurity. The ice retreated and, as it did, revealed which of them remained unchanged by the pressure, the scraping, the gouging, the attachment, the cracking, the melting. Not many.

A man boarded this bus wearing a green jacket and dirty jeans. The bus continued toward the top of the hill, which is wide and runs from south to north, as most large features in the area do, because the last glacier to leave pulled south to north as it retreated. The driver of the bus recognized this man, believed he was the same one who'd refused to pay a fare in a past still present in the driver's mind. The man had a pit bull with him, brought the animal on the bus, and let it stretch out on the seats next to him. The driver asked the man to get his pit bull off the seats, and the man, Isaiah Kalebu, twenty-three years old, told the driver to shut up and keep driving. Passengers began yelling at Isaiah, telling him to put his dog on the floor. Isaiah told them to shut up, too. Everyone needed to leave him alone.

The son of an immigrant, Isaiah now began berating the driver for being an immigrant. He moved toward the front of the bus, stood over the driver, told him, "You are a fucking servant." Told him, "If you don't learn how it works here, you should go back to Mexico." Soon the passengers who had been yelling at Isaiah changed course, and a pattern that had been repeating itself for the last two years repeated itself one last time. People within range of Isaiah's fury became alarmed, including the bus driver, who hit an emergency alert button several times and then pulled the bus over. People separated themselves from Isaiah, most of the passengers fleeing out the bus doors. The difficult, threatening person was left behind, isolated, and then the police arrived. They talked to Isaiah, found no cause to detain him within the letter of the law, and sent him on his way.

18

As funeral preparations were being made in St. Louis, Detective Duffy and her partner, the improbably named David Duty, narrowed on a single suspect. Local television had been describing the crime as one of the worst authorities could remember, and Detective Duffy had found herself chasing leads, and hoping for a break, with unusual intensity. "What he did to them made me want to find him," she said. It seemed clear to her, from interviews with Jennifer and from the evidence, that the crime was motivated not by the women's sexual orientation but by their gender. She worried he might do it again. She worried he might simply disappear. "A lot of people get away with a lot of shit," Detective Duffy said.

A sketch artist had been sent to see Jennifer first thing and had produced an image that led to many tips. None led anywhere. Scores of on-file prints were run against prints found inside the red house. None of them matched. Video was collected from stores and gas stations in the area, and Detective Duty wandered the homeless encampments around South Park, including one self-governing camp calling itself Nickelsville, the name intended to remind Seattle's mayor at the time, Greg Nickels, that he was presiding over a period of vivid inequity, similar to the time when Hoovervilles lined the city's southern edge. At Nickelsville, Detective Duty learned that a man roughly matching the police sketch had been denied entrance the night of the attacks, for "obnoxious behavior and no current identification." It was interesting, but it didn't give Detective

Duty a suspect he could lay hands on. A meeting was held at the South Park Community Center to try to calm neighborhood residents, whose windows, even amid the string of exceptionally warm nights, were now uniformly shut. "All of them were open before this," said Judy Mills, fifty, who'd been in South Park for fifteen years. She lived alone and was presently sleeping between two golf clubs and two guns.

The break came on a Thursday, the day before Teresa was buried and four days after the attacks, when Detective Duffy received a call from the state crime lab. A woman on the other end of the line told her DNA from the South Park crime scene matched DNA collected just over a year earlier as part of an unsolved break-in investigation in Auburn, a suburb in a valley southeast of Seattle. There was a surveillance video associated with that crime. Detective Duffy drove straight down to Auburn to have a look.

The video had been sitting in a police evidence locker since the break-in occurred, and it showed images of an unknown man wandering around the service entrance to the Auburn City Hall on the evening of March 20, 2008, looking for a door that might open, finding one, breaking in, and then leaving within a few minutes, empty-handed, his pit bull in tow. An officer just three months out of the police academy had investigated and did a rather thorough job considering nothing was stolen and little damage was caused. He even went so far as to send traces of blood left on a broken lockbox to the state crime lab. At the time, they'd produced no DNA matches, and no other fruitful leads emerged, so the surveillance video was stored away and the DNA sample kept on file, just in case.

Detective Duffy drove back to Seattle and had the video prepped for release. It went to officers in a special bulletin. Then, on Friday morning, as Teresa was being buried, and not long after the bus rolling through the suburbs south of Seattle had made its emergency stop, the video was released to the public. Seattle's television stations put it on the noon news; blogs and newspaper Web sites kept it up all day. Within a couple hours, the police received a call from Isaiah's mother. "That's my boy on the video," she told Detective Duty. "Don't shoot him." Detective Duty asked the woman if she was sure, and she replied, "Mister, I know my own boy. And I recognize his dog." She didn't know where either of them might be.

Another call came in from a police officer who'd responded, earlier that morning, to the emergency alert from the public bus rolling up the hill south of Seattle. He recognized the man in the video as the same unruly passenger he'd detained and then released. The police soon broadcast an alert to all public bus drivers in King County, and within a few hours James Gayden radioed from a route he was driving and said, "I think the guy you're looking for just got off my bus." He'd been a driver for about seven years and on that day was assigned to drive the 74 Express, which originates in downtown Seattle and heads northward toward Magnuson Park, a small peninsula jutting like a bent thumb into Lake Washington. The park is 350 acres, home to a large off-leash dog area and plenty of places where a person can rest comfortably in warm weather, unnoticed.

The man who'd just gotten off Gayden's bus had on a winter jacket and long pants, which was odd because the temperature that day was in the nineties. He was unkempt and tired looking, too, and so stood out from the students and downtown professionals who normally ride the route. As he exited, his odor caused Gayden to recall working night-owl shifts. "I picked up a lot of homeless people," he said. "And it's just a certain smell you get from people who haven't bathed in a while." The man didn't pay, telling Gayden, "I don't have any bus fare."

The police swarmed the area. Officer Leon Towne, who happened to be inside Magnuson Park when the call went out, spotted Isaiah first. "I stepped out of my car," Towne said. "I stayed right next to it, and as he gets close enough, I address him. I advised him to secure his dog to a fence—a post that he was next to at that point—and he did. He continued to approach the car. He came right up to the front of the hood." At that point, Towne's backup arrived.

Towne asked Isaiah for identification. Isaiah said he didn't have any. Towne put Isaiah in the back of his patrol car and took him straight downtown, to Detectives Duffy and Duty, and as he drove, he, too, noticed the odor. "Like he had been living on the streets for a while," Towne said. As he sat in the interview room, Detective Duffy watched Isaiah on closed-circuit video. He appeared calm, though at one point he bit his nails, which she interpreted as a sign of anxiety. "I got him some water," she said. "I think he said, 'Thank you.' Very respectful." He asked her, "Hey, can I take my socks off?" He said, "Sorry I smell."

Detective Duffy has a dead-level gaze, a slight rasp to her voice, and a confidence honed in interviews with suspects of all kinds over the years. She also has what she calls "the gift of gab," and she led with this. Sensing that Isaiah had a soft spot for his pit bull, she started talking to him about her Rottweiler, Tug, who'd just passed away. Isaiah didn't take the bait. "He just point-blank said, 'I'm not into this conversation.'" He asked for a lawyer.

They made him change into a jail uniform, took pictures of his clothes, noticed bloodstains on them, and also noticed he wasn't wearing any underwear. This provoked in Detective Duffy a euphoric feeling of things clicking into place. A pair of men's boxers had been found at the red house, and she'd thought them an important enough lead to get in touch with Jennifer, even though she was in St. Louis for the funeral. "I hated to interrupt," Detective Duffy said, "but this was so important." She'd sent a picture over e-mail, and Jennifer had confirmed: the boxers weren't theirs. The man who attacked them must have worn them and then left without them.

"We knew we had the guy," Detective Duffy said. Isaiah looked like the man in the video from the old Auburn case, and he matched Jennifer's description of the man who attacked them. There would be fingerprint and footprint evidence to explore further. With Detective Duty, she took Isaiah to Harborview for a court-ordered blood draw so that his DNA could be definitively connected to the crime scene, and then they took him to jail. In transit, they asked him what he liked to do for fun. He replied that he liked to read, particularly chemistry and physics books.

19

T he line to view Teresa's coffin stretched down the block, some people waiting quietly for over three hours, many of them never seen by the Butz family before. Strangers had been calling the family home, too. People who'd lost children of their own. People who knew Teresa and wanted to connect. People who simply wanted to offer condolences.

Later, at the funeral service, the ten remaining Butz siblings stood and sang Amy Grant for their sister, all of them back at St. Stephen Protomartyr Catholic Church, the place where Teresa first met Jean and Rachel, both friends now there as well, to say good-bye. Norbert senior and Dolly sat in the pews, and Jennifer sat in the pews, too, held and supported but not spoken of in prayers and eulogies as the woman Teresa had been planning to marry in two months. "It's just not what that was about," Jennifer said. "I know people who were in the seats—that were there from Seattle—they were upset about it. I wasn't upset about it, because part of loving and accepting Teresa was loving and accepting the constraints of her family. And they were good people, and they are good people, and they loved me."

After the funeral was over, Norbert junior said, "I got on a plane." He was headed back to Seattle, to the dark theater, "because there were a lot of people that were relying on me." That, and he needed to give some structure to his day, needed to do something familiar, purposeful. "When your world explodes," Norbert said, "and nothing makes sense, and reality is not real, you do begin to feel like the world is spinning and you're going to be flung off it. I think a human instinct is to do something that feels really natural, and really, really safe, or you feel like you're going to die. You're not going to make it through. You know, people say 'Breathe, take a breath' when someone is in distress. 'Breathe, take a breath.' Well, you know, singing is breath. It's breath. It's taking breath after breath after breath after breath. You can't sing unless there's been a breath taken, and that feels—for me, that was a natural—is a natural way to get back into my body. I have not died. I have not been flung off the face of the earth. The universe is not crashing."

Performing made him feel more sane, and it was not enough. He had a rule about not drinking during shows, and now the rule was suspended. "A bit," he said. "Not a lot. It was just a few shots here and there. And I wasn't sleeping. I didn't sleep for a long, long time. So I got sleep medication. And sleep medication is always enhanced; there's always a little high to get before you fall asleep if you mix it with Ketel One, or Maker's Mark, or something. And so, before I knew it, I had really sort of painted myself into a bad corner."

Jennifer and some of the Butz family went, after the funeral, to Sundecker's, a bar in the old part of town, the part of town you can still get your arms around. Not the sprawling neighborhoods that ring St. Louis and stretch beyond comprehension toward plains stretching beyond comprehension. Not the big, hulking rest of downtown, with its mammoth stone buildings inscribed with ambitious intentions, where the etching on the municipal auditorium declares, "A temple on whose altar is everglowing the flame at which patriotism may be rekindled," and where "To our soldier dead" is engraved atop a giant memorial commissioned as a necessary reminder at the close of World War I and then finished, on the eve of World War II, as B-17s were already rolling off the Duwamish assembly line.

This bar in the old part of town was a favorite place for Teresa, tucked in a two-story brick building just below the Martin Luther King Bridge, where a neon Budweiser sign sits above the front door, an old-school sign bearing the Anheuser-Busch logo from back before the company sold out and Teresa took—and then let go of—great umbrage. The Budweiser comes in bottles, six for the price of five if you buy the metal bucket full of them, and the claim to culinary fame is humble: great, house-made ranch dressing. The view from the wooden deck out back is of railway tracks and the Mississippi River and, on the other side of the river, power lines and grain silos. On the Sundecker's side, ivy grows up the iron Martin Luther King Bridge supports, and the bridge rattles as cars and trucks race over, and classic rock rattles out of the Sundecker's speakers. On the afternoon of Friday, July 24, 2009, Jennifer was there, seated at a big table of family and friends. "I remember we laughed more than we cried," she said. "And that was good." Her cell phone rang, unnoticed, and went to voice mail. It was Detective Duffy, who'd been the one to go back inside the red house and gather Teresa's wedding dress and wedding ring for Jennifer and who now had a message she'd been itching to leave. "I can't tell you that feeling," Detective Duffy said. "That's why I do this job."

Later, Jennifer checked messages. "And I got up," Jennifer said, "and I hear her voice on the phone, and she says, 'We have him.'"

Jennifer told the people at Sundecker's.

"Joy," she said. "People were just so happy."

She watched, took in the scene.

"It was a good moment," she said. "Because I knew I could go back home."

Two weeks later, Isaiah pleaded not guilty and was held, pending trial, on $10 million bail. A month after that, on September 12, 2009, the day Teresa and Jennifer were to be married, another memorial. This one was private, in Seattle, at the venue the couple had booked for their wedding, the Tyee Yacht Club on Lake Union, a place where Teresa once worked as a caterer and where Carley and Carmen had shown up some evenings to help her clean so they could all go out and party sooner.

The centerpieces on the tables would have worked for a wedding but now did a different duty, treelike metal stands holding photographs of Jennifer and Teresa together, smiling hugely, arms around each other. Sun poured through the windows as it set over the hills of the city and, beyond the hills, to the west, the Olympic Mountains. People milled about with bottles of Bud. A friend shot video. Expressions were pained, dazed, angry, unsure of how to be, and the same range of emotions crossed Jennifer's face as she helped with final preparations. A breeze billowed curtains that had been pulled aside. A guitar strummed, warming up. Sunflowers sat in glass vases. This was to be a celebration and a farewell. Jennifer's mother was there, along with her grandmother, now ninety-three. So were Jean and Rachel. Jennifer's vocal jazz teacher from Roosevelt High School, Susan Bardsley, came too, but left after about forty-five minutes. "It was too painful," she said.

Teresa's pastor spoke, acknowledging at the start a room filled with questions. He asked that the evening become "a fun and holy journey of remembrance, and gratefulness, and thankfulness, and celebration." A gospel choir had been invited, the Total Experience Gospel Choir, the best-known choir in Seattle. They sang about sharing the weight of a burden, and then Pastor Patrinell Wright, the choir leader, told the people at the memorial, "I know more than most of you think I know about this whole situation."

People laughed at first, not knowing what she meant, not knowing how to react. "Because," Pastor Wright continued, "we had already experienced this. My friend, in Tacoma, was one of the victims too."

Ten days before Teresa and Jennifer were attacked, Isaiah's aunt, Rachel Kalebu, died in an arson at her home near Tacoma, just south of Seattle.

Also killed in the fire: J. J. Jones, a former quarterback for the New York Jets who had fallen on hard times, lost his home in foreclosure, moved to the Pacific Northwest, and then moved in with Rachel to help her care for two sick and elderly family members. "That's the type of person she was," Jones's son told detectives. "She cared for those that somebody may not wanna care for." After the elderly relatives had passed away, JJ stayed on, living in Rachel's basement as a boarder. Detectives didn't have conclusive evidence, but they now suspected Isaiah in the deaths of Rachel and JJ, too, all of it suggesting a terrible, unchecked deterioration in a young man who'd never before been convicted of a felony.

"So," Pastor Wright said, "we're all in this together. But we shall overcome together . . . So we're just gonna turn the Tyee Yacht Club into a synagogue, sanctuary, church—" She was interrupted by cheers. The choir jumped back into a song.

Tony Butz stood next, one of only two of Teresa's siblings who had chosen to attend. Norbert Leo Butz was the other. Dolly and Norbert senior did not come to this memorial. "To know my sister is to know that she was born in 1969," Tony began, and then he told an abbreviated version of her childhood. Her nicknames. The scissors she took to her already-boyish hair. Next, Rachel rose and spoke directly to Teresa about how she was going to miss her. The outfielders backing up when Teresa got up to bat. How inside she was all goo. How this day had been circled on Rachel's calendar for some time, and inside the circle the words "Butz Getting Hitched." Jean talked about "Teree." Her swagger. Her laugh. Her clap. The way her heart seemed "a little homeless" before she met Jennifer, and how, after she met Jennifer, "everything was different, Teresa was different . . . I heard in her a hard-won sense of finally being worthy of receiving love."

Norbert Leo Butz stood, guitar strapped to shoulder, and as he strummed talked about how he and Tony were "the lone representatives of the Butz family," how he was struggling to keep it together. With Jennifer backing him up, they sang a favorite song of Teresa's, about the crooked road to love. Then, because it came to him, Norbert sang another one, "It's a Hard Life Wherever You Go," by the folksinger Nanci Griffith. "Teresa always loved this song," Norbert said. "And I didn't know that I was going to sing this, but I just feel like I want to. So here goes."

The song is a tour of intergenerational violence, learned hatreds, limited possibilities. In Belfast. In Chicago. In the writer's own soul and psyche. Norbert sang it steely, angrily, sorrowfully, clear. "If we poison our children with hatred, then the hard life is all that they'll know."

Jenni Butz, Tony's wife, talked about how into dreams Teresa had been. How she once asked, "What does it mean when your father turns into a braunschweiger and you bury him on the beach?" How she bought Teresa a dream interpretation book to help. Carley read from the letter Teresa sent her from her trip across the country, and then a blind woman who worked in the same building as Teresa talked about their friendship, built partly around love of rival baseball teams.

A player from Teresa's softball team talked about the game they'd played in Teresa's honor after she died. "We got ten-runned and the game ended early, so, you know, we didn't win that night," she said. "But it wasn't the end of the season. A couple weeks later, we actually had our softball tournament, and goddamn it"—and here she appeared to give a glance, concerned and then instantly unconcerned, at the pastor—"we won the whole thing." The win was for Teresa. They established an award in her honor. "It's a little, tiny league," the woman said, "but it's our league."

Jennifer sang "Heavenly Day" by Patty Griffin, the song she and Teresa realized they both loved before they realized much else. As she sang, scars were clear on her neck, raised red welts still healing. Then Jennifer said she wanted to speak to Teresa. She thanked her. She was supposed to be doing vows with her on this day, Teresa standing there in the simple, lace-edged, cream-colored dress she'd bought on sale for $70, including tax. In Teresa's ears would have been two pearl drop earrings the couple had been given for free when, after finding the dress, they'd wandered through the jewelry store where Jennifer's grandfather once worked. "I can't let the fiancée of Sid Leavitt's granddaughter walk out of here without something," a salesperson told them. Back at the red house, Teresa had worn the earrings with shorts and a T-shirt, flipping them around, admiring them in a mirror.

Jennifer offered a new vow. "I promise to live," she said, and people stood, cried, cheered. "I promise to love. I promise to give. I promise to laugh. I promise to sing. I promise to dream. And I promise to forgive. Teresa Butz, you were the best thing that ever, ever happened to me. And you once told me that you were lovable but you were leavable. And so I want you to look around this room right now. We will never leave you. None of us."

She then told two stories about Teresa. One was from two months before Teresa was killed. In a dream, Jennifer saw Teresa wearing a little black cocktail dress with sequins on top, along with a pair of three-inch heels that she could somehow dance in all night. Teresa was on a stage, holding a microphone and singing—which was not her usual, the singing—and then she began dancing, mostly with her shoulders, a move Jennifer used to tease her about. She was swinging the microphone from its cord while she danced, and Jennifer woke up laughing and told Teresa the dream. "Oh, I love that," Teresa said. "I am gonna do that. I am gonna swing that microphone." Jennifer loved this response.

The other story was from about two weeks before Teresa was killed. Jennifer got a call from Teresa, who wanted to know, "Where are you?" There was a mouse in the house on Rose Street, and Teresa was terrified. Jennifer was at her grandmother's, but she came right over. With Teresa standing on the couch, and later atop the coffee table, Jennifer chased the mouse around and finally caught it in a Tupperware container. "Jen, what are you gonna do?" Teresa asked. "Are you gonna kill it?" Jennifer said, "It breathes, can't kill it, so we're gonna get it outside." Together, they slid a piece of wood under the overturned Tupperware, carried the animal out of the house, took it some distance away, let it go, and then went back inside, where Teresa said to her, "Jen, you're the bravest person I know."

"I might have been able to save her from a little mouse," Jennifer told the people at the memorial. "But I am standing here today because of bravery that I can't even describe to you, and I will forever be grateful. Teresa Butz, you are the bravest person I know."

20

L ater, Teresa's pastor announced, "We've got the holiest of all music coming up, '80s and '90s!" Soon there would be dancing. But before the dancing, a prayer.

In the prayer, in passing, Teresa's pastor mentioned evil. That evil happens, and when it does, it mars beauty.

It was, in a way, the continuation of a discussion begun many weeks before that night, when Jennifer had gone for a walk with him along Alki Beach, not far from a brunch place Teresa loved, not far from where the Duwamish enters Elliott Bay.

Teresa's death was even more recent then, and Jennifer had asked the pastor searching, basic questions. She wondered, "Why do these things happen?"

Just asking that particular question was a new step for her. "It was my first conversation where I started to talk about some of the empathy I had for Kalebu," Jennifer said.

She wasn't so interested in answers that involved evil or original sin.

What she wanted to know was this: "What happened to him? How does somebody become this guy?"

Isaiah

21

I saiah Kalebu, before he became much of anything at all, experienced a mother, a father, and the rhythms of the family they created. Beyond that close periphery, other forces nudging each of them in turn.

The father fled to Seattle in 1980, escaping civil war in the Republic of Uganda, a country not two decades out of colonial rule. He was twenty-three years old, adventurous and ambitious, and he rarely talked about the brutality he'd witnessed. When he did, he confided this: his own father had been shot dead, in front of him, by agents of the Idi Amin regime, and some of his family members raped as part of a campaign of violence that took the lives of hundreds of thousands of Ugandans.

At a summer party in 1984, this man met a woman who was, like him, pressing on. The woman was a child of rape. She was African American. When she was three years old, a court took her from her mother's home in Washington State, and within a few years she found herself in a foster home in Oregon. She reported being beaten there with extension cords and pots. When she was thirteen, an aunt found her. "Explained who I was," the woman said, "and who she was, and how I got put into foster care and stuff." The woman was returned to her mother's house, where her mother pretended she was still an infant, bathing her, rocking her, wanting to sleep with her at night. She left as quickly as she could. At sixteen, the woman was pregnant with her first child. At twenty, she was at the summer party in Seattle, where she met the man from Uganda.

He was twenty-seven and seemed to her to be "very quiet, nice, serious, educated, and going places." By winter, she was pregnant with his child. Their son, Isaiah Kalebu, was born the first day of August in 1985.

Isaiah behaved like an ordinary baby. He seemed happy and energetic, and records reflect a pregnancy and delivery that were, in the words of one examiner, "uneventful."

His family of origin, as reports later called it, proved challenging. Isaiah's father was not around for much of his infancy, having departed for California, where he was studying to be an electrical engineer, aiming to become a high-achieving professional like others in his family who had sought refuge in the United States. He did not expect visits from his newborn son or from his newborn son's mother—this was not the arrangement. He visited them when he was back in Seattle on breaks from engineering school.

As a consequence, until he was six, Isaiah rarely saw his father and was effectively raised by a single mother who already had a daughter from her earlier pregnancy. The daughter, Deborah, was five years older than Isaiah, and Deborah's father, too, was absent. The three of them lived— mother, daughter, son—in a series of small apartments in North Seattle, supported by work Isaiah's mother found as a teacher's aide and by help from Isaiah's father when it came. One of the last North Seattle apartments they inhabited was on a quiet street lined with trees and Craftsman homes. The street slopes gently toward a public high school, a public pool, and a public ball field where, on a clear day, there is a direct view of the volcanic peak of Mount Rainier, framed by two of Seattle's major hills, each sloping toward the other, overlapping in the flattening of distance.

When Isaiah was two months old, he was brought to the emergency room at Children's Hospital in North Seattle with what was determined to be a "superficial burn" near one of his eyes. "I was smoking a cigarette," his mother told me, "and I picked him up, and I had the cigarette in my mouth and I burnt him on his eye—on the corner of his eye. And they thought it was child abuse. But they found out that it was just a mere accident." This is how the state came to have its first direct intervention in Isaiah's life, at age two months. After an investigation, the State of Washington declared "patterns of parental supervision adequate" in Isaiah's household. The case was closed.

When Isaiah was about three months old, his mother was called to identify the body of her own mother, whom she hadn't seen in a long time. "She was going through her schizophrenia," Isaiah's mother said. The body floated in the frigid salt waters of the Salish Sea, at the current-swirled juncture where Puget Sound becomes the Strait of Juan de Fuca and then the Pacific. Eventually, the body washed up on San Juan Island, a short distance from Canada's Vancouver Island, in "an unrecognizable condition," according to records, and was buried in "a pauper's grave."

Isaiah's mother believes a significant number of her maternal relatives lived with serious mental disorders. Her family tree is "replete with mental illness for at least four generations," court records say, and she herself has endured chronic depression.

In 1987, when Isaiah was eighteen months old, his mother attempted suicide and was hospitalized. While she was recovering, Isaiah was taken in by his father's sister, Rachel Kalebu, who lived to the south of the city. Isaiah's half sister, Deborah, was taken in, too. Later, a report on Isaiah's childhood would be ordered by a court, and it would say of this early episode of trauma and dislocation for Isaiah and Deborah, "It is not clear that anyone noticed what either child felt, or if there were any changes in their behavior."

Over the next two years, the young Isaiah, described in court records as "a sweet, thoughtful, and loving child," was in the emergency room frequently, often for ear infections. He had surgery on his tonsils and adenoids. Tubes were placed in his ears. He and Deborah returned to living with their mother after she returned from her hospitalization, and Isaiah's father continued his occasional visits. By 1990, when Isaiah was five, his mother was pregnant again. That same year, Isaiah began kindergarten at a public school near the apartment.

When he was in first grade, his mother gave birth to her second daughter. Around the same time, Isaiah's father, recently graduated from engineering school, began living with them. "Suddenly, in a matter of months, an infant and the father entered the family," says the report on Isaiah's childhood. It then repeated a refrain that runs through its findings: "There is no record or information by either parent as to how Isaiah reacted to any of these major events."

The report was written by Dr. Maria Lymberis, a psychoanalyst and forensic psychiatrist who teaches at the University of California, Los Angeles. She is a busy woman who, in her mid-seventies, still attends spin class four days a week and sees patients. Dr. Lymberis spins in part because, as she put it in her thick Greek accent, "modern science has proven there are only two ways to help neuronal regeneration. Your brain will produce new neurons if you learn new things, and if you do aerobic exercise." She does both, in large quantities.

One result is her work in forensic psychiatry, which she became interested in through years of conducting investigations into psychiatrist-patient relationships gone wrong. In 2011, two decades after the five-year-old Isaiah started elementary school, Dr. Lymberis, in part because of her forensic experience, was hired by a Seattle court. Her task was to help determine whether any "mitigating" factors warranted authorities seeking life in prison for Isaiah, rather than the death penalty, as punishment for what he'd allegedly become, and done, as an adult.

———————

Dr. Lymberis scoured hospital, school, court, employment, and police records totaling thousands of pages. Many of these records are available to the public. Some of them are not. She read transcripts of interviews with Isaiah and his family of origin. She conducted her own interviews with his mother, father, and half sister, Deborah. What she found in Isaiah's family was an environment that grew increasingly dysfunctional as he aged. His mother's depression was "highly stigmatized" by his father, Dr. Lymberis wrote, and the developmental needs of the children were not effectively engaged by either parent, in part because both parents had "their own deficits in emotional self-regulation."

Both parents have said trouble grew out of the collision of cultures from which Isaiah and his siblings were born: a refugee from Uganda trying to co-parent with a woman raised, in hard conditions, in the United States. "For their culture," Dr. Lymberis wrote of Isaiah's father and his family, "the task was survival by will power and hard work, and the goal was to successfully meet expectations for social success." If a child was suffering, her findings and other court records suggest, Isaiah's father believed it the child's responsibility to become tougher. If a child was seen to be misbehaving, the punishment, from Isaiah's father, was corporal. If Isaiah's mother objected, as she often did, she too could be subject to violence from the father.

What exactly traces to culture and what to character is impossible to untangle. Isaiah's father talked to Dr. Lymberis about his relationship with his son, but he refused to talk to the Seattle police ("Wouldn't have anything to do with us," Detective Duffy said) and was not seen at his son's trial. He never responded to attempts at contact for this book. Still, this much is known: plenty of cross-cultural relationships present challenges, as do relationships of all sorts, and not all cross-cultural relationships produce the particular dysfunction of Isaiah's family.

As Dr. Lymberis explored this particular dysfunction, she connected many of Isaiah's parents' issues to their unique needs, which left them with limited space for focus on other things. "Such limitations," she wrote, "proved to be malignant for the psychological development of Isaiah, who was already psychologically very vulnerable." He had been born to survivors of extreme adversity. They did not prove to be safe harbors for each other. As a consequence, he grew up amid his own extreme adversity.

When Isaiah's parents were married, in September 1992, Isaiah was seven years old, a voracious reader who enjoyed riding bikes and playing video games. His older half sister, Deborah, was twelve. At his parents' ceremony, Isaiah was the ring bearer. Deborah cried, she reported, "because I knew it wasn't going to work out. I had a bad feeling."

This was not without cause. Four months earlier, Isaiah's father had been arrested by the Seattle police, late on a Friday night, for domestic assault. Such arrests are today described as "murder prevention" in Seattle law enforcement circles, and generally this is meant to refer to the fact that domestic abusers, left unchecked, can end up killing their spouses. The phrase can be heard another way as well. Witnessing parental abuse and experiencing unchecked child abuse are both common experiences among people who, as adults, visit violence upon others.

It was Isaiah's mother who had summoned the police in this instance. A few days afterward, she appeared in court and declined to pursue a no-contact order against Isaiah's father. Not long after that, assault charges against him were dismissed. But two decades later, Isaiah's mother described the incident to a social worker, who wrote, "She got in-between the father and their son, Isaiah (then 7), because the father was trying to spank him with a stick. She states that Isaiah was just a little boy. The mother relates that she confronted the father at this time about hitting her daughter, Deborah, and told him never to do that again."

When this same social worker spoke to Isaiah's father, he confirmed the basic facts of the 1992 incident and expanded on his motivation. "He states that Isaiah 'had bad manners,'" the social worker wrote, "and he wanted to 'spank him with a stick.' The mother interfered with the father, and a fight ensued. The father states, 'We got into a shoving match.'"

In the police report for the incident, Isaiah's mother is described as having a bump on the back of her head. It was caused, she told the police, when Isaiah's father pushed her and, falling, she hit her head on a door latch. It also describes Deborah saying she was pushed down by Isaiah's father. Both mother and daughter declined medical attention. Isaiah's father spent one night in jail, then returned home.

Incidents like this are what Dr. Lymberis referred to in her report as "a pattern of chronic, severe marital conflict" in the marriage of Isaiah's parents. "Characteristically," she wrote, the fights revolved around the way Isaiah's father was disciplining Isaiah, "which included using physical beatings with 'broomsticks, belts, and sticks.'" As Deborah put it, "I didn't see a real father-son relationship." As Isaiah's mother put it, "He was rough on the kids . . . As far as dealing with the schools and playing with the kids and stuff, that didn't happen." She complained that her husband spent most of his time working, or fixing cars, and that when home he treated the children, and her, like servants.

Reports of Isaiah's first years in public elementary school show him performing decently, but with two or three weeks of absences each year. After his father returned from California to live with the family, they also note Isaiah becoming "more and more withdrawn, secretive, and noncompliant." Isaiah had to change schools a number of times in the following years as his family moved out of the apartment on the quiet street in North Seattle and into two different suburbs south of the city. Around the same time, his mother had another child with Isaiah's father. It was a boy, and he arrived when Isaiah was eight years old. Then, when Isaiah was ten, his parents purchased a house atop a wide hill called West Seattle, not far from where the hill rises up from South Park.

The house is a modest one-story bungalow with a finished basement, a chimney, and a detached garage, set on a corner of Elmgrove Street, a street that also runs through South Park, two blocks north of South Rose. The hill that holds the home on Elmgrove, as well as the rest of West Seattle, is part of what geologists call a drumlin field. That is, a cluster of rises sculpted by advancing and retreating glaciers during the last ice age. The particular drumlin on which Isaiah now lived is so wide that its best views are not at its top but rather on its steeply sloping sides, and this is also true for a number of the other major hills in Seattle, where one likewise finds modest homes spread atop high flats that offer no particular vista. The house on Elmgrove was near a public elementary school and a large playfield and also near a cross street from which, looking north on a clear day, one can just make out the top of the Space Needle poking up above the running concrete and, above the needle, sky. Several blocks to the east, a park overlooking the Duwamish River valley.

During the moves and school changes that brought Isaiah to the house on Elmgrove, his teachers had registered certain concerns. At one elementary school, they described him as "very active" and "difficult to settle down." Deborah remembers noticing this about her brother, too. She and others in the family chalked it up to his just being a boy. The school did not. It made contact with Isaiah's mother more than ten times, sent daily reports home, tried a variety of interventions. "There was no major improvement in Isaiah," Dr. Lymberis wrote, "and he never got any help." She believes his behavior troubles at school represented only "the tip of the iceberg" of what he was dealing with. She also believes his experiences at home were magnified by the fact that he was quite intelligent and therefore well able to comprehend the gulf between what was and what could be.

Isaiah's family knew he was very smart. They would say, "Oh, you've been here before," conveying something akin to the idea of an old soul. This was one reason they never saw any legitimacy in the concerns expressed by schoolteachers about Isaiah's performance. Deborah said Isaiah showed his intense curiosity not just by reading everything he could get his hands on but also by watching educational programming on television and taking in "anything electronic, anything about planes." He wasn't violent as a child or during his adolescence, his mother said. "He didn't get in trouble," she told me. "He didn't steal, he didn't do drugs, he didn't do anything that would cause him to be picked up by the police." Dr. Lymberis found no sign of "conduct disorder," a persistent character trait that is believed by some to arise in childhood and inexorably worsen, in adulthood, into antisocial personality disorder or sociopathic behavior.

Isaiah liked to ride his bike. He liked to play basketball. At the same time, he was shy. He needed glasses for reading, but at school he wouldn't wear them because other kids made fun. Instead, he hid them. "Isaiah was bullied at school quite a bit," his mother said. "He was in his own world. He didn't communicate with the other kids, and so they bullied him."

He was scrawny back then and not well able to fight back. "There were these two girls who were twins," his mother said, "and they would just constantly torment him . . . They would call him skinny, ugly, black—because Isaiah had a darker skin complexion, like his father. They were just awful." When Isaiah told his mother about this, she went to his school and confronted the twins, who she believes felt superior to Isaiah in part because they were lighter-skinned African American women, like herself. After she confronted them, Isaiah's mother said, "they stopped messing with him."

By 1994, Isaiah's teacher was worried about "academic progress in all areas" and described him as "not organized." The teacher said Isaiah "often times arrives at school very angry" and that he "gets in trouble at recess and on the bus" and "is very aggressive." He was around nine years old. Alerted by the school that teachers believed Isaiah had ADD, his parents ignored the idea. "We didn't believe that's what was going on with him," his mother said. "He never had any kind of learning disability. He was teaching me stuff I didn't know . . . Isaiah taught me math. He knows the map of the world before I did. He's very intelligent."

That same year, Isaiah's mother showed up in an emergency room with stab wounds to her leg. She told doctors she had stabbed herself, out of anger, because of her husband's abuse, which she found demeaning and humiliating, particularly because it was happening in front of their children. Dr. Lymberis, based on her investigation, wrote that Isaiah's mother went to the ER because Isaiah's father "threw her down the basement stairs and stabbed her two times in the leg. This violence started over Isaiah having a hard time doing his homework." She said Isaiah's mother "was seen five times for accidental stab wounds," was diagnosed with major depression, and was referred for counseling. Isaiah's mother told me, "I don't want to get into that one, but I didn't stab myself." She added that it wasn't Isaiah who stabbed her. Then she said, "I told them I did it. I just didn't want to cause more problems than there already was."

Soon after this, Isaiah's mother became suicidal again. "I had given up," she said, "because I was tired of the way I was being treated." She was in the ER for that, too, as well as for problems with her back that ended up requiring multiple surgeries and narcotic pain medication, including Vicodin, Soma, and, eventually, methadone. Around this time, one teacher at Isaiah's school described him as "bright-eyed, fun-loving, and well-mannered," while another described him as "quite a puzzling student to me, so capable and yet so elusive." Isaiah soon left that school and soon left another school, too. By fifth grade, a teacher wrote—"quite prophetically," Dr. Lymberis noted—that Isaiah's challenges urgently needed to be addressed before it was too late. He'd been tardy and absent a lot, seemed easily frustrated and unable to concentrate. Perhaps trying to reach Isaiah's parents by first agreeing with their assessment of his intelligence, this teacher wrote, "Isaiah's diverse abilities have become obvious. But his frustrations are something that must be addressed. His intelligence and abilities are not in question, but his ADD has increased his frustrations and, of course, affect his self-concept along with socialization endeavors. We must talk to consider these aspects for Isaiah's sake, before he 'turns off' completely and we'll lose a very special young man." The note was written in 1995. Isaiah was ten years old. His parents did not engage the plea.

That same year, the Seattle police were called to their home on Elmgrove Street because of an assault in which Isaiah was described as the victim. More detailed records of that incident have since been destroyed by the Seattle police as part of their regular purging of old records.

By 1997, Isaiah was at yet another school, where testing found him learning disabled and eligible for special education services, with problems using written language and math. Isaiah's mother recalls being summoned at some point for a conference about Isaiah's abilities, which she couldn't believe. She said she made Isaiah write an apology note to his teachers on the spot and that they were amazed by his fluency and ease of expression. "He said, 'Mom, these teachers are so stupid, they think that I can't read or write, so if they want to believe it, let them believe it.'"

What was not expressed verbally, at least as far as any available school records indicate, was what Isaiah was witnessing at home. His mother's back troubles continued, and worsened, requiring a series of spinal fusions that left her to walk hunched over and led to her permanent use of narcotic pain medication, which was supervised by her doctor to prevent abuse. "She has been through hell and back," Deborah said. The reports of domestic violence continued as well. In 1997, Isaiah's mother told the social worker, her husband attacked her in the living room. "I was having problems with my back," Isaiah's mother told me. "And he knew it, and he just kicked my feet from under me, and I fell on my back on the floor, and he got on top of me and was bending my legs up to my neck, knowing it was hurting, and that's when Isaiah intervened, and he pushed his father off me—pushed him across the room. He was protecting me."

That fight began, Isaiah's mother said, because Isaiah's father told her to stay in her place. She responded by asking, "What place is that?"

She stood in one part of the room. "Here?" She moved a few feet away. "Here?" In response, she said, he attacked.

Records created by the social worker show Isaiah's mother describing a similar incident in 2001. "She states that the father got mad at her," the social worker wrote. "She states that the father then kicked her legs, sat on her, and punched her in the back. She relates that the father attempts to hurt her back because he knows that she suffers back pain from previous injuries." Medical reports support the mother's account, the social worker wrote, quoting from a primary care provider's records: "Most recent attack was on Saturday night, 7-21-01, when he punched her in the lower back, sat on her while she was lying on her stomach, and also stepped with his boot on her right thigh." The doctor noted tenderness in Isaiah's mother's back, neck, shoulder, and thighs; contusions on her thigh, back, and arms; and swelling on her right thigh.

She described another loss of footing around this time, this one less literal. Isaiah's father was the sole breadwinner in the family because her back injuries were becoming a disability that kept her from working, and so access to money had become another battleground. "The mother relates that the father has always controlled the finances," the social worker wrote. "She relates that the father has three checking accounts and her name is not on any of them. She states that the father gives her $60 a week and tells her to buy groceries for five people."

Isaiah's father was a Seventh-Day Adventist, a religion brought to Uganda by missionaries, and this faith was another thing he turned to for assistance. A core fear for him, Dr. Lymberis wrote, was that Isaiah would "become like his mother." Trying to prevent this, he used "discipline, threats, and control," and when that didn't work to his satisfaction, he tried religion.

When Isaiah was twelve, he was sent to a Seventh-Day Adventist school near Auburn, in the valley southeast of Seattle. He finished eighth grade there and then was sent to Auburn Adventist Academy, the boarding school next door. "Dad caught him smoking a cigarette and sent him off," Deborah said. "Kinda drastic, huh?" Auburn's civic motto is "More Than You Imagined," and Auburn Adventist Academy is located near the Green River, farther upriver than the spot where Teresa would come to buy a condo, miles from where the river becomes the Duwamish. A mural at the main entrance to the school describes its surroundings: pastureland, evergreen trees, soft purple light falling on a close Mount Rainier at sunset. The grounds of the academy are surrounded by a black metal fence, and its one-story tan-brick buildings are arranged around a grassy quad. There's a hangar-like gym with a half-dome roof of corrugated metal. Nearby, a small runway owned by the school, which offers some pilot training to its students.

The approach to the academy is notably less pastoral than the academy itself: mobile home parks, an Air Route Traffic Control Center run by the Federal Aviation Administration, stretches of Muckleshoot Indian Reservation land on which casino signs flash, pawnshops with names like Cash America. When Isaiah first arrived in this landscape as an eighth grader, he'd become friends with Kayla Manteghi. "He was really sweet," she said. "Very nice." Kayla also remembers a dry sense of humor that took her a while to figure out. "He would crack jokes," she said, "but not smile."

At home, Deborah had been one of the people Isaiah would come to with new things he'd learned while reading in his room in the basement, or watching lectures on the University of Washington's cable channel, or nature programs on the Discovery Channel. Sometimes she'd be with friends and brush her little brother off. "I feel so bad," Deborah said. "I would be like, 'Yeah, leave him alone, he's crazy. He's a weirdo.' He would say weird stuff, but it wouldn't be *weird* stuff. It would be, like, things he learned on TV. He'll just come talk to you about it." Politics. The abilities of swordfish. For Deborah and her friends, it was way off topic. "Don't nobody care," Deborah recalled herself saying. "We're just trying to hang out."

She told her friends, "Oh, that's just my brother."

And, to her brother, "Isaiah, get out!"

Now he was gone, off to the boarding school in Auburn. Around the same time, Deborah moved out. "I left home at seventeen," she said. "Never went back."

Boarding school was difficult for Isaiah. "You have to understand," Deborah said, "he's one of maybe five black people in this whole Adventist school, which—he has to live there on top of it—and all kinds of things going on. I know for a fact he went through hell. As an adult, I would ask him, 'How was school when you went there?' And he would say, 'If you only knew the things I went through.' But he would never tell me in detail." His English teacher, Mary Kobberstad, said he was "quiet, reserved" and "had a difficult time fitting in." She remembers him bringing up the challenge of being one of the few nonwhite people at Auburn Adventist. "He sometimes pulled the race card on us a little bit," she said.

Isaiah's mother said she wasn't listed as a contact on the school paperwork, just Isaiah's father and his father's sister, Rachel Kalebu. The school principal at the time, Keith Hallam, recalls Rachel as a prominent figure in Isaiah's life. "A mother's love in an aunt's heart is what I saw," Hallam said. Court records reflect the absence of Isaiah's mother on school forms and say this "effectively cut Isaiah's mother out of not only Isaiah's day-to-day life" but also "any knowledge of her son's academic progress." Still, Isaiah's mother said, she went to the school regularly to bring Isaiah clean clothes and give him money, and he would come home to stay with his parents on weekends.

At the home on Elmgrove Street, even with their son away most of the time, "the parents continued to fight over Isaiah," Dr. Lymberis wrote. "The mother and Isaiah wanted him to return home, but the father continued to refuse." At one point, Isaiah's mother said, they went to marriage counseling, and Isaiah's father "told the counselor right in front of me that we would have to get a divorce, or else one of us would end up dead. And that scared me. And it scared the counselor." She said they had separate sessions after that.

Isaiah's mother doesn't remember exactly when, but sometime in these years Isaiah asked her why she cried so often. She decided to tell him something she had kept from him, something that made it hard for her to believe, years later, that Isaiah had committed the crime for which he was put on trial. A child of rape, Isaiah's mother now told her son that in her teenage years she herself survived a rape. "I was raped at knifepoint," she said. "And Isaiah knew all this, and it disturbed him desperately. It bothered him badly."

The year before she met Isaiah's father, she told me, she was attacked by a man who offered her a ride to help her find her schizophrenic mother and Deborah, who had gone out together and were missing. "He just put the knife to my throat," she said, "and then he made me have oral sex with him, and then he raped me in his bedroom." He set the knife on the bed near him during the rape, and she put her hand on it a few times, thought about using it, "but didn't want to kill nobody," she said, "so I just kept putting it down and got through it." She thinks Isaiah might have been about fifteen years old when she told him this. "It made him mad where he just destroyed his room," she said.

Around this time, Isaiah was expelled from the Adventist academy for showing a small knife to a prospective student visiting the campus. Afterward, he was homeschooled for six months. It was 2001. In late February, an earthquake near the state capital of Olympia shook the entire region, a release of built-up pressure from ongoing, unseen friction beneath the surface, the same rattling that pushed the South Park Bridge further toward the need for intervention, an intervention that, in the end, did not come quickly enough. "That summer," Dr. Lymberis wrote, "his father took him on an extended trip to Uganda. Isaiah was very impressed with the way his father and family lived, especially that they had servants and that the people looked up to the U.S."

This is the longest period of father-son time noted in any available record of Isaiah's relationship with his father, and Isaiah returned motivated to reenter high school. He was sent to another Adventist academy, this one in Kirkland, another Seattle suburb distant from his parents' home, though in the opposite direction, to the northeast. It was not a boarding school, so Isaiah often rode the public bus from the poorer southern end of the city to this well-to-do enclave on the other side of the two floating bridges that span Lake Washington, bridges that connect to neighborhoods where people like Bill Gates reside. Off an exit near the end of one of these bridges, and up a road that winds through evergreen trees, are the low beige buildings of Puget Sound Adventist Academy. Kayla Manteghi, having left Auburn after eighth grade for this school, remembers rekindling her friendship with Isaiah when he arrived. He promised to protect her from guys at school who were treating her badly, "always looked out for me," she said. Yearbook pictures from Puget Sound Adventist show Isaiah, now a junior, dunking a basketball in front of onlookers, smiling in a class picture wearing a sweater with a loose turtleneck, standing with a group at a formal dance, dressed in a suit. The pictures also suggest this school was similar in racial makeup to the Adventist academy in Auburn. Isaiah's class was small, only nineteen people in all, and in the yearbook pictures he is shown amid mostly white faces.

That winter, a few months after he turned sixteen, Isaiah was home for Thanksgiving break when, late on the evening of Thanksgiving, his father, then forty-four years old, called the Seattle police. When officers arrived at the house on Elmgrove, Isaiah's father told them he'd been arguing with Isaiah over Isaiah's "eating whatever he wants without regard for anyone else in the house." Specifically, he was mad that Isaiah drank too much eggnog. Isaiah's mother said her husband threw the remaining eggnog in Isaiah's face. Then the fight escalated, with Isaiah's father telling his son to get out of the house. Isaiah's mother "got betwixt her son and husband," the police report says, trying to prevent anyone from leaving. In response, Isaiah's father pushed his wife and asked Isaiah, "What are you going to do, beat me up?"

Isaiah was no longer a scrawny kid. He is described in this police report as six inches taller than his father, six feet one to his father's five feet seven. In his high school yearbook photographs, he appears well built, with broad shoulders and a strong chest.

In response to his father's question about whether he was going to beat him up, Isaiah replied directly, "Yes."

Father and son then pushed each other, the shoving match ending when Isaiah's father changed course and called the police. Isaiah was arrested, spent the night in juvenile detention, and was released. Likewise, his father was arrested, spent the night in the King County Jail, and was released. Neither pursued charges against the other.

A few months passed, and then the police were called again, this time by Puget Sound Adventist Academy in Kirkland, where there had been an altercation between Isaiah and another male student. "The episode started," Dr. Lymberis wrote, "because the other student would not stop crying over his mother being in the hospital." The student now works as a mental health professional in California, and he remembers the encounter. Like Isaiah, he had transferred to Puget Sound Adventist Academy because of problems at his previous school. Like Isaiah, he had challenges at home, his revolving around a mother living with multiple sclerosis. "Basically, I grew up with my mother slowly deteriorating," the former classmate said. "I was very emotionally vulnerable." He didn't know Isaiah well when the fight began, didn't know anything at all about Isaiah's family background. They were just two near strangers who found themselves at odds inside the student lounge that day. He remembers Isaiah saying something about his mother, though he doesn't remember what it was exactly, and he doesn't remember much after that.

Likely, he said, Isaiah's comment had something to do with his crying over his mother's hospitalization for MS. Isaiah was not one to outwardly express emotion over such things, although he, too, had a mother who had been repeatedly hospitalized. "In all of the records I reviewed," Dr. Lymberis wrote, "there is hardly any record that Isaiah ever expressed feelings about the chronic conflict and violence in his family, about the physical beatings by his father or his mother's depression and suicide attempts, or about other aspects of his traumatic and difficult childhood." All that Isaiah outwardly expressed was a powerful instinct to protect his mother from his father, an increasing frustration at his circumstances, and a tightly compressed, building rage.

Whatever Isaiah said that day, the other student responded by throwing a pillow at him. "And then," the former classmate of Isaiah's said, "I basically started walking toward him. Isaiah got up off the couch, started walking toward me, and that's all I remember. The next thing I remember is my PE teacher standing above me." Isaiah's classmate was coming to, after being knocked out by Isaiah. "He got me good," the former classmate said. "It was like a one-hitter type of deal."

The principal at the time, Doug White, said it took a while to calm Isaiah down. "It was hard getting him under control, I think," White said. "He was very emotionally upset and mad." Kathy Fridlund, then the school's development director, remembers calling 911 and then feeling upset when Isaiah was led away in handcuffs. She thought that was beyond what was required. So did others on campus. She shared a picture she took of Isaiah playing baseball during a student-faculty field day, his face intent, bat in swing. "Just total determination to connect with the ball," she said. She also recalls Isaiah, upon his return to school after the arrest, offering an apology to the student he knocked out.

Told what was going on with Isaiah at the time of the fight, that former classmate of his said, "I can sympathize with him . . . That's difficult to hear." At the time, however, it was not sufficiently heard by anyone, and nothing more was done about the fight. "It is of note," Dr. Lymberis wrote, "that the records show that when the vice principal tried to contact Isaiah's parents numerous times, none of them responded."

The student whom Isaiah hit declined to pursue any charges, having seen the fight as "consensual," a consequence of two young men headed toward hurting each other, each arriving at his destination without interference or self-correction.

22

By now, the state had intervened in Isaiah's troubled family life in three distinct ways over sixteen years. It had deemed his parental supervision "adequate" after he was brought, at two months of age, to the emergency room with a burn near his eye from his mother's cigarette. It had expressed concern, in the form of repeated attempts at intervention by Isaiah's public elementary and middle school teachers, but none of those attempts at intervention had been successful. Finally, the state had appeared at Isaiah's homes and at his private Adventist school in Kirkland, in the form of summoned police officers, for incidents of domestic violence and for the fight Isaiah had with another student. There had been repeated nights in jail for Isaiah's father and, once, a Thanksgiving night in juvenile detention for Isaiah. But none of these incidents ever resulted in anyone's pursuing formal charges in court. Now, slowly, in the sixteenth year of Isaiah's life, the path to the social worker began.

The social worker's relatively brief investigation was conducted under court order and was brought about by a further deterioration in the relationship between Isaiah's parents. In May 2002—as Jennifer was moving on from her breakup with Ann in New York City, as Teresa was settling into her new condo in Renton—Isaiah's father filed for a restraining order against Isaiah's mother, describing a turbulent marriage in which "we have been keeping and sleeping in separate bedrooms for the last six years." In other words, since Isaiah was ten years old. Isaiah's father complained that late on a recent Wednesday night his wife had come into his bedroom in the basement of the house on Elmgrove Street while he was reading and asked him, "Why have you been ignoring me?" He told her it was to avoid fighting. "This," he wrote, "went on into a critical discussion of my views, beliefs, and parenting style. We talked about compromise, and I told her that certain principles, I could not compromise. At this point she was getting quite agitated . . . She said I was destroying the family and would not get what I wanted."

He suggested they end the discussion, according to his typewritten account. She expressed more anger and then left. "I locked my door," Isaiah's father wrote, "and tried to go to sleep." About twenty minutes later, he wrote, his wife came to his door wanting to continue the conversation and, when he would not, "decided to bash the door in. She came in and continued to yell at me, telling me to come out of from under the blanket and finish the fight, she claimed, I had started. She poked and prodded to provoke me to get up. Due to previous similar occurrences, I was scared of many things. I covered myself and concentrated on keeping myself calm to avoid getting into a physical exchange. After about 10 minutes with no response from me, she quieted down, went out of the room, and stood just outside the door. She stayed there for another 10 or 15 minutes with an occasional verbal assault and then she went back upstairs." The previous week, Isaiah's father wrote, there had been another dispute, this one over whether his wife had made dinner for him. "She accused me of wanting to have everybody become my servant," he said. Isaiah's father claimed his wife "generally intimidates and threatens the kids if they follow my view if and when it differs from hers." He said she had a "deep rooted anger management problem" and that she was abusing alcohol and drugs, including "strong prescription pain medications (Soma, Vicodin, etc.)." He wanted his wife kept out of their house and his workplace by court order for over a year, and he wanted custody of the three children still in the house: Isaiah, his younger sister, and his younger brother. Isaiah's father wrote, "Please help!"

He filed this request at 3:27 on a Friday afternoon. Within less than ninety minutes, the court denied it and dismissed the case without setting any hearing. Isaiah's father had said a lot of things in his filing, but none of them established clear evidence of domestic violence against him by his wife. At that point, the arrest records connected to Isaiah's father suggested the opposite might be true.

That summer, Isaiah turned seventeen. Two weeks after his birthday, the police again arrived at his family's home in West Seattle, this time late on a Thursday night, in response to a hang-up 911 call. They found Isaiah's father with three lacerations on the left side of his neck. There were also scratches in his beard line, on the right side of his face, and on the top of his left hand. They found Isaiah's mother with an abrasion on the back of her left shoulder and a scratch on the top of her head, "and ligature (cord) marks were observed in her wrists."

The police spent two hours at the home on Elmgrove Street, listening to Isaiah's mother and father give accounts of what happened. Their stories overlapped significantly but differed as to who was the instigator of each round of violence. The father, listed in the police report as five feet seven and 180 pounds, said it was instigated by the mother, who was listed as five feet eight and 130 pounds. In the end, the police arrested both of them and took them to cool off in jail. Once out, both headed to court for restraining orders and a divorce, producing filings full of recriminations that detailed years of marital violence, coercive control, and cruelty.

Each accused the other of manipulating the truth to gain advantage. Isaiah's father said the most recent fight began, like the previous one, with his wife's coming into his room in the basement. "She got into the bed and we chatted for a little while, and I went back to my reading," he wrote. "After about five minutes she said she was bursting to tell me something. I asked her to go ahead and tell me. She expressed her disappointment in that here she was, a beautiful woman laying in bed with me and I was ignoring her. I tried to explain that I liked to read to unwind before going to sleep. That I did not want to be with her as I was very tired and just wanted to go to sleep. She was silent, then after a little while she got up and left. A little while later she came back down and demanded an explanation. She quickly became belligerent and combative. She slapped me across the face and scratched or cut my neck with some object in several places, like she wanted to puncture a vein. I thought she was going to kill me. She continued to hit me and kick me. I laid back down hoping she would calm down and go back upstairs. But she just continued on with a verbal attack." He went to bandage his neck, he said, and his wife continued berating him, threatening to get relatives to come and hurt him, threatening to keep him from sleeping that night. When he picked up the phone to call the police, he said, "she snatched the phone out of my hand and threw it against the wall." In his telling, he tried to use another phone, and she broke that one, too. He tried to crawl out of a window, and she went outside to confront him there. He crawled back in, left through the front door, and went to their 1986 Chevrolet Astro van. She got in the van with him. He drove to a corner store and called the police from a pay phone, and when she realized he'd gotten through to the police, she drove away in their van, leaving him there. He said that in the past she had used "knives, hammers, stereo speakers, and any loose object available" to harm him and that she once got "mad about something" and pushed his desk computer onto the floor.

Isaiah's mother agreed the fight began with her climbing into her husband's bed uninvited. "I don't see any problem getting in bed with my own husband," she told a judge at a hearing that was recorded on old cassette tapes. In a narrative of the incident that she filed, she wrote in longhand, "I went in and laid down beside him and waiting for a few moments before saying anything. I then ask him, 'Why are you ignoring me?' He responded by saying, 'I don't have to stop reading just because you are here. You don't sleep with me on a regular basis. Leave me alone.' I got upset and left the room crying. I came back and ask, 'Why do you treat me like this? Why are you so mean all the time?' He responded by getting up yelling at me, and he then got in my face and head-butted me. I push him away and said, 'Don't you head-butt me again.' He did it a second time at that time. I grabbed his neck with my right hand and held on, telling him, 'I told you not to do that to me.' We struggled and he ended up pushing me down on the bed and bending my legs upward towards my neck. I push him off somehow. He grabbed me, slamming me into the laundry room cabinet where I got a hole in my back. I broke free and went for the phone, telling him I'm going to call my brothers. How would he like it if a man does to him what he is doing to me?" She couldn't reach anyone on the phone. She started pulling his clothes out of the closet, telling him to just get out. "He refused. I then went to call the police. He grabbed the phone and threw it against the wall of his bedroom. I ran to the downstairs office phone. He pulled the phone cord from the ceiling. I went upstairs to call and he pulled the cord from the wall. He then wrapped the cord around my arms in front and left." She added that after a judge kicked her husband out of the house in response to the incident, her husband had the phone disconnected. "All bill and bank statements are in his name," she wrote. "I don't have access to anything—a big form of the control I have suffered over the 18 years of being with this man."

In court, each expressed worry that the other would respond in anger to the revelations and requests for intervention. Isaiah's mother expressed a particular concern that her husband would take the children to Africa. In response, the court ordered that he surrender their passports.

Isaiah's father moved to a motel and then to the Tacoma home of his sister, Rachel Kalebu. He began listing a post office box as his address in court documents. He stopped paying the mortgage on the family home in West Seattle, which was then foreclosed on, causing Isaiah's mother to move to an apartment with the children. Court records suggest this apartment was in a complex of buildings that look out on a large embankment holding up the western end of Seattle-Tacoma International Airport's runways, a grimy place set between the airport and the same highway that hems in South Park.

Around this time, something called Family Court got involved in the dispute between Isaiah's parents. It's a department of King County Superior Court designed to assist families going through difficult proceedings and, in doing so, perhaps save on court costs—and, by extension, taxpayer money—while better protecting the interests of children. Family Court was asked to investigate the domestic violence allegations coming from each of Isaiah's parents and, after that, to recommend a course of action to the judge handling their divorce. A social worker was assigned to help in the investigating.

The social worker's report, which was completed in October 2002, noted that Isaiah's father complained to her at least five times about his wife's "bitching" and that he also admitted to being arrested twice for incidents involving Isaiah. "This behavior," the social worker wrote, "appears to indicate a lack of empathy on the part of the father toward his children, in addition to a lack of consideration for the mother's wishes. These behaviors, viewed in totality, are indicative of a pattern of control and violence that exemplifies domestic violence." She recommended that Isaiah's father "complete a domestic violence treatment program, and a respectful parenting course." She suggested that Isaiah's mother "would benefit from mental health counseling to assist her in learning how to remove herself from violent situations rather than respond in an aggressive manner." Finally, she singled out Isaiah, then just over two months past his seventeenth birthday, for special consideration. "It appears that the oldest son has endured a great deal of the father's abusive behavior," the social worker wrote. "This son would also benefit from mental health counseling in order to help him deal with the experiences he has endured at the hands of his father." This never happened.

"A major missed opportunity," wrote Dr. Lymberis.

Had someone tried, at public expense, to get Isaiah into mental health counseling, it's possible the system itself would have missed the opportunity, too. "A patchwork relic" is how a presidential commission, established just a few months before this social worker's suggestion, described the nation's mental health apparatus. In any event, the opportunity was missed, and the legal battle between Isaiah's parents dragged on, in a local court system that, like others around the nation, was itself suffering from neglect.

A major issue was inadequate funding. Soon, current and former Washington State Supreme Court justices would launch a campaign for more money called Justice in Jeopardy. This campaign would have the misfortune of arriving a few years before the Great Recession.

In the fight between Isaiah's parents, Isaiah's father began asking Family Court to reconsider its negative assessment of him. "Is that too much for a male to ask?" he said, through a lawyer, in one filing. He also complained that his wife's demands for child support were too great, and as evidence of this he said Isaiah had recently been sent home from his private high school "for lack of funds." Other records show that Isaiah, having left the Kirkland academy and returned to Auburn Adventist for his senior year of high school, ended up living in the school's dorms for a time but wasn't allowed to attend classes because of his parents' lack of payment. "Isaiah's education should not be used as a bargaining chip for more income," Isaiah's father wrote. "If the respondent really cares about his education, she should get a job, even part time, and send her contribution directly to the school, like the rest of us do." Whichever parent was actually using Isaiah's education as a bargaining chip, the immediate result was more turbulence for Isaiah.

Isaiah's mother filed income statements showing minimal resources and filed notes from her doctor supporting her contention that she was in no position to work. "My physical condition has now deteriorated to the point that I will need additional surgery on my back," she wrote. "I am now physically unable to perform any substantial gainful activity. My only job skill is working in a pre-school." She said she could no longer lift more than two pounds or stand or walk for extended periods, which made it impossible for her to work at a preschool. She said she was presently driving a van that had to be started with a wrench due to disrepair and that her husband's claims of physical victimization were absurd. "Petitioner is a large, threatening man and I find it amazing that he is suddenly scared of a woman who he has aggressively attacked and beaten over the years," she wrote.

Another assessment was ordered by the court. While the deadline for the report approached, Isaiah moved in and out of several more schools. He ultimately graduated from Auburn Adventist Academy and began looking at colleges, including one well on the other side of the Cascade Mountain Range from his parents, an Adventist university in Walla Walla, Washington. That's where Kayla Manteghi ended up going to college, and she remembers one day running into Isaiah on campus. It was a quick conversation. But, she said, "he seemed the same to me." Isaiah attended only two quarters at Walla Walla University, the fall of 2003 and the winter of 2004.

In September 2003, the second report on Isaiah's family was completed. As it was being prepared by the social worker, on an "expedited" basis, his father's progress in domestic violence treatment and the respectful parenting class was evaluated. That progress was found wanting. Almost a year after being ordered into these programs, Isaiah's father had failed to do much more than complete one intake form, though he "did admit to pushing and grabbing the mother," according to his domestic violence caseworker and therapist. Interviews with all the "minor children" in Isaiah's family were also conducted for this second report from the social worker, but by now the "minor children" designation excluded Isaiah. He was eighteen, considered independent from the family that raised him, ready to exercise his free will in society at large.

Consequently, only Isaiah's younger sister and brother were called in to Family Court for a session with the social worker. Isaiah's younger brother, then nine years old, was interviewed first. He was noted to be relaxed, friendly, and dressed appropriately. He made good eye contact as he spoke about beginning a new school year, movies, and playing basketball. "When asked about his relationship with his mother," the report states, "he told the evaluator, 'She always listens to me and doesn't get mad,'" although he did note she was making him do some chores, like folding clothes and doing the dishes. When asked about his relationship with his father, he said, "I wish he wouldn't take things so seriously." When asked what he meant, he said, "I don't know, I just think he gets mad a lot and we always have to explain things to him." He spoke of his parents' fighting often before their separation, said his father had not been nice to his mother. When asked what three wishes he would like to have granted, he said, "To live in a house, for my parents to get along, and for me to have a happy life." He also spoke of his older brother, Isaiah, and how Isaiah had just started college, which meant Isaiah was getting to live away from home in a dorm.

Isaiah's younger sister, then eleven years old, was interviewed next. She, too, seemed relaxed and made good eye contact, though she spoke more softly than her younger brother. When asked what her parents' separation had been like for her, she looked on the positive side. "It's okay," she said, "because before this my dad used to hit us sometimes." When asked for her three wishes, she said she wanted to continue living with her mother but also wanted to spend some time with her father and that she wished for her parents to stop fighting.

Seven years later, after much else had happened, and as another school year was beginning, Isaiah would have a chance to field a question about three wishes. By then, however, the context would be quite different. Isaiah's first wish, he told a psychiatrist who was examining him at the request of his public defenders: "Not being in jail." His second: "Perfect health." His third wish: To become "smart enough to know what the best thing to wish for would be."

23

I n the fall of 2003, Isaiah was simply trying to make it through college. It proved difficult. It was not long after the social worker completed her assessment of his family back in Seattle that Isaiah dropped out of Walla Walla University. By the fall of 2004, he was attending Pierce College at Fort Steilacoom, a community college not far from the Tacoma home of his aunt, Rachel Kalebu. He didn't get any further than two semesters.

That same year, a judge ordered Isaiah's father, who was still working a well-compensated job as an engineer, to pay $1,000 a month support to his mother and to pay off Isaiah's private high school tuition bills, one of which totaled $5,000. In the meantime, Isaiah's mother was to apply for Social Security disability benefits. By the end of that year, Isaiah's father had sent a letter, through his lawyer, telling Isaiah's mother that he understood she'd been denied disability benefits. The letter told her to start looking for a job and keep him apprised.

In early 2005, Isaiah, now nineteen, was arrested, charged with misdemeanor theft, and then released after shoplifting two CDs from a Kmart that was a ten-minute drive from his aunt Rachel's house. A couple months later, Isaiah's parents were back in court arguing over money, including the tuition still owed to Isaiah's private Adventist high schools. Isaiah's father filed invoices from the schools that had notes at the top saying, "MUST BE PAID TO GET TRANSCRIPTS." He told the court he couldn't afford to pay until the financial support to Isaiah's mother was either decreased or ended. The court continued the requirement that Isaiah's father pay support to Isaiah's mother, in order to give her more time to appeal her disability denial. As a result, Isaiah's transcripts were effectively held hostage to their continued disagreement.

Not too long after this, Isaiah was living with his mother and went with her to the grocery store. While shopping, Dr. Lymberis wrote, "he had a spontaneous, out-of-control episode of sobbing. His mother noted that 'he was a mess.'" It is the first account of any outward expression of vulnerability that Dr. Lymberis could find. In that grocery store, Isaiah complained that his aunt and his father "were on him all the time" and that the lack of transcripts was hindering his attempts to return to college. "His mother knew Isaiah could not get his transcripts because his father had not paid the high school the past-due tuition of $5,000, but Isaiah was not saying that to her," Dr. Lymberis wrote. "She also noted that Isaiah had applied to pilot school because no transcripts were needed for entrance to that school." While he was crying, Isaiah's mother told me, she noticed him "stammering, stuttering—and he never had a stuttering problem before."

It's unclear when, exactly, pilot school became a goal of Isaiah's. Perhaps he'd remembered the pilot training program at Auburn Adventist, or maybe the roar from the airport runways near his mother's latest apartment. Whatever the immediate motivation, he'd applied to learn to fly at a technical college, his childhood fascination with planes now an adult pursuit. Isaiah did well in his pilot training program, earning As and Bs, feeling hopeful. "That was his dream," said his older sister, Deborah. "He loved it. He felt free. He just wanted to travel. Eventually, his goal was to make lots of money so he can build him a house on a island somewhere, and just live peaceful and free. That's what he always used to tell me. That's all he wanted. He loved the sky. And he would work. And I know that flight lessons are very expensive, and he would spend all of his money for those flight lessons, until he found out he was color-blind. And that destroyed everything."

The flight school, at some point, had required Isaiah to take a vision test as part of his physical. Until then, not one person in Isaiah's life had noticed his color blindness, including Isaiah. Now, in his early twenties, he learned that he would never be a pilot.

He had tried, by what will he had, to escape the fetters of his experience, only to find them still clinging, too tight for his resources. For Isaiah, this was a cataclysmic disappointment. "That's where everything went downhill," Deborah said. "That's where it starts."

Danger to Self and Others

24

There is a fault that runs directly beneath this city. People ignore it and go on with their days, though it is widely known that if it were to slip, years of pressure cracking loose in an instant, much of the fill beneath Seattle's industrial south could liquefy and revert toward its primeval disposition, muck washed around by tides. This same fault runs near the mouth of the Duwamish, perpendicular to the river's flow. The last time it moved, land on one side of the fault jumped twenty feet, disrupting the river for a time, until its northward tendency—the tendency helpful to humans casting things out to sea, and to salmon seeking wider waters—carved out a new path. This fault will jump again, interrupting commerce, relationships, migrations. For all the modern science, for all the scans that have begun to show the hidden movements beneath observable events, this is all that is certain.

Much of Isaiah's youth was spent on a hill above this crack in the earth. The home in which his parents fought was above it, and after the police came to the house on Elmgrove Street for his parents' last brawl as husband and wife, after the home was foreclosed on by the bank amid divorce proceedings, after the Family Court social worker recommended counseling for Isaiah that never materialized, after Isaiah dropped out of two colleges and learned he was too color-blind to become a pilot, something was observed to be rising within the young man. It might well have been rising for some time.

All that is known for sure is that Isaiah remained bereft of helpful intervention, even as it became increasingly apparent that the part of him now surfacing needed assistance. He was an adult, not only in the eyes of his family, but also in the eyes of the law, and he was expected to contribute to society or face consequences. He was having trouble with both expectations. In 2006, he was pulled over for a broken taillight on a road not far from his aunt's house. When the officer smelled pot, Isaiah was arrested, based on the law at the time, for illegal possession of marijuana. He was found to have a glass pipe and a few grams with him in the car, and he told his mother and sister he was using pot to quiet negative voices in his head. He bounced between their apartments and his aunt's house and between something like twenty different jobs over two years, getting fired from places like Bel-R Greenhouse and Interstate Plastics. In court filings connected to his theft arrest, he'd listed his employer as "Abercrombie."

During this period, Isaiah was sometimes described as a smart and dedicated worker. Other times he was described as disorganized, slow, sad, chronically tardy. Sometimes he was responsible and straightforward, and sometimes he was dishonest, manipulative, willing to take surprising risks. At Interstate Plastics, where one employee remembered him talking about his dream of flight school, Isaiah claimed to be able to drive a forklift. He appeared to have no experience with one, though, driving a forklift around, a co-worker said, like "a wild man." When he was fired from that job for being late one too many times, he called his boss to thank him for being "the best of all the bosses" he'd had. "I thought that was strange," the boss later told Dr. Lymberis.

Isaiah tried to use his mind to escape the troubles in which he found himself. It didn't always work. He'd told the officer who arrested him for marijuana possession that he didn't know anything about an outstanding warrant for his arrest, but he did know and a few minutes later admitted as much. The warrant was for the misdemeanor theft charges that had been filed against Isaiah a year earlier, for shoplifting those CDs from the Kmart. His aunt, Rachel Kalebu, had posted bail to get him released on those theft charges, and Isaiah had never resolved them, triggering the warrant. When he was arrested for marijuana possession, he was arrested for the outstanding theft warrant, too. Again, Rachel Kalebu posted bail for him.

"She loved like God loves," Deborah said. "No matter what you'd do, she'd kinda forgive you." This was her role in the family, the reason she was referred to as Mama Ray by the wider Kalebu clan. "Mama Ray takes in strays," Isaiah's mother told Dr. Lymberis. "Discarded people. The broken ones." She had played this role for Isaiah's mother and father when they needed it. She had played it for her elderly mother and aunt when they were dying and needed home care. She played it for J. J. Jones. She played it for Isaiah in his childhood, and now, with Isaiah's parents still caught up in their divorce proceedings, she continued to play it for him in his adulthood.

After the marijuana arrest, Isaiah attended some court dates, completed Alcohol and Drug Information School, as required by the court, and began to pay down hundreds of dollars in fines in small chunks: $20.38 one month, $28.88 the next. Sometimes he was helpful around the homes he inhabited, buying his mother groceries or babysitting Deborah's kids, and sometimes he was emotionless, zombielike, impossible to communicate with, and speaking of wrongs done to him, of hidden codes and plots. Sometimes he had money, and sometimes he didn't. He took out a $400 payday loan from a Tacoma business called Advance Til Payday, failed to pay it back, and ended up with another court proceeding, this one in small-claims court.

Isaiah later described this period to Dr. Lymberis as "the worst time of my life," worse than anything that happened before or after. A number of his older relatives died during these years, including his paternal grandmother, known as Je-Jah, whom he'd been close with and whom Aunt Rachel had been caring for at her home. He developed the first significant relationship of his life with a woman Deborah said he met riding the bus, but then the woman got pregnant. Isaiah strongly wanted children and a family of his own, spoke of hoping to become a father. But the woman did not feel Isaiah could financially support her, so she aborted the pregnancy. After that, Dr. Lymberis wrote, "he was sleeping 10–12 hours a day, felt depressed, lost and demoralized."

He had been taught to disintegrate, to become a man by keeping this separate from that, to be successful by not engaging, or displaying, the effects of his traumatic childhood, to push back on anything that felt like a challenge to his self-perception. "When I'm pushed, I push," he later told Dr. Lymberis. "It is always me against the world, and I'm not going to lose." No one ever successfully intervened to suggest a different path. No one with expertise ever spoke to him about the pressure building, the way, unaddressed, unintegrated, it would continue to build, push against him, and leak out when it couldn't be contained. "It was a constant," Dr. Lymberis said. "It was leaking out, and destroyed his capacity for adaptation, even when he was given a chance." Unable to attend college, keep a job, or start a family, and tangled up in the effects of this disintegration, Isaiah now adhered to a new feeling, a feeling that, to outsiders, had no connection to his present reality. "He started thinking he was God," his mother said. He also began talking about himself as the king, the creator, the president of the United States. He felt omnipotent, "in the zone." He went to his room in his mother's apartment and paced back and forth for hours. Words burst out of him as if under incredible pressure, following a logic those around him couldn't trace.

There were still periods of engagement with the world others saw, with forces Isaiah admitted were more powerful than himself. These periods came in and out, an intermittent signal amid the noise. One day in 2007, Isaiah called a court and paid $28.57 toward an old speeding fine that had grown, with late fees, to about $185. In these moments of relative clarity, Deborah would ask him what was going on. "He'd be like, 'I have a problem with authority. I'll get another job. I'm just looking for the right job. I want to fly.'"

He was flying, regularly. Into delusions. Into extended periods of sleeplessness. Into rages over things like his car getting towed from a spot in front of Deborah's home. "He went up to the place," Deborah said, "and instead of handling it professionally, all I know is that my mom called me and said, 'Deborah, Isaiah just said that he's about to go kill everybody up in the tow yard.'" Isaiah's mother called to warn the tow yard, and nothing ended up happening, except that when Isaiah's mother eventually paid to get the car out, Isaiah told her he didn't want the car anymore. Deborah found that odd.

Not long after that, Deborah went over to her mom's place on the way to return a shirt at the Southcenter Mall. She saw her mom. She saw Isaiah. "Mind you, everything is fine," Deborah said. It was early in the morning, and after she returned the shirt at the mall, she brought them all breakfast from Burger King. "Me, Mom, and Isaiah are the only ones there," she said. "We eat breakfast, the Burger King I brought, and I was like, 'Okay, I gotta go, you guys.'

"So, I give him a hug. 'Love you, see you guys later. You coming to the house later?' You know, small talk. He's like, 'Yeah, I'll come through.' You know, talking. 'Bye, Mom, love you.' Out the door, right? The very next morning, I get a call. I'm getting ready for work. He calls me, he's like, 'You're a terrible mother. I'ma take your kids, and I'm gonna get custody of them, I'ma ship 'em off to Africa. Matter fact, I'ma call CPS and get those kids taken away from you. You don't deserve to be a mother.' Like, I don't even know who this is, though, on my phone at this point. I'm like, 'Who is this? Isaiah?' So I'm looking at the number. I'm like, 'What's wrong with you?' 'Yeah, yeah, something's wrong with me, huh? You're the crazy bitch.' He's cussing me out, telling me he's gonna take my kids. I don't know where it comes from. Just out the blue, right?"

She had been out of the house during her parents' most explosive fights, during the beginning of their divorce and custody battle, during the father's complaints about the mother's "bitching," during the father's talk about how the kids should be taken away from the mother, during the court order that the father surrender his children's passports over concerns he would take the kids to Africa. She hadn't heard what Isaiah heard in those years.

Deborah called her mother to ask what was going on. Her mother didn't know, told her Isaiah had just left. So Deborah went to work. Her job was running a cash register at a Dollar Tree store not far from her mom's place, which was at present an apartment in a city just south of the airport but still along the same high drumlin field that holds West Seattle. The city is called Burien, and much of it is a sprawl of gas stations, car dealers, and fast-food restaurants. The apartment is near a public high school and the Burien Transit Center, a four-story concrete park-and-ride where the parking stalls on the rooftop level are watched by cameras, and the view is of Seattle-Tacoma International Airport being watched by its air traffic control tower. Watching over this entire vista, from the public buses coming and going at the transit center to the airplanes landing and taking off at the airport, is the dormant volcano. Lest it be missed on cloudy days, it is also depicted, in painted relief, on the transit center's sides.

Through the front windows of the Dollar Tree store, Deborah spotted Isaiah walking through the parking lot. She called her mom, said, "Mom, I see this fool right here." This was how she referred to Isaiah when he was being thickheaded. "I'm on my register, but I could see him," Deborah said. "I'm like, 'I'm getting off work anyways, it's time for me to go.' So I'm like, 'Mom, come get me right now at the job. Come pick me up, because Isaiah's up here and he's walking like he's RoboCop, the Terminator.' Like, he's got this blank look, and he's just marching. Blank stare. Like he's on a mission, but I don't know what for."

Their mother drove to the Dollar Tree. Deborah got in the van. They drove into Isaiah's line of sight, shouted to him, "Isaiah, get in the car! Isaiah! Isaiah!" He kept on walking, toward the transit center, as if he were about to get on a bus. "Lord and behold, if he did not—if he could walk through that car, he would have. Mom literally backed up her car because that's how blank stare he was." Deborah was mad at this point, still upset about Isaiah's threatening to call CPS on her that morning and still wondering what was wrong with him, so she jumped out to confront her brother. "So he's walking, and I'm like, 'You got a knife in your hand? Isaiah!'" She jumped back in the van and with her mother drove to the Burien police station. The police looked for Isaiah but didn't find him. "They did nothing," Deborah said.

It was around this time that Isaiah's family became well acquainted with the phrase "Danger to self or others." Something was clearly wrong with Isaiah. "I kept trying to get him into mental hospitals, but he wouldn't go," his mother said. "And he was bigger than me. I couldn't very well drag him to the hospital." That, and he was now over eighteen, which meant that legally, except under specific threatening circumstances that were not yet present, Isaiah would have to drag himself.

His mother, who thought he was a danger to both himself and others, became frustrated by the standoff. "I told them, I said, 'Do you want him to hurt someone before you help him?' And that's exactly what happened."

25

I n 1955, more than half a million Americans were housed in mental hospitals. Many of them were there for no particular reason, other than that someone with a certain amount of power found them strange, or inconvenient, or of the wrong skin color. Conditions in these institutions could be hideous, and protesting one's confinement could be taken as proof of one's instability. It was an open question as to whether this system was creating more insanity than it was purportedly treating, and at the urging of reform-minded psychiatrists President John F. Kennedy closed the question by, effectively, closing down the institutions.

The community treatment movement began, with promises of increased respect for individual rights and an emphasis on tailored outpatient therapies whenever possible, all of it to be backed by the latest science and huge increases in federal spending. Mental hospital populations began falling, helped along by a 1975 Supreme Court ruling that declared it unconstitutional to involuntarily commit "a non-dangerous individual who is capable of surviving safely in freedom by himself or with the help of willing and responsible family members or friends." This, over time, evolved into a commonplace legal standard that, with some variations from state to state, prohibited involuntary psychiatric detention of any individual unless that individual posed "danger to self or others."

By 1980, the population of American mental institutions was down to around 155,000 people, a fraction of the number just two and a half decades previous. It has been calculated that by 1994, adjusting for population growth, about 92 percent of those who once would have been institution-alized were not. The problem was that new treatments weren't as much of a breakthrough as thought, and in any case federal funding sufficient to the challenge of community treatment never materialized. The Vietnam War intervened, requiring attention and money. An oil crisis came, requir-ing attention and money.

Over the decades that passed after President Kennedy signed his 1963 Community Mental Health Act, whenever crises arrived, whenever bud-gets had to be cut, expensive programs designed to help a marginalized and stigmatized population, now dispersed throughout many communi-ties and possessing little political clout, tended to be the first to get the knife. Dreams of widespread education about psychological instability did not materialize, either. Nor did dreams of services capable of responding rapidly to any individual in crisis. By 2008, when Isaiah found himself in crisis, multiple presidents had been warned that the system put in place by President Kennedy was failing because of neglect and was riddled with disparities and limitations. The same presidential commission that had described America's "patchwork relic" of a mental health care system had, in its final report in 2003, called for a "fundamental transformation" of the country's entire approach to people in psychological distress. It imagined a system in which, "at the first sign of difficulties, preventive interventions will be started to keep problems from escalating." This commission was called the New Freedom Commission on Mental Health, and it reported to the then president, George W. Bush, who created it intending to fulfill a campaign promise. However, the commission had the misfortune of competing for attention with the aftermath of Septem-ber 11, 2001.

No "fundamental transformation" ever occurred. Instead, in the years after the New Freedom Commission's final report, the burden of handling people in psychological distress fell increasingly on families without the capacity to help and, when those families inevitably reached their limit, onto local police, emergency rooms, courts, and, finally, prisons, which had effectively become the new mental institutions, except without the mission to provide restorative treatment. It has been pointed out that there's strong irony to these developments. It was the shameful confinement of psychologically disturbed Americans to prisons that, after being exposed in the 1840s by a woman named Dorothea Dix, led to the creation of mental hospitals and institutions in the first place. According to the Treatment Advocacy Center, which has highlighted this irony, the mentally ill population of America's jails and prisons now far outnumbers the population of its surviving mental hospitals.

At the time when Isaiah found himself in need of help, the vast majority of Americans facing psychological distress were, as always, nonviolent, far more likely to be victims of crimes than perpetrators, far more likely to harm themselves than anyone else. But whether they were among the vast, nonviolent majority or in the small minority with violent tendencies, if they were poor, like Isaiah, they found themselves encountering a public mental health system that was in a state of collapse. If they were African American, like Isaiah, they were "unlikely to receive treatment" from this system at all, another federal report found, and in the event they did receive treatment were "more likely to be incorrectly diagnosed." Then the financial collapse of 2008 and, consequently, even more cuts to programs that might help people like Isaiah.

Deborah didn't know anything about this history. She didn't know that she and her family lived in a state that had recently received a D grade for its public mental health services from the National Alliance on Mental Illness, nor did she know that this put Washington State exactly in line with the rest of America, which as a whole had received a D grade, too (with the alliance's report describing a country in which people needing treatment "are allowed to falter to the point of crisis" and in which "the outcome of this neglect and lack of will by policymakers remains often horrendous"). What Deborah knew was that her brother was acting weird and that at first she was having a hard time taking it seriously. She'd minimized it all, telling herself he was just mad, frustrated about pilot school and his job situation, and would get over it. At the same time, she was becoming increasingly scared. The last time she'd seen him, he was heading to the Burien Transit Center with a knife.

"A couple days pass," Deborah said, "and he comes to the house"—her house, which at the time was in White Center, part of the drumlin field and about midway between West Seattle, where Isaiah had grown up, and Burien, where his mother now lived. Deborah's home was in a low-income housing development, and it was where Isaiah was spending most of his time in those days. He knocked on her door, but by the time she got downstairs, he had kicked it in. She screamed at him about her children, that he was waking them. "Now, mind you," Deborah said, "it's not like, 'I kicked in your door and I'm about to freak out and fight you.' He kicked in the door, walks through the kitchen, like, 'What'd you cook?'"

She lost it. Her children's father came downstairs. Isaiah slammed a six-pack of beer on the floor, and the beer shot everywhere. Deborah said, "You have beer in your hands? You've been drinking? You don't drink!" She knew he used weed from time to time, but she also knew he didn't like to lose control like this. Isaiah was foaming at the mouth, she said. "I can't forget it." Her children's dad put him in a full nelson, restrained him, and suddenly he seemed to snap out of it. Given no choice but to pause and calm down, Isaiah did. "He just releases," Deborah said. "He just relaxes and is like, 'I'm sorry.'"

Deborah was not feeling calm. She called her mom, began throwing Isaiah's clothes out on the back porch and then in the trash, was furious. Their mother came, didn't know what to say, told Isaiah to get into her minivan, a new 2004 Ford Freestyle. Deborah, feeling bad about her furious reaction, started pulling clothes out of the trash and putting them in a box for him. He tossed the box out of the minivan, told his mom to drive off. She did, so Deborah threw the clothes back in the garbage. Later, Isaiah's mom ended up missing a payment on her new vehicle in order to buy Isaiah some new clothes. Still, Deborah assumed the stress and the disappointment of flight school were mostly to blame for Isaiah's behavior. She told herself Isaiah would never hurt her. She didn't have a vocabulary for what might be going on with him psychologically, much less a method to effectively respond.

"These are acquired skills," Dr. Lymberis said. "You are not born with it."

Not long afterward, Isaiah came by Deborah's house with some cuts on one hand. He explained the cuts by saying his dog bit him, but Deborah didn't believe him. Now she thinks they were actually from Isaiah's break-in at the Auburn City Hall, which is not far from the Auburn Adventist Academy he'd attended and also not far from Auburn Station, a transit center where public buses come in from all over.

Isaiah's paths of distress, and his paths of crime and violence, seem to have regularly circled back onto the paths of his childhood: back to Auburn, back to the Burien Transit Center, back to places reachable by long public bus rides across stretches of suburbia, rides like the ones that got him to Puget Sound Adventist Academy as a teenager.

"Maybe a week later," Deborah said, "he's like, 'Mom, I've got a place.'" Deborah had kicked him out, and now he would be leaving his mom's apartment, too. Isaiah's mother got in her minivan with Isaiah and his pit bull, and Isaiah directed her to a large house on Seattle's Capitol Hill, not far from downtown. It was a huge, two-story Craftsman with a finished attic, bigger than any place Isaiah's family had ever lived. They arrived at around 10:30 a.m., but the house was already occupied, by a small financial services business. Isaiah walked into the business with his dog, announced that he owned the place, and began firing people. He looked around, opened cupboards, peered in crannies. He explained that he was an African king and that the home had been stolen from him during the sugar trade of the nineteenth century.

When the police arrived, Isaiah's mother begged them to take her son to the hospital instead of jail. She explained that several members of her own family had serious mental disorders and that Isaiah's sister had recently kicked him out because of his sudden personality changes. Isaiah's mother now believed her son had what her own mother had: schizophrenia. However, she told the police what was true: up to this point, Isaiah had never been diagnosed with anything. In fact, he had never seen a psychiatric professional of any sort. The police escorted Isaiah to Harborview Medical Center, where emergency psychiatric evaluations are conducted, and where Jennifer would be brought a little over a year later, and where Isaiah, after his arrest on charges of attacking Jennifer and Teresa, would then be brought by Detective Duffy for the court-ordered blood draw. It is a Gotham-like complex of medical towers, some art deco, some afterthought, that occupies multiple city blocks and receives, on its helipad, trauma cases from all over the Pacific Northwest.

"And here we go," said Dr. Lymberis. "When the family turned to the system, the system had the same dynamic as the family." The system was under financial stress. It was under time pressures. It had dysfunctions and limitations. No one could pay enough attention. Which was all well-known to people within this system. For decades, commissions at the state level, just like their counterparts at the federal level, had presented papers urging change, action, bigger fixes, more funds. "But, you know, everybody's too busy with their own narcissism, and with the narcissism of the country, to really address problems," Dr. Lymberis said. "So here we are."

In Washington State, 2008 brought the elimination of a thirty-bed ward at Western State Hospital, the largest publicly financed psychiatric hospital in the region, which had already shrunk considerably in recent years. Money saved by the ward closure was supposed to be invested in better community treatment programs, but that investment was effectively canceled out by recession-spurred cuts to those same programs. This contributed to an ongoing problem in which the system for handling people in acute mental distress was essentially locking up. Many other states faced, and still face, this problem. Like a number of those states, Washington addressed it by "boarding"—that is, strapping to gurneys in local emergency rooms—people deemed in need of psychiatric commitment but for whom there were no rooms available in any psychiatric hospital. In 2008, more than eight hundred people were held in this manner in the county that encompasses Seattle, kept in hallways or empty rooms in hospitals like Harborview, for various and unpredictable periods, waiting, often untreated, in a purgatory that local officials considered inhumane. By 2013, the year before the state's supreme court ruled this practice unconstitutional, the number of Harborview boardings would be up to nearly one thousand.

The month Isaiah was brought to Harborview, March 2008, saw forty-three people being boarded. They were not all at the hospital at once, nor were they all there for the entire month, but the number means that on March 28, 2008, when Isaiah was brought in, there were likely one or two people already strapped to gurneys at Harborview, in urgent need of involuntary commitment but waiting, in states from untreated to insufficiently treated, until a psychiatric bed opened up somewhere.

"During the evaluation," Dr. Lymberis wrote, "Isaiah actively tried to present himself as sane." Deborah, who was called during the evaluation by a Harborview doctor, described the same thing but in different language. "He done gone into this Harborview," Deborah said, "and talked to the man so cold where the doctor called me like I was the crazy one." Deborah couldn't believe it. She said she begged the doctor not to release Isaiah, explained that his family had become scared of him. She said the doctor told her Isaiah had not been deemed a danger to himself or others, so he would be sent on his way.

The particulars of the Harborview evaluation, Dr. Lymberis wrote, involved Isaiah denying "any depressive or psychotic symptoms, admitting only that, in the last two months, he has become more enlightened. He was 'being in the zone.' He refused to discuss any of the details of what actually brought him to the hospital." The hospital recorded Isaiah's family history of schizophrenia, but it diagnosed him with something different. It said he was in a manic state of bipolar disorder.

A hospital psychiatrist wrote that Isaiah's behavior "strongly suggests he is not capable of being in behavioral control due to his mania, that his decision-making is extremely poor," and that "his impulsivity creates an imminent risk." Isaiah had bothered other patients, had been combative with the hospital staff, and had claimed that people there were going to hurt him. Lithium was recommended should he be hospitalized against his will. However, the decision as to whether Isaiah would be held for a seventy-two-hour evaluation was not the hospital psychiatrist's to make.

Like other states, Washington uses a system of Designated Mental Health Professionals who are called to evaluate whether people like Isaiah—people brought to emergency psychiatric centers because of concerns about their behavior but who express profound disagreement with their diagnosis—should actually lose their civil liberties by being involuntarily committed. They have a hard job, balancing individual rights against community safety and applying a static law to dynamic mental disorders, often with little background information about the individual in question, all with the knowledge that in either direction, hold or release, there will be challenges in getting the individual care.

In Isaiah's case, the DMHP determined that Isaiah did not meet the state's criteria for involuntary commitment, which had been loosened and fine-tuned several times over the years but still revolved around the idea of danger to self or others. During the events that had brought Isaiah to Harborview, he had not described or evinced any intent to imminently harm himself or anyone else. He'd just falsely claimed to be an African king with the power to fire strangers from their jobs and had been a handful for hospital staff who he believed were wrongly detaining him. So, as Isaiah's own public defenders later wrote, "Ten hours after arriving at Harborview, Isaiah was released without medication, without prescription, and without follow-up aftercare."

He was twenty-two years old.

Records suggest Isaiah returned to the financial services firm, but the police scattered him off. By the next day, he was back at his mother's apartment, where she demanded that he begin taking medication or move out. This infuriated Isaiah, a not-uncommon reaction among people in the grip of a serious mental disorder and rejecting their diagnosis.

Detective Duffy saw this "all the time" when she was working as a nurse. There was a psychiatric unit on the eighth floor of her hospital, and there she learned that most of the time, if people don't want to take prescribed medication, "you can't force them. And, usually, if you finally get them on a regime, the meds make them feel quote-unquote not normal, or lethargic, or fuzzy, and so they feel that if they don't take their meds, they feel more normal." When, because of financial issues, her hospital lost its floor for treating patients in acute mental distress, Detective Duffy said a lot of the disturbed patients ended up on the street. "And that's what you see," she said. "You look out there now, every street corner there's somebody that could use help, mentally." Her investigations often end up involving people in this situation, either as victims or as perpetrators of violent crime. "So, I don't know what the answer is," she said. "More mental health facilities that are better funded? But I just don't think it's going to happen." The reason: "Money." Which doesn't make good sense to her, because she constantly sees the high cost of inaction and lack of investment. "I don't know why people don't see it," Detective Duffy said. "It's so expensive."

In Isaiah's case, the tendency to reject medication might have been heightened by what records suggest his father had taught him: that the correct response to personal trouble is merely increased will and anything else is failure. When Isaiah's mother, after his release from Harborview, said she wanted him to take medication, Isaiah told her to get out. Of her own home, the apartment in Burien. He told her, "You're dead to me."

His mother asked him what he was talking about. "Just leave," Isaiah told her. "Enjoy your last day on earth." His mother became scared, grabbed a pair of scissors to defend herself. "You're no match for me," Isaiah told her, according to a police report of the incident.

Deborah was present for this altercation and fled with Isaiah's mother and Isaiah's two younger siblings to the minivan. "Our family is in a whirlwind at this point," Deborah said. Someone told Isaiah to stay put. Someone told Isaiah to be out by the next day. In response, Isaiah grabbed a backpack and his dog and left, walking past the minivan and flashing a knife with a six-inch blade as he did so.

Deborah and her mother followed Isaiah. He was headed, once again, for the Burien Transit Center and its depiction of the volcano. Isaiah's father was summoned, and when he caught up with his son, Isaiah said to his father, "My family has forsaken me. You'll never see me again."

In a sense, the last part was true.

Isaiah having disappeared from their sight, the family called the police. The police searched for Isaiah but didn't find him. By the next day, Isaiah was back at his mother's apartment, smashing the windshield of her new minivan with a rock. She watched from a window of her apartment as he went around the vehicle breaking more windows, as if they were the barrier he needed to shatter to solve his predicament.

"Stop that," she shouted.

"Go fuck yourself," he shouted back. She told him to leave, and he kept shouting at her, "You're all dead." His words suggested they were his enemies now, that in his mind, at this moment, they were what was persecuting him.

Isaiah's mother called the police, Isaiah left, and the police searched the area again but failed to find him. After that, his mother and his two younger siblings were driven in a patrol car to Deborah's place, where it was thought they'd be safer.

Deborah remembers how proud her mom was of her new minivan, the one she'd skipped a payment on to get Isaiah new clothes, and how much its destruction hurt her. "That was something that she got on her own without her husband," Deborah said. "It meant something to her. And the look—I'd never seen my mom look like that before. It was so sad. I wish I could take it away."

Soon, Isaiah was out in front of Deborah's place. He'd run there from his mom's. "All of a sudden you hear all this glass breaking," Deborah said. He'd thrown a rock through the window of her front door. He was standing in a grass field across the street from her house, a field on the flat top of a drumlin, no water view, no dramatic relief, just the tips of the Olympics above the distant horizon where the hill begins to drop off. Isaiah was shouting, "Come on! Come on!"

"You would have thought we was gang members or something," Deborah said. Beyond the shouting and threats, there was something very off about Isaiah. "It was like his soul was gone," she said. "His eyes were like black." He was jumping as he shouted. "I've never seen a human jump that high off grass," Deborah said. "No trampoline, no nothing." Isaiah had his dog with him. He sometimes described it as a service animal, and its name was Indo, a common slang for marijuana. When Isaiah's family came out to try to calm him, he removed Indo's leash and told the dog to attack. When it didn't, Isaiah began swinging the leash, which had a chain on the end, at his mother. "He had no idea who I was," she said. "And at that point, I knew he was in a psychotic break." The chain hit her head.

"Once my mom hits the ground," Deborah said, "we lose it. I lose it. My kids' dad loses it. So we're, like, trying to tackle Isaiah. We have to get him down. 'Cause this is not my brother right now. I swear. I believe in people being possessed and all that stuff, and I don't know what took over his body, but we're gonna get it out. 'Cause, like, you just knocked Mom down with a dog chain, and you would never hit Mother. You would never hit Mom. I don't know what's in you right now."

Deborah is a big woman and not easily intimidated. "When I was younger," she said, "if I got in a fight, it was with a boy. I won every time." There was a nosy neighbor watching it all unfold—"Bless her soul," Deborah said—and now Deborah shouted at the nosy neighbor to quit watching and call the police. Then she jumped on her brother.

"I just tackle him," she said. "I just jump on Isaiah, and I'm just laying on him." He shouted at her to get off. He growled. He foamed at the mouth. "Have you ever seen somebody, like, you can look straight through them?" Deborah asked. "In their eyes? It was dead. You know what I mean? Like a doll . . . That's how he looks." Her children's father came to help hold Isaiah down, and once Isaiah was under control, Deborah lay down near him.

"And I start rubbing his head," Deborah said. "I'm rubbing his head, and I'm like, 'Isaiah, why?' Just, 'Why?' Just, 'Talk to me, I love you so much, just tell me. Isaiah, what happened?' And he just gets this joker smile on his face . . . But still that same look, that dead look . . . He's just cheesin'. I'm like, 'Isaiah, I love you. I'm not mad anymore. I don't hate you right now. I'm not mad you hurt Mom.' All I feel is just love, like I gave birth to him myself . . . And I didn't, but I basically helped raise Isaiah, okay? So when we're laying on this ground, it was so hurtful, but it was just peaceful. It was almost like nobody was there. And it was like, 'Isaiah, just tell me, what happened? Why are you doing this? Are you okay?

I love you. I love you. I love you.' And I kept repeating that. 'I love you. I love you, I love you, I love you.' A million times until the police got there."

The police arrived, and two days after he'd been released from Harborview, where his mother had hoped he'd be treated, Isaiah was loaded into a police cruiser and taken to jail, where he could not be well treated and where his twisted path into, out of, and then back into the criminal justice system began.

The day after this arrest, Deborah and their mother went to see Isaiah. He was awaiting arraignment, charged with felony harassment and malicious mischief. Deborah asked him, "Why did you do that?" Isaiah, she said, replied, "Because you tried to have me committed. I'm not crazy. You guys tried to have me committed."

Deborah's next step was to call back the doctor at Harborview and tell him what happened. "But he wouldn't take none of my calls," Deborah said. She admits she wasn't being her most polite self. "I'm not gonna lie," Deborah said. "I have never been so ghetto in my life. I was cussing. I was cursing. Because I was so mad."

Like her mother, she asked, "Why do you have to wait until someone dies, or gets critically hurt, before they do anything?"

Offered a brief sketch of the history and the current state of the law, she said, "I get that. I can understand that. 'Cause I sure wouldn't want to be committed just because someone thought so." And then, "Jesus, what are we gonna do?"

26

Fifteen days later, Isaiah, wearing a red prisoner's uniform, his hands cuffed behind his back, stood before the King County Superior Court judge Brian Gain. The date: April 14, 2008. Through a glass window at the back of the courtroom, his mother and Deborah watched as a deputy prosecutor immediately requested that Isaiah be sent to Western State Hospital, the state's main psychiatric hospital, for an evaluation. Isaiah's public defender said she'd spoken with Isaiah about the likelihood of this happening, and he'd told her it was fine.

Isaiah began shaking his head.

"I did not agree to that," he said, in a clear and slightly perturbed voice. "I'm not crazy. I don't feel like I need an evaluation."

A few days earlier, as Isaiah waited in jail for this hearing, the last item in his parents' divorce had been settled. Isaiah's mother was now on disability, his father no longer required to make support payments to her. Whether Isaiah's high school tuition debts were ever paid remains unclear, though at this point it didn't matter much.

It had been about six years since the divorce began, and about the same amount of time had passed since the Family Court social worker recommended Isaiah get counseling. Over that time, the paperwork on his parents' divorce had become a stack nearly a foot high, and no counseling had occurred. Now, finished with its dealings with Isaiah's parents, King County Superior Court was turning to the matter of the new charges against their son, whose relatively thin stack of paperwork would soon eclipse theirs.

Judge Gain, whom Isaiah was now standing before, was the chief judge at the Regional Justice Center in Kent, a city just south of Seattle and just north of Auburn Adventist Academy. He has salt-and-pepper hair and at times sports a thick black beard and mustache befitting a mariner. In the right cap, he could be imagined captaining one of the countless fishing vessels that sail annually out of Seattle's protected harbors to the frigid waters of Alaska in search of cod and halibut. He served in the army in Vietnam, graduated from Loyola Law School in Los Angeles in 1972, and worked variously as a public defender, a King County deputy prosecutor, and the city attorney for Bellevue, just east of Seattle. All judges are elected in nonpartisan races in Washington State, and in 1992 he ran for and won a spot on the King County Superior Court bench. During that campaign, he emphasized his work on behalf of crime victims and said he considered himself part of the community's continuing response to domestic violence. He also said he considered it his job to safeguard civil liberties, impartially apply the law, and "treat all litigants with dignity and respect." He's faced five elections since 1992 but has never been challenged for his seat.

A typical day in Judge Gain's courtroom could bring as many as fifty new defendants like Isaiah, part of a heavy churn that feeds concern about an underfunded, overstretched judiciary. It's a concern mirrored in other states, but it's been particularly acute in Washington State, which, at the time Isaiah was standing before Judge Gain, ranked last in the nation in terms of state spending on local courts. Less than one half of one percent of the state's budget goes to court funding, leaving individual counties trying, with uneven results, to cover the remaining costs. To help ease the burden this system creates, the chief justice of the Washington State Supreme Court, Barbara Madsen, has at times volunteered as a first-appearance judge. "If you have five minutes with these defendants, you're doing good," she said in 2011 on a state public affairs show. "I was just sort of praying that nothing happened that would prove that I made a mistake on a release decision, for example." She wondered how the full-time judges do it, comparing it to air traffic control. "If the planes crash midair, it's because you didn't see the blip on the radar screen," she said. "It's really kind of terrifying, honestly . . . So few resources, so little time, and so many criminal defendants."

Judge Gain wouldn't speak about the specifics of Isaiah's case. He said he saw "no benefit." But he did say, in two letters to me, that cases like Isaiah's are "a particular challenge." Here, at this first hearing with Isaiah, he had a twenty-two-year-old defendant who had not yet been convicted of any felony and who didn't, at this moment, want a psychiatric evaluation. The defendant was being accused of serious violence and threats of violence, but in a court of law these are only accusations until proven.

The prosecutor was presenting the defendant as so mentally ill that he needed to lose certain civil liberties and be involuntarily committed, but, as Judge Gain wrote in his letter, "resources for the criminal justice system to address mental illness are extremely limited." In addition, he said, "Western State Hospital is already stressed because of lack of resources and the volume of cases they are asked to examine." Like the Designated Mental Health Professional at Harborview, Judge Gain was in the position of knowing that whichever way he sent Isaiah, hold or release, there would be challenges in getting him care.

Judge Gain asked to read the charging documents. They were handed up, and as he began reading, Isaiah suggested he wanted to fire his public defender, a woman named Mary Ellen Ramey. Two jail guards stood close behind Isaiah, one wearing blue plastic gloves. Isaiah then turned to Ramey, who had been keeping her distance from him. "Was I unclear?" he asked. She replied, in essence, that he was. "I said that I did not want an evaluation," Isaiah said. "I'm saying it now, again." There was a full minute of silence as Judge Gain read through the details of Isaiah's alleged violence and threats against his mother and sister, the release from Harborview, the smashing of the minivan windows, the promises of death, the swinging of the dog chain, his mother falling, his sister tackling him.

"Mr. Kalebu," Judge Gain asked, "are you required to take some medication?"

"I am not," he said.

"Have you been prescribed medication?"

"I have not."

Judge Gain paused for a few seconds. He scratched his left ear.

"Have you ever received any treatment for mental health issues?"

"I have not."

Another pause as Judge Gain read further into the charging documents, a pause that lasted another full minute, after which Judge Gain looked up and said, "I'm going to send you down to Western State."

Isaiah said he wanted his mother, who was still watching from behind the glass window, to speak. The guard with the gloves moved closer still. Judge Gain denied the request.

"I have a question," Isaiah said.

"Yes, go ahead," Judge Gain replied.

"When I appeal all this, and it gets bumped up to a higher jurisdiction, who do you think they're gonna rule in favor of?" He laughed a little at this, as if chuckling at the judge's stupidity. "What do you think's gonna happen?"

Isaiah's mother stood, put her hand over her mouth, pressed close against the glass separating her from the courtroom.

"They're going to want to know what your mental health issues are," Judge Gain said.

"Exactly, exactly."

Isaiah was smiling now, head cocked, confident, as if he'd put the judge in checkmate. The guard gestured silently to the judge, asking whether the judge wanted him to physically remove Isaiah from court.

"You can appeal if you'd like," Judge Gain said.

"I will," Isaiah said. Then, leaning toward the judge, he added, "My best recommendation for you is to start saving all of your money, liquidating all of your assets, because by the time we're done, you won't be able to buy and sell shit."

The guard's gesturing became more intense.

"Mr. Kalebu," Judge Gain said, "anything else you'd like to tell me?"

"No, that's about it."

"You just confirmed that you need to have somebody tell me what your mental health issues are."

A thirty-day evaluation was agreed upon by the judge and the lawyers.

"Thirty days it is," Isaiah said. "See you guys in a month. That's plenty of time to save up, right? Better sell your house. Better sell your car."

"We'll see you, Mr. Kalebu."

The hearing concluded, clocking in at almost exactly five minutes. The guard began pulling Isaiah away.

"Better sell all your stuff," Isaiah said. "I ain't gonna lose!"

Western State Hospital is on a groomed campus that's a roughly seven-minute walk from the community college Isaiah had dropped out of three years earlier. Once at the hospital, Isaiah was a "constant behavioral management problem," according to a report written by a state psychologist, Dr. Gregory Kramer. Isaiah was angry, demanding, threatening, "but not violent."

In Dr. Kramer's opinion, he was also inappropriately focused on wrongs done to him by his family. He paced constantly. He jumped on and off a table with no explanation. He was placed in restraints for two days, during which time he verbally harassed a female staff member assigned to monitor him. When asked the date, he said it was March 29. It was as if time had stopped on the day his mother confronted him about the need to take medication. In fact, it was a month later, April 30, 2008.

In the world outside, the reality of the financial crisis was beginning to register, the first Bush stimulus package having passed a few months before in a $152 billion attempt to avert recession. Soon, taxpayers would be receiving "stimulus checks" to encourage consumer spending. The collapse of Lehman Brothers was five months away.

Isaiah's aunt was contacted, and she told Western State doctors about Isaiah's family life. "His upbringing was difficult due to neglect and abuse," Dr. Kramer wrote in his report. "And he developed a lot of anger." Isaiah told Western State that his childhood was "rough" and that he had "beatings" and watched his parents fight. He talked about being sent away to boarding school, about his parents' divorce, about his father's upbringing in Uganda and recent remarriage, about his color blindness and its consequences for pilot school, about the roughly twenty jobs he held in quick succession after that. "He reported that sometimes he quit and sometimes he was fired," the report states. "He described his frequent employment changes as resulting from him having higher standards than others because he does not lie, cheat, or steal. He denied ever being married and reported no children 'that I know of.' He denied any history of significant relationships, three months being his longest reported relationship." He said he "rarely" used marijuana, specifying less than once a week, and that he used no other drugs, though he did say he sometimes became depressed and cried when he drank too much.

"According to his aunt," the report states, "Mr. Kalebu's father's cultural upbringing did not include acceptance of mental disorders." Isaiah described his mother as a "drug addict" who abused painkillers, echoing his father's allegations in the divorce proceedings. He described himself as being "in the zone" the last few months and at first denied he'd been taken to Harborview. Later, he admitted he had been taken there and also admitted that he sometimes fired people. He described his mood most days as "ecstatic" and said it sometimes got him in trouble.

Like Harborview, Western State diagnosed Isaiah as bipolar but said more evaluation was needed to determine other aspects of his mental disturbance. It also stated that Isaiah was not competent to stand trial because of his rigid thought processes and that he posed "an elevated risk for future danger to others" because of his lack of insight into his mental disturbance, his alleged violence, his rough upbringing, his "early maladjustment," his employment issues, his lack of relationships, his resistance to treatment attempts, his impulsivity, his negative attitudes, and his expected stress upon release. It recommended a process called "competency restoration," which is essentially a prolonged involuntary commitment at Western State. It also recommended the hospital be granted authority to force Isaiah to take psychotropic medications if necessary.

Judge Gain agreed but not before having another exchange in court with Isaiah. On May 15, 2008, a hearing was held to review the Western State recommendations, and Mary Ellen Ramey, Isaiah's lawyer, told the court she had no evidence with which to rebut them. Judge Gain said that based on the Western State report, competency restoration "is the only option I have."

"May I speak, please?" Isaiah asked. "May I please speak?"

"Sure," Judge Gain said.

"I feel that I am competent for trial," Isaiah said. He then proceeded to say some seemingly odd things. "I feel that I knowingly committed the crime," he told Judge Gain. Such an admission could negate the need for a trial, but Isaiah went on, sounding as if he were still hoping for a trial and, maybe, exoneration. "I feel like for me to explain my actions, I would like to be able to face my accusers and explain them in a rational way," he said. "I have valid reasons for them. And, if I go back to Western State I will not have the opportunity to explain myself. I would just simply ask for the opportunity to explain myself."

As a legal strategy, this did not make a lot of sense. But if there is some psychological sense to be made of it, perhaps what Isaiah was saying is that his current self—this disjointed, unmedicated, allegedly incompetent, but very confident self—could see that by going through "competency restoration," it would lose the opportunity to explain itself. It wanted to remain itself, and explain itself, now.

"You will have an opportunity," Judge Gain said. "But I am going to sign the order."

"May I ask why it is that I'm found incompetent?"

Judge Gain told Isaiah to talk to his attorney. The next day, while waiting in the King County Jail to be transferred back to Western State, Isaiah attempted suicide by tying clothing around his neck. He was given some Ativan, placed in isolation, and then sent for competency restoration.

Competency restoration is not long-term treatment. It is not psychotherapy. It was not a venue for exploring Isaiah's deep rage and disappointment or their sources. It was not what Isaiah's elementary school teachers thought he needed thirteen years earlier or what the Family Court social worker thought he needed six years earlier. Many of Isaiah's statements while at Western State, particularly the ones Dr. Kramer found too focused on blaming his family, could be interpreted as invitations to this kind of exploration. But these were not invitations Western State was prepared to accept.

Competency restoration is simply what it says, the restoration of a person's ability to meet the minimum legal standard of competency. That is, the ability to understand the charges against oneself and assist one's attorney. This, as Judge Gain suggested in his letter, is one of the many problems with handling complex psychological challenges through the court system. The court system doesn't have the time, or the mandate, to make more than a narrowly targeted effort. The focus is on preparing a defendant for questions of guilt and punishment, not on preparing a troubled person for recovery and, perhaps, integration back into society.

The major vehicle Western State used for achieving competency with Isaiah was forced medications, first the antipsychotic Zyprexa, then the mood stabilizer lithium. He had been quite angry when he returned to the facility from court, glaring at the doctor who greeted him. "His speech was rapid and he was difficult to interrupt at times," the report on his competency restoration noted. "Some grandiosity was apparent." He described his suicide attempt as a "plea for help" but didn't want to talk much more about it, saying it was "a moment of weakness that I would rather not dwell on." He complained he was being treated poorly, "demanded rule books so that he could see what the rules were and where they were written," described his public defender as "not on my side," and spoke about his ability to think rationally as a "super power considering the world we live in where nobody thinks rationally and logically."

Zyprexa, the Western State report explained, is "an antipsychotic also sometimes used to treat acute mania." During the two days after it was prescribed for Isaiah, he got in fights with other inmates and had to be sent to the hospital for his injuries. Eventually, he was tapered off the Zyprexa and put on lithium, which doctors thought improved his mood somewhat. His speech slowed down. He was less impulsive. The mania seemed to be gone, but the grandiose thinking lingered, and the denial of any mental disorder was still present. "Overall," Western State reported, "he appeared more emotionally stable."

Again, Isaiah was diagnosed as bipolar, this time with the notation of some "possible Narcissistic traits, including an apparent sense of entitlement, arrogant behavior, and grandiose sense of self-importance." He also was described as "a relatively intelligent individual with no obvious intellectual or cognitive defects" who now, in the opinion of Dr. Kramer, met the minimum legal standard for competency. The date of his opinion: July 11, 2008. Isaiah was now a few weeks shy of his twenty-third birthday.

On August 6, competency restored, Isaiah was back before Judge Gain. His bearing was different from before, more slouched than coiled, his face slack. The joker-like grin was nowhere to be seen. Asked by Judge Gain about his mental health, Isaiah replied, "I am calm." His speech was also different from that in his earlier appearance, more molasses than geyser, his tone more remote. "I'm fine," Isaiah continued. "Competent." Asked by the judge whether the medication was helping, he replied, "Uh, yes."

Isaiah's lawyer, Mary Ellen Ramey, pronounced a "total turnaround" and urged Judge Gain to release Isaiah to his aunt, Rachel Kalebu, pending trial, "with any conditions that the court would impose."

The prosecutor immediately pointed out the weakness in this plan. It was a family member's demand that Isaiah take medication, the prosecutor reminded the court, that led to Isaiah's being arrested and brought before Judge Gain in the first place. If Judge Gain were to release Isaiah, the prosecutor recommended strict conditions.

Judge Gain essentially agreed with this assessment. Isaiah would be released on the condition that he have no alcohol or illegal drugs, possess no dangerous weapons, have no contact with his mother or Deborah, establish care with a community health center, attend all appointments, take all medications as instructed, and provide his medical records to the court so that Judge Gain could monitor his treatment if need be. "I don't want to be back in a circumstance where he's not taking his medication," Judge Gain said, perhaps recalling a warning in Dr. Kramer's report. It called Isaiah "an above average long-term risk for future danger to others" and said his competency would warrant reevaluation "should he stop taking his medication and decompensate."

On August 21, 2008, after a successful one-day visit with his aunt, Isaiah was set free on his own recognizance. It was now a few weeks after his twenty-third birthday. In the span of four months, he had run a route that is typical in a system that routinely fails people like him, a route that led from his mother's care to the police, from the police to the emergency room at Harborview, from the Harborview emergency room back to his mother's care, from his mother's care back to the police, and, finally, from the police to jail. Once in jail, Isaiah had been sent to the courtroom of Judge Brian Gain, from Judge Gain's courtroom to Western State Hospital, from Western State Hospital back to Judge Gain with a finding of competency, and then, with certain conditions, back into the community. This is not the community treatment apparatus that President Kennedy envisioned when he signed the Community Mental Health Act in 1963. It was now the fall of 2008. Teresa and Jennifer had been engaged for two months.

27

What Isaiah still didn't have was a relationship with someone who had time to hear his whole story, someone who could sit alongside the young man, talk with him, look with him into his experience, its beginnings, its possibilities. Instead, he continued to be seen in pieces. That is, whatever piece of him seemed most pressing to whatever particular authorities had to deal with him at a given moment. "They only see a section of the elephant," Dr. Lymberis said. "So, to one person it looks like a snake. To another person, it looks like—I don't know—a tiger or whatever, and it's because the picture they have is very limited. But if you put the whole thing together, that is when the whole thing comes to life." Isaiah also didn't have a clear recognition that he needed help, which made things more complicated. Western State called his insight into his mental disorder "limited" and had cautioned in its final report to Judge Gain that Isaiah's ability to be compliant with medications was unknown, because he'd never once taken them without being forced. But the prospect of his establishing a relationship with a community treatment provider did offer some hope. Maybe it would be an opportunity for a more comprehensive encounter.

"In the treatment of people with severe chronic mental illness," Dr. Lymberis wrote later, "medication is necessary, often life-saving, but it does not result in meaningful adaptational change unless it is linked to effective and meaningful psychotherapy." Theoretically, this possibility, or something like it, now awaited Isaiah.

Theoretically. In actuality, community treatment clinics like the one Isaiah established care with are chronically underfunded and overworked, with treatment providers paid significantly lower salaries than providers in the private sector, who generally see people with health insurance or the ability to pay out of pocket. The name of Isaiah's publicly funded provider: Cascade Mental Health Care. There, initial intake paperwork noted Isaiah as depressed, socially isolated, and suffering from mood swings, irritability, anxiety, aggression, grief, and emotional trauma. He was given a prescription for Zyprexa and lithium, the same medications he'd been prescribed at Western State. When Isaiah showed up for his first session, on September 11, 2008, he was back to denying any mental disturbance whatsoever. He said he wasn't depressed, anxious, or experiencing any sort of psychosis. He was noted to be angry and gave "testy, short, and curt answers." He also expressed displeasure at having to be involved in community treatment at all. He had been free on his own recognizance for exactly three weeks.

Isaiah's blood could have been tested to see whether he was taking his lithium as prescribed. It wasn't. Instead, a blood draw was ordered for Isaiah's next visit, set for early October. Isaiah didn't show for that visit. Nor did he appear for his scheduled visits in November or December. By the beginning of 2009, nine months before Teresa and Jennifer's wedding date, Isaiah had spent more than three months out of compliance with Judge Gain's order that he attend all of his Cascade Mental Health Care appointments. "Neither the provider nor his aunt informed the court," Isaiah's public defenders wrote years later. "Nor did the court seek verification of Isaiah's mental health medication and treatment compliance." Such lack of communication and oversight is not unusual, given the demands on the mental health and criminal justice systems and the limited resources they are provided. In this case, the lack of communication and oversight continued for a total of eleven months. It went on, Isaiah's lawyers later wrote, "even though Isaiah had fourteen scheduled court hearings during that period."

During this same period, the Washington State Legislature was struggling with a $9 billion shortfall caused by the financial crisis, which had now become the Great Recession. In an echo of the national mood, voters in Washington State opposed increasing taxes. At the same time, they demanded more effective government services. Similarly, major businesses in the state wanted tax breaks and were embracing tax dodges while at the same time demanding a better-educated workforce and massive improvements to the transportation infrastructure. To meet these contradictory demands, Washington State's elected leaders, like many others around the country, began cutting their state's own safety net, including mental health funding. Simultaneously, the federal government's spending for mental health declined. As a result, over the two-year budgeting cycle that began in 2009, funding for mental health services in Washington State dropped by $24 million, and sixty more beds were lost at Western State Hospital. This phenomenon was repeated all around the nation, to the point that the National Alliance on Mental Illness, in a 2009 report, described a system "in crisis" that was creating "a vicious cycle that destroys lives, and creates more significant financial troubles for states and the federal government in the long-run."

Due to what the report described as "our country's utter neglect of its most vulnerable citizens," the United States again received a D grade for its mental health services. "The lack of improvement over time brings into sharp relief our complete failure to take charge of an ineffective system and begin to transform it," the report stated. "It need not be this way."

It continued this way. Isaiah did show up for an appointment on January 7, 2009, at Cascade Mental Health Care, but on that day he was angry, argued with his treatment provider, expressed displeasure with his medication, and tried to negotiate some other alternative. He particularly didn't like taking Zyprexa. "The clinician, hoping to 'prevent him' from stopping his medication, agreed to lower the dose without having checked any blood levels," Dr. Lymberis wrote. The same clinician noted that Isaiah going off his meds "would be a disaster."

Isaiah never returned to Cascade Mental Health Care. "Very little is known about Isaiah's activities between January 2009 to late June 2009," his public defenders later wrote. He was barred by court order from contact with his mother and Deborah. He was out of work. He was living with his aunt, but, Dr. Lymberis wrote, "during that time he was isolated, only taking walks with his dog every day."

Beyond his aunt, his family feared him. "His personhood and humanity were lost to the illness," Dr. Lymberis wrote. "Isaiah became his illness." On top of this, restraining orders against him by his mother and sister, she wrote, "were experienced by him, in his damaged state, as worse than abandonment."

He could still pull it together, though. Could still, at times, do what his father had taught him: tough it out. On April 24, 2009, Isaiah appeared in court for a pretrial hearing in the case revolving around his alleged threats and violence against his mother and sister. His hair was cut in a short, tight Afro, and he was wearing a brown leather jacket over a gray dress shirt. His demeanor was tense but controlled. With Mary Ellen Ramey standing next to him, he pleaded guilty to the harassment and malicious mischief charges. Then, when told he would have to provide a DNA sample as part of his plea, he withdrew the plea and asked for a new lawyer. A trial was now inevitable.

Two months later, Isaiah's aunt picked up the phone at her house in Stonewood, a suburban development shaded by evergreen trees just south of Tacoma. Signs at the development's entrance feature a twisting river carved in wood and painted in light browns. She called the local human services department and reported that Isaiah was off his medications, that he was showing symptoms of his mental disorder. When human services staff arrived, they observed Isaiah to have "very controlled, pressured speech, and an intense stare." He denied he had any psychological disturbance, telling them it was his aunt who was delusional. Isaiah's tendency to turn things around, and to blame the women who were sheltering him, was still present.

Court documents state that human services "was unable to determine any grounds for detention of Isaiah." The department wouldn't comment on the case, citing medical privacy rules, but presumably Isaiah was again ruled not a danger to himself or others because the next day he was out with his dog, roaming a park near his aunt's house.

Cirque Park is mostly flat and wide open, holding ball fields, a skate park, an off-leash area for dogs, and, in one corner, a wooded hill with gravel trails. In an area of the park that requires dogs to be on leashes, Isaiah was seen flouting the rule in an inventive manner. He had attached a leash to Indo, but then he'd let go of the leash so the pit bull could wander about freely, dragging the leash behind him. When an animal-control officer told Isaiah to hold on to the leash, Isaiah "flipped him off and then made sexual and derogatory remarks and started to approach him," according to court records. Isaiah then "started to follow him around the parking lot and only stopped when police arrived."

The police officers found an upset Isaiah, who had "the large pit bull in one hand and a golf club in the other." It was a Wilson 3 iron, a type of club that J. J. Jones, Rachel Kalebu's roommate and an avid golfer, kept around the house. The police had with them Tasers and nonlethal bean-bag guns, tools that departments have been buying and deploying with increasing frequency as they confront disturbed individuals who need restraint and psychiatric help rather than lethal force. The officers told Isaiah to put the golf club down. Isaiah did. They asked him why he was harassing the animal-control officer. Isaiah said it was an expression of free speech.

They asked Isaiah for identification. Isaiah refused. They threatened Isaiah with arrest. Go ahead, he told them.

The officers told Isaiah to place his hands behind his back and let go of the dog. Isaiah refused. They warned him to comply or be tasered. Isaiah refused to comply.

"Tasers were deployed," the police report states, "but not effectively." Isaiah picked up the golf club. Indo became agitated. The officers then shot Isaiah with nonlethal beanbag rounds, tasered him again, took him into custody, and charged him with obstructing law enforcement and resisting arrest.

The following day—Tuesday, June 30, 2009—Isaiah appeared in the courtroom of the Pierce County District Court judge Pat O'Malley. During the weekend that had just passed, Gay Pride weekend in Seattle, Teresa and Jennifer had gone out shopping and returned with Teresa's $70 wedding dress and those pearl earrings.

Judge O'Malley is a genial, soft-spoken man who, like Judge Gain, has seen the law, and the force it wields, from a number of sides. Born in Minneapolis, he attended college at the University of Minnesota and then enlisted in the navy, where he served as an officer for three years. "I was in firefights," Judge O'Malley said. "And there's some things that are just plain unavoidable. That just happen. When your number's up, it's up. So. Do you try to prevent that? Absolutely." The cruelty and capriciousness of life must be tempered by justice. After leaving the navy, he went to law school at Gonzaga University in eastern Washington and then worked as a public defender, a labor lawyer, an elected Port of Tacoma commissioner, and a county council member. In 2002, he was elected a Pierce County District Court judge with 54 percent of the vote. In the years after, he never faced a challenger.

About eighty cases a day move through Judge O'Malley's courtroom, roughly ten an hour. "Hello," he said as he opened court on this day, audio of the proceedings digitally recorded. "Have a seat, everybody. Where would we like to begin? Let's see. How many do we have in the jail, total? A lot? Okay. Let's start with one in the jail . . ."

A Mr. Booker appeared, charged with driving while his license was suspended. He pleaded not guilty and was released pending further hearings. A Mr. Owen appeared, charged with vehicle prowling. He'd missed a recent hearing because of the flu, he said. "Remember what we talked about, about who you hang around with," Judge O'Malley told Mr. Owen before encouraging him to keep up with classes he was taking at a technical college. A Mr. Zalzibar appeared, having been picked up on a very old charge of driving while under the influence. Judge O'Malley said a few words to Mr. Zalzibar in Spanish, leaving the rest up to an interpreter, and then released Mr. Zalzibar, finding that the day the man had just spent in jail was enough punishment for such an old offense and good behavior since. About forty minutes and five other cases later, Isaiah's name and case number were called. Someone whispered to Judge O'Malley, "His aunt's in the courtroom."

"Oh," Judge O'Malley said. "Mr. Kalebu, your aunt's in the courtroom. How about if you move up one pew?"

"I can see her," Isaiah said.

"Oh, you can see her? Great. Well, she's been here for quite a while. I'd say at least an hour. So, pretty nice of her to come. Thank her when you get out, okay?"

"Yes, sir."

The charges against Isaiah were announced: obstruction and resisting arrest. Isaiah, through his public defender, pleaded not guilty. No mention was made of the unmedicated context in which the charges arose.

"Okay, thank you," Judge O'Malley said. "I'm just reading the declaration now."

Judge O'Malley read the declaration of probable cause, which outlined Isaiah's standoff with the police in the park. A few seconds in, he sighed audibly in an otherwise silent courtroom. About forty-five seconds in, he issued a concerned "Hm" and kept going, the courtroom still silent, waiting. "Wow," Judge O'Malley said after about a minute. "Well, I'll find probable cause. Fortunate something really bad didn't happen that day. Ugh. So. Conditions?"

Judge O'Malley wanted to know what conditions the prosecutor would like imposed should the judge decide to release Isaiah until his next hearing. The prosecutor asked for $1,000 bail and noted that Isaiah had an open matter in King County (the case in Judge Gain's court) as well as a bit of a warrant history (connected to the misdemeanor theft and marijuana possession charges from a few years back).

"Well, it doesn't look like there are any—or maybe there are. What's the F-column mean again?" Judge O'Malley was struggling with the antiquated patchwork of computer systems still used by all trial courts in Washington State. Judges have been asking for improvements to these systems for more than a decade. Meanwhile, the state that birthed Microsoft and later, at Microsoft's urging, allowed the company billions of dollars in tax breaks has struggled to find the money to upgrade its trial courts' case management software.

The antiquated system was unable to tell Judge O'Malley what conditions Judge Gain had released Isaiah on, even though it would have been quite useful for Judge O'Malley to know that those conditions included compliance with mental health treatment and no new law violations. "We're dealing with hundreds of people a week on a relatively limited amount of information," Judge O'Malley said. "So that's it." (Judge Gain, who later would not be able to easily pull up details about Judge O'Malley's interaction with Isaiah, told me in one letter, "Unfortunately, only in the movies and TV is the criminal justice system omniscient.")

———————

As Judge O'Malley peered into his insufficient computer screen, Isaiah's public defender noted that Isaiah was a longtime resident of the area, that a family member was present, that Isaiah was currently on state welfare, and that he had a minimal conviction history. The public defender also told the court that Judge Gain had released Isaiah on his own recognizance, which was true, narrowly speaking, and he asked Judge O'Malley for the same treatment in this case.

Judge O'Malley thought for a moment, and then he spoke: "Like I said, it's fortunate something—it didn't deteriorate." He perused Isaiah's computer record some more. "Where do you live?" he asked. "Do you live with yourself?"

("What I'm trying to do while I'm talking with people," Judge O'Malley told me later, "I'm trying to get some connection with them. I'm trying to understand them, if you will.")

"I live with the lady you see right there," Isaiah said. He was referring to his aunt, Rachel Kalebu.

("He appeared to be very articulate and grounded," Judge O'Malley said later. "There's no hostility in his tone or manner . . . His aunt was there vouching for him.")

"Okay," Judge O'Malley said to Isaiah. "And are you going to school? Or, what do you do?"

("We're not psychiatrists," Judge O'Malley told me. He didn't know, at this point, about Isaiah's mental disorder. The computer system couldn't tell him about it, and the charging documents didn't mention it, focusing only on the part of the elephant they were concerned with, the confrontation with law enforcement.)

"I am not in school at the moment," Isaiah told the judge. "But as soon as I have the financial means to, I will be."

"Okay," Judge O'Malley said. "Well. I'll tell you what, I'll release you on your personal recognizance."

"Thank you very much."

("I think I made the best decision I could at the time," Judge O'Malley later said. "Had I had additional information—we all can look back at many facets of our lives and say, 'Wow, had I known this, I would have done this.' That's the uncertainty of life. This job, unfortunately, has an element of uncertainty and risk that you just sort of have to accept. We have more people in jail in the United States than just about any country in the world. We're not going to be able to put all these people in jail, and statistically something like this can happen. Obviously, I feel sad, but I think the same with Judge Gain: he did the best job he possibly could under the circumstances.")

At the hearing, Judge O'Malley then said to Isaiah, "You're a smart guy, use your good sense." He was still perusing Isaiah's computer record. "What I see here is a pattern . . . It's a pattern there that I hope you address before something happens that you can't fix like today."

"Yes, Your Honor."

An elderly, weak voice now rose from the courtroom, Rachel Kalebu's voice. "Thank you, Your Honor. He's my nephew. My nephew has bipolar."

"I can't hear you," Judge O'Malley said.

Someone closer to Judge O'Malley said, "He has bipolar."

"Ohhhh," Judge O'Malley said. "Oh, okay."

The limited history that Judge O'Malley was seeing on his computer screen now began to make a little more sense. Even so, he didn't have any evidence that Isaiah was currently, at the present moment, a danger to himself or others, so there was no option to involuntarily commit him. "Couldn't have done that," Judge O'Malley said later. "There was nothing there. That was out of the question." Also, Judge O'Malley believes that jail is "the worst place in the world" for people diagnosed as bipolar. "From what I've read in the literature, it intensifies their condition rather than alleviates it, so they're worse when they're released," he said. That in turn increases the chance they'll end up right back in court, where, he believes, the cycle continues.

Judge O'Malley now asked Isaiah and his public defender to wait a moment. He still had a chance to reverse his earlier decision.

("You have to make a decision every couple of minutes," he told me later. "The prosecutors are all just saying, 'Put 'em in jail.' The defense lawyers are all just saying, 'No, he's fine.'" Helpful information is lacking. "It's just an antiquated system," Judge O'Malley said. "So, clearly, if one could improve the communication between these different spheres, or these different, like, kingdoms, that would be a huge step. Because information is really a critical aspect of it, I think." However, easy communication between the kingdoms is not the reality. So he listens, reads at the same time, goes through the file, tries to figure out what happened. If he takes too long in doing this, he falls behind and the whole system backs up—a system that, because of budget cuts, has fewer people to keep it running at a time of increased need. "Even if you're tired, or you're hungry, or you're thinking about your mortgage payment—it's just all those people," he said. "Until you see it . . ." He trailed off. His days frequently end with his arriving home, drained. "I just come home, and I go up to our—we have a big walk-in closet, I close the door, and I just lay on the floor for twenty minutes, half an hour," Judge O'Malley said. "It's just a place where it's quiet." Other times he goes running, and still other times, Judge O'Malley said, "I've just driven into the garage in the car, and I just stay in the car . . . You don't want to be around people. You just don't want to be around people. I have not met a judge that has not had that feeling.")

Judge O'Malley took some time with this last encounter with Isaiah, though. He feels strongly that psychologically disturbed people need to be better handled by the criminal justice system, has pushed, without success, to get a mental health court in his county that would allow more flexibility in dealing with disturbed people accused of misdemeanor crimes.

"Are you taking your medications?" Judge O'Malley asked Isaiah.

"Yes, Your Honor," Isaiah said.

"I want to encourage you to take those medications," Judge O'Malley said. "Because, I think what happens is, you know, not good things happen when you're not doing that. And usually, a lot of times, people who suffer from that, from bipolarism, they don't take the medi—they're okay, and then they don't take the medications, and then they, you know, their chemical composition changes in their brain, because they don't take the medicine, and then they get back into behavior that, you know, like I said, fortunately—you know, you got tasered here."

"Several times," Isaiah said.

"Yeah," Judge O'Malley said. "That's pretty painful. Okay? So please just take that medicine, okay?"

"Okay."

"All right, that's our deal."

The deal struck, Isaiah was free to go. Judge O'Malley said to Isaiah's aunt, "Oh, I'm glad you told me that." She told him how she'd had to call the crisis line because of Isaiah that past Sunday. She also said Isaiah was in treatment at Cascade Mental Health Care, perhaps because she didn't know Isaiah had been skipping appointments. Isaiah was encouraged to keep going to treatment. He said nothing in response. "Thank you so much," Isaiah's aunt said.

"It's okay," Judge O'Malley replied. "It's part of the job . . . Thank goodness you told me, because it doesn't make sense." He said Isaiah would be released from jail that evening, around 6:00.

"Take care of yourself," Judge O'Malley told Isaiah's aunt.

"I will, Your Honor," she replied. "Thank you."

The whole proceeding lasted about five minutes and thirty seconds, and then Judge O'Malley went on to the next hearing, a Mr. Butoric, who was charged with misdemeanor theft.

Court records indicate that when he was not at the hearing, Isaiah told jail medical staff treating him for Taser burns that his aunt was "delusional" and that he was scared for his own safety. "The medical staff did not obtain his prior mental health records," Dr. Lymberis wrote, "and did not realize that his perception of both his aunt and his behavior with the police were grossly abnormal."

28

U nfinished business related to the old theft and marijuana possession charges kept Isaiah in jail for six more days. Then, two
days after Isaiah's release his aunt, Rachel Kalebu, showed up
in Pierce County Superior Court seeking a restraining order against her
nephew. She asked that Isaiah be ordered to "take his medicine," that he
return her computer bag, and that he stop destroying her property, such
as her dishes and her computer. "I am a prisoner in my own home," she
wrote. She said Isaiah was "defiant" and "disrespectful," that he had
"threatened to hurt me" and "to also hit me." She told the court that she'd
recently called a mental health crisis line. "They advised me to evict him,"
she wrote, "and ask for restraining him."

Instead of triggering intervention, Rachel Kalebu's statements about
Isaiah's behavior, and her request for a restraining order going forward,
triggered nothing but further isolation for Isaiah. With his aunt at her
limit, Dr. Lymberis wrote, "Isaiah lost his last meaningful emotional
attachment and support. By then everyone in the family agreed that the
solution was to let the state take care of him. For Isaiah, this translated
as: he was now discarded and no longer a member of his family. This situation proved to be a catastrophic development."

The next day, Rachel and JJ were killed in the arson. Detectives in the
area later reported to Seattle detectives that Isaiah, who had been sleeping in a wooded part of the neighborhood since his aunt kicked him
out, had parked his bicycle near the crime scene, walked up, and was

watching with other onlookers when detectives recognized him and began asking some questions. He readily answered. Television footage shows Isaiah looking calm and wearing a mismatched tracksuit, black on top and red on bottom. Deborah, who also came to the scene, remembers Isaiah being strangely unfazed. "If I was living in a house that was burned to a crisp," she said, "my reaction would be devastation. His reaction was, 'Hey, guys, what's going on?' Your house is burned to a crisp, and you have no reaction? So, it kind of made me think, like, 'Why?'" The police suspected Isaiah might have committed the arson, and when they interviewed him, they offered him mental health treatment. He refused, according to records. Later, detectives came to believe that J. J. Jones was struck in the head with a golf club before the house was set on fire. They found a Wilson 3 iron at the scene. Jones's son, speaking to a detective, said that JJ had encouraged Rachel to kick Isaiah out of the house "several times."

29

Because Isaiah had been displaced by the fire, the Red Cross offered him a voucher to stay at the Western Inn, a cheap motel near Interstate 5 where rooms were $59 a night. The Red Cross also gave him a prepaid debit card to cover minimal food expenses. Isaiah stayed three nights at the Western Inn, and while he was there, a hotel manager said, he destroyed his room.

He checked out on July 13, 2009, and that day was back in Judge Gain's courtroom for a pretrial hearing on the charges of threatening his mother and sister more than a year earlier. Eighteen months had passed since his mom had taken him to the house that held the financial services firm and then urged the police to take him to Harborview. Isaiah, for this appearance before Judge Gain, was wearing a black V-neck sweater over a collared shirt and tie. A deputy prosecuting attorney told Judge Gain about Isaiah's recent charges in a neighboring county for obstruction and resisting arrest and alluded vaguely—because details were not in hand—to the fact that Isaiah had recently been investigated, but released, in connection with an arson. The deputy prosecutor admitted he could not immediately prove that Isaiah was violating the judge's order to get treatment but expressed concern that the run-ins with law enforcement suggested Isaiah had become "unstable." He asked for $50,000 bail. Judge Gain denied this request, noting that Isaiah had come to court as required.

"Although," Judge Gain said, "I am concerned about all of this. So, I'm gonna set a review for approximately three weeks, and I'd like an update from his mental health provider." The date for the review: August 3, 2009. "Assuming that he's complying with his medication and any other recommendations, that will be the end of it."

Isaiah walked out of Judge Gain's courtroom with his new public defender, Theresa Griffin, who was becoming scared of him.

Before Rachel Kalebu died in the fire, she had been calling Theresa Griffin at all hours, saying she was unable to control Isaiah, that he was just locking himself in his room. "I can't help you with that," Theresa Griffin had told her. "I don't represent you. I represent him." This was precisely the complaint from Isaiah's family: no one seemed to represent them and their concerns. When Isaiah's aunt went so far as to show up at the public defense headquarters in downtown Seattle looking for help, they called Theresa Griffin, and again Griffin told her to look elsewhere.

Then, when Isaiah's aunt was killed in the arson, Griffin realized she was a potential witness in that case and because of this would have to withdraw as Isaiah's attorney. "He was not happy about that," Griffin said. She remembers riding in a courthouse elevator with Isaiah and trying to calm him, saying she knew he was upset. "He said, 'No, I'm not upset. I'm outraged.'"

The next day, Isaiah showed up at his father's downtown office building. His father had recently turned fifty-two. When security called asking if they should send Isaiah up, his father said no. He didn't want that. Instead, he went down to the lobby, met his son, and walked to the nearby Rem Koolhaas–designed public library. "I had mixed feelings about seeing him," Isaiah's father said to Dr. Lymberis. "I was afraid he'll set the dog on me and was looking for the camera of the library." He had urged one of Isaiah's public defenders to see that Isaiah was kept in jail rather than released. He'd also urged this public defender not to tell Isaiah about the request. Apparently, Isaiah found out. "I had never seen him so angry," Isaiah's father said. "He was wearing dark glasses and kept questioning me: 'Why did you tell the attorney to keep me in jail? Why? Why?'" Isaiah's father replied, "I don't think you are okay. In jail you are safe. We cannot make you take your medicine. I want you to be in a safe place where you can be managed, controlled."

Isaiah's response was short, direct, and furious: "Dad, things happen. Life is short. Mama Rachel died and you don't know who will be next."

Then he left.

Isaiah's father, worried, talked to security in his office building. They suggested he call the police, which he did. He said the police told him they couldn't do anything, because Isaiah hadn't threatened him directly. He thought of hiding out somewhere but then determined, "I can't run from my son." So he took the only recourse he saw left to him. He prayed.

"That last time I saw him," Isaiah's father told Dr. Lymberis, "he was not my son. He was ready to explode. He was full of rage."

It was a rage that had never been explored. To the extent it had been engaged by mental health professionals, the engagement was so sporadic it could barely be called such. It was instead more like topical ointment on a mortar wound or a Band-Aid on a fault line. Isaiah's attitude toward treatment didn't help, but Dr. Lymberis saw Isaiah's encounter with his father as something different from outright rejection of all help. What she saw was one last attempt at doing something that might be ameliorative. "He sought out his father," Dr. Lymberis wrote, "in a desperate attempt to find meaning and purpose as he was falling further into the pit of his illness." He didn't find that.

On Friday, July 17, 2009, as Teresa and Jennifer were preparing to spend a weekend together, Isaiah was again in Judge Gain's courtroom, beneath the dropped ceiling and fluorescent lights, as Theresa Griffin formally withdrew as his defense attorney. After that, she had a meeting with Judge Gain in his chambers at which, she said, she made it clear she thought Isaiah had killed his aunt. "I was very, very fearful for myself," Griffin said. "He really liked me, and I really liked him, but he was really dangerous." She thought Isaiah was schizophrenic, one more provisional diagnosis to add to the list. "I felt that he came with completely different personalities at different times and kind of came in and out of them," Griffin said, "like a young man who was just starting to go into schizophrenia." She added, "It was really sad that somebody didn't help that kid."

Griffin found it "shocking" that Judge Gain didn't revoke Isaiah's pretrial release after the Tacoma arson. "I just could not believe that the judge did not take him in," she said. "Had he taken him in on Friday, that girl would be alive today." Though Judge Gain sees "no benefit" in talking about the specifics of Isaiah's case, his office said, in a letter to a newspaper eleven days after he last released Isaiah, that "it must be remembered that each one of us is presumed innocent when we are brought before the court." This echoed what Judge Gain had said when first running for superior court in 1992: a judge has to balance community safety, individual rights, and the letter of the law. The letter from his office added that release decisions are "some of the most difficult decisions faced by judges." As of that Friday, Isaiah had yet to be tried on the charges of threatening to kill his mother and sister and had not even been arrested in connection with the deaths of his aunt and J. J. Jones by arson. Judge Gain was also unaware that Isaiah had been noncompliant with his mental health treatment for at least the past seven months. "Many a judge will tell you that they see defendants every day who at some time will probably commit additional crimes," Judge Gain said in a letter to me. "Which defendants, and the timing and severity of the crimes, the judge has no ability to discern."

That Friday night, Isaiah was back riding a public bus through the distant suburbs. He'd made the long ride from Judge Gain's courtroom, about twenty miles south of Seattle, to the Bothell transit station, about twenty miles north of Seattle. It was around 9:00 p.m.

A man getting off the bus at the park-and-ride saw Isaiah, dog in tow, trying to steal his silver mountain bike, which had been locked to a park-and-ride fence.

"What makes you think you're going to steal my bike?" the man asked Isaiah, according to a police report.

"I'm coming up," Isaiah replied.

The man flagged down a police officer in a patrol car at the park-and-ride. While the man was doing this, Isaiah set the bike down and got on a bus, a familiar refuge. The officer told him to get off the bus and sit with Indo in a bus shelter. Isaiah complied.

At first, he denied trying to steal the bike. Then Isaiah told another officer, "Okay, I took it." He was informed the case would be referred to King County prosecutors for a theft prosecution. The bike was noted to be worth $200. Then Isaiah was released at the scene.

It was late at night. He had nowhere to go. He'd destroyed his last home, a hotel room provided by the Red Cross. His aunt was dead, her house destroyed, too. His mother and sister now seemed to be his enemies. In any case, restraining orders barred him from their homes. His father wanted him jailed.

He slept in parks at times like this, his mother said. Or he rode the bus, like in high school, a thick clutch of multicolored transfers in his pocket. Of this period, Isaiah's lawyers later wrote, "Isaiah wandered homeless for days, accompanied only by his dog and his delusions, until he encountered Teresa Butz and Jennifer Hopper."

Threshold of Competence

30

Seattle's main courthouse was built nearly one hundred years ago, out of granite pulled from quarries north of the city and marble shipped from Alaska. Five stories high, wrapped in decorative Ionic columns and other motifs of ancient authority, it was a beaux arts declaration dropped into a state not thirty years old. When its doors opened to the public, the Duwamish River had just been straightened.

The city grew. Courthouse floors were added, six of them piled atop the original five at the dawn of the Great Depression, cheaply, all wooden windows and gray brick. Later, a towering attic was set atop those six additional floors and, inside this attic, a jail where inmates waited behind three-story arching windows with mountain views, guarded by copper eagles along the roof's cornice. Also inside this attic, a bakery, the source of inmate-made bread and enticing smells that wafted downward into the courthouse until a time when the jail became too small and was relocated, its former top-floor cells transformed into offices for elected officials, the bakery closed.

In the 1960s, the look of the courthouse was deemed out of step with "modern" architecture and an intervention conducted. Marble wainscoting was ripped out and replaced with concrete panels. Ornate hanging lamps in the shape of acorns were replaced by economical, tubular fluorescents. The original grand entrance became a loading dock. The Olmsted-inspired park the grand entrance had opened onto became neglected. On the courthouse exterior, aluminum walls were hung in vertical stripes over rows of windows on the eastern and western facades, the intent being to create a more sophisticated look while dampening traffic noise and moderating courtroom temperatures by limiting sunlight. Some of these aims accomplished, the aluminum walls then aged into a dismal, streaked brown. In 2001, the earthquake. It caused so many things to go wrong in the courthouse that the need for a seismic upgrade, long ignored, was un-ignored. The foundation was re-poured. Shock absorbers were laid through-out the structure, in the form of X-ing braces that can be seen cutting through the views of many windows not covered in aluminum.

The sum of it all, on approach from the street, is deranged, an aes-thetic that shifts repeatedly, often within a few square feet, from ancient to "modern" to braced-against-calamity, a hall of justice doubling as a monument to the way insane outcomes can be created slowly, over time. Around the perimeter, scavenging seagulls and desperate citizens wan-der the park that fed the grand entrance before the grand entrance became the loading dock, and people in the throes of legal argument file in and out of two newer, less-grand entrances, one of which, after the financial collapse of 2008, had to be frequently closed because of budget constraints.

In the lobby, a charcoal-drawn mural spans several walls and evokes a different perception of time than the building's exterior, a perception in which history doesn't weather and fade, and therefore no excavation of the past need be conducted to understand the present. Instead, all happens at once. There is place—the hills and waters and rivers of King County—and in this place exists, simultaneously, all that it has experienced: the land verdant and denuded, longhouses and skyscrapers, the courthouse in its many incarnations, the Duwamish, the white settlers, Chief Si'ahl, weary loggers, dirty miners, the lumbering B-17, laden cargo ships, marching unions, Bill Gates hunched over a boxy desktop computer, antiglobaliza-tion protesters, and, in the center of the central panel, Martin Luther King

Jr., who, in 2005, by legislative order, became the namesake of this county, replacing the original namesake, William Rufus King, a slave owner and, briefly, before his death after a few weeks in office, vice president of the United States under Franklin Pierce. The mural's artist calls his technique "memory drawing."

In the spring of 2011, a special summons issued from this courthouse to residents of King County, part of the drive to impanel a jury in the matter of *State of Washington v. Isaiah Kalebu.* Three thousand summonses went out, an unusually high number, because it was believed it would be difficult to find people who hadn't heard what Isaiah was accused of doing in South Park on July 19, 2009.

It was also believed, correctly, that a large number of those receiving summonses would beg off. On April 25, 2011, Judge Michael C. Hayden, a sturdy man then in his nineteenth year on the bench, called his eighth-floor courtroom to order so that he, two King County prosecutors, and two public defenders could go through what Judge Hayden described as "the very voluminous written and electronic hardship requests we got." Judge Hayden was sixty-two at the time, born in North Carolina and raised in northern Virginia by a father who was a newspaperman. At Dartmouth, he majored in psychology and political science. He also met a woman he intended to marry, and five days after graduation they moved to Seattle together. Her family had lived in Washington since before it was a state, her great-grandfather having worked as an early superior court judge and, before that, as a lawyer whose private practice was interrupted by the Great Seattle Fire of 1889. "Had to save all his law papers by rolling them down a stairwell in a rolltop desk," Judge Hayden said. That desk is now in a local museum. In Seattle, Judge Hayden's wife found work as a teacher. He worked as a service manager in a camera store and then decided to go to law school. Spent sixteen years in private practice defending major automakers like Ford and Chrysler and then grew tired of that work. "The billable hours," he said, "the headaches." He liked to ski, but in the early 1990s "I did a somersault that I did not intend to do on the ski hill. Landed on the back of my head, and I contused my spinal cord pretty high. At C-3, 4. And I was paralyzed from the neck down for some period of time and thought that I was paralyzed for life. But I had a recovery that no one could explain. The doc said, 'I don't know why you survived the accident. I don't know why, a year later, you could walk. I don't know why you can ski again. But you can.' And once I recovered, I thought, 'You know, if I can survive that, and come back, what's the little obstacle of changing career paths?'"

His wife kept saying she'd be a teacher even if no one was paying her. Being a judge seemed as if it might be that kind of work for him, so in 1992 he ran for and won an open seat on the superior court bench. "Not a landslide by any stretch," Judge Hayden said. But he was never once challenged for his seat afterward.

The hardship requests Judge Hayden and the lawyers were reviewing on this day came from people who, not even having set foot in the courthouse in connection with *State of Washington v. Isaiah Kalebu,* had written to say they couldn't serve, a cross section of personal misfortune and the pressing business of life. An eighty-three-year-old woman with hypertension, hypothyroidism, and an adrenal mass was excused, along with a large number of other people whose doctors attested to maladies including heart conditions, upcoming surgeries, incontinence, dementia, fibromyalgia, and MRSA. "How is she still alive?" asked a prosecutor, after reading one potential juror's list of ailments.

It took days to go through each and every hardship request. There were people with cancer and people caring for people with cancer. People reporting Alzheimer's, ALS, kidney failure, brain injury. "High blood pressure, asthma, anxiety," Judge Hayden said during one marathon session. "Let her go." Presented with the case of a man who reported deafness and memory loss, Judge Hayden empathized: "My wife says the same thing about me." That man was excused. For someone reporting sleep apnea, he offered, "Might suggest that juror come in right now. We could cure any sleep problems." For a person with difficulty sitting: "I can appreciate that."

There were financial hardships, too, for people whose jobs wouldn't pay them during a lengthy trial and who couldn't get by on the $10 a day, plus mileage, that King County offers its jurors as compensation. It's an amount criticized as insufficient by a succession of Washington State Supreme Court chief justices, an amount Judge Hayden finds "embarrassing." Equally embarrassing, he said, is when jurors are asked to consider donating their $10 a day back to the court to help fund child care at the Regional Justice Center in Kent. One potential juror expressing financial hardship on this day was a man who worked on hourly wages for Chase Bank. "Chase Bank has plenty of money right now," Judge Hayden said, and it was true: the bank had recently swallowed up Washington Mutual, a locally grown behemoth that inflated with the boom and then imploded with the crash. "But it doesn't mean he does." The Chase employee was excused. A person working for McDonald's was excused for similar reasons. A human resources worker at a local community college was excused for needing to manage upcoming layoffs. Then there were the previously scheduled commitments: a European cruise, a honeymoon in the Dominican Republic, the birth of a baby. One man was excused for being dead. One woman was excused for being the mother of a murder victim. A doctor at Harborview was excused. An army reservist was excused. A number of full-time college students were excused. A teacher was excused after reporting being the only person able to lead a school's upcoming dissection of fetal pigs.

Still, when the remaining jurors arrived at the courthouse for the beginning of in-person examinations, it was a tight fit. "This court was not set up with the facilities, the technology, in order to bring in this large number of jurors," Judge Hayden explained to a crowd of citizens that included employees from well-financed, spaciously headquartered local companies such as Amazon, Microsoft, and Boeing. "So, we've been doing the best we can." He apologized for the long line getting through courthouse security. He explained he was about to give an introductory talk to all the potential jurors presently in the courtroom, as well as to other potential jurors watching by video feed from the first-floor jury assembly room. On another floor, four other courtrooms filled with potential jurors waiting for Judge Hayden to deliver the exact same speech to them later.

"Without your service," Judge Hayden began, "our system of justice would quickly grind to a halt." He quoted Thomas Jefferson. He outlined how the idea of juries for accused criminals came to be embedded in the Sixth Amendment. He told of recently hosting a group of lawyers and judges from the former Soviet republic of Georgia and their interest in this practice. "For them, the jury system and our system of justice is a dream," he said. "For us, it's a reality, but it's a reality that we have to guard on a daily basis in order to protect what we should never take for granted. You're here in that tradition."

Judge Hayden then told the potential jurors that after filling out an initial questionnaire, everyone would reconvene for a process called voir dire. "I've heard various interpretations of that French term," Judge Hayden said. "It may mean to speak from the heart."

Among those listening to him was JoAnn Wuitschick, a human resources consultant for the University of Washington. She was forty-six at the time. "I remember vividly getting this summons," JoAnn said. The language struck her: "You have been chosen . . ." Not long after Judge Hayden's speech, she read the questionnaire's vague description of what happened in South Park that night in 2009. Nothing sounded familiar. "In 2009," she said, "my mom had been re-diagnosed with breast cancer. Stage 4. It was very serious. My focus was completely inwards, and toward her."

Michelle Abercrombie, then thirty-six and a staffing manager at a

Seattle software company, hadn't been tracking the news in the summer of 2009, either. "I just don't pay attention to any of the stuff that's on TV," she said. "Which I guess could be good, because sometimes media isn't always correct."

Likewise with Jamie Dellaringa, then forty-three and doing business analytics for Costco. She had no problem filling out the questionnaire. "It was so easy for me," she said, "because I am not a TV person. I do not watch the news. I don't want to know about the news. I try to keep it out of my life because it's always bad." She figures that if she ever needs to know about something urgently, "someone's gonna tell me about it."

Also listening to Judge Hayden, and also headed for the jury box: A former preschool teacher. A health-care administrator. A retired Boeing engineer. An employee at the state's Department of Health and Human Services. A computer programmer for Microsoft. An electronic products developer who was a veteran of several small start-ups. A marketing manager for a local community college. A security systems salesman. An administrator for professors working on pulmonary research. And an army veteran who explained his job this way: "I have a cart. Like, I build wheelchair ramps for senior apartments and stuff. I repair the roofs, et cetera." Asked whether serving on a long trial would be a financial hardship for him, the man said, "Probably knock me off a few bucks, but I'd be doing my civic duty, I guess."

31

A year and nine months had passed between Isaiah's arrest for the South Park attacks, as they had come to be known, and this sifting of potential jurors. During much of that time, the mystery of his mental state preoccupied his lawyers, prosecutors, and Judge Hayden. It continued to elude easy grasp. Numerous pretrial hearings and motions tangled with the question of what, exactly, possessed this young man who, now twenty-five years old and having no means to pay the $10 million bail, was passing time in a jail two blocks uphill from the courthouse.

An underlying dynamic for these discussions was set early, by Isaiah himself. It was the same dynamic that had vexed his family, the police, Harborview, and Judge Gain. It was the challenge of a man who does not want to be seen as having challenges, who manipulates for advantage, who suffers severe discomforts yet seeks to create discomfort in others, who deals with distress and disintegration by reaching for ever more forceful means of control, and who harbors, beneath all of these attempts at coping and containment, a chilling rage that erupts when they fail.

Only a few months after Isaiah was arrested, a hearing was called because he was at odds with one of his public defenders. He was facing the death penalty, so his attorneys had been working on a "mitigation report," the process that led to the hiring of Dr. Lymberis. Isaiah didn't like how things were going. He told Judge Hayden he wanted public defender Michael Schwartz to be removed from the case, in part because Isaiah had come to mistrust Schwartz. One issue was that Schwartz kept pushing for Isaiah to be examined by Dr. Lymberis, and Isaiah kept resisting. "It has gotten to the point where he simply does not want to communicate with me any further about the case," Schwartz told the court. Schwartz also suggested there was "an underlying issue here having to do with Mr. Kalebu's mental health status."

Judge Hayden made it clear to Isaiah that the choice of defense attorney was not entirely his to make, because he was being defended at public expense. He also explained that Isaiah would not necessarily get a better lawyer if Schwartz, a capable and experienced defense attorney, were excused. Judge Hayden addressed Isaiah as "sir" as he outlined what was in Isaiah's control and what was not in Isaiah's control. He said, "I'd hate to see you give up a very seasoned trial lawyer who is experienced, and very good at what he does, and then have the Office of Public Defense appoint you another one, and you look back with some remorse. You know, buyer's remorse. I traded something in, I traded the car in, I find out I like the old one better than the new one."

With this, Isaiah changed course but not tone. "I'm prepared to go forward," he announced. "Provided my expectations are met, I will not have an issue with Mr. Schwartz . . . But if my issues continue, we'll return and have to do this again."

This became a constant refrain in Isaiah's relationship with his trial, this way of relating in which he was constantly trying to flip the power dynamics of the courtroom, attempting to run the proceedings, attempting to run his defense team in directions contrary to their advice (and, sometimes, in directions contrary to his own previous declarations). He refused to accept that others might know better, kept trying to turn a losing hand into a winning hand. He seemed a captive of his own grandiosity, paranoia, and shifting mood, though he did not see it this way. As he would tell Dr. Lymberis when he eventually assented to an examination with her, and as he'd already suggested to Judge Gain back in 2008, "It is always me against the world, and I'm not going to lose."

At times, Isaiah's grandiosity and paranoia faded, but even then the instinct to manipulate remained. It seemed near foundational. Perhaps it was a foundation laid early. Perhaps it had become a final defense, a last means by which he was not going to lose, even if his manipulative strategies, in the context of a courtroom, ended up creating confusing situations for everyone, particularly those seeing him for the first time.

Judge Hayden continued, praising Isaiah's lucidity, perhaps testing whether deference could pay behavioral dividends. "You certainly appear intelligent and thoughtful," the judge said after Isaiah had withdrawn his request to fire Schwartz. Then Judge Hayden checked in on something he'd heard from the jail about Isaiah's not being willing to come to court for this hearing, a hearing Isaiah himself had triggered. "An outright lie," Isaiah said. "I will come to court. I have no intention of not coming to court."

A few months passed, and Isaiah was back in front of Judge Hayden, wanting to fire Schwartz again. Judge Hayden cleared the courtroom so that Isaiah could explain the situation. Things were dragging on too long, Isaiah said.

In jail, in advance of this hearing, Isaiah had made himself familiar with the Rules of Professional Conduct for attorneys. About two years earlier, when he'd been sent to Western State Hospital by Judge Gain and was feeling dissatisfied with his public defender, something similar had occurred. Then he'd demanded rule books, Western State reported, "so that he could see what the rules were and where they were written." Now he was arguing to Judge Hayden that his attorneys weren't keeping him well enough apprised of developments in his case. Later, he would tell a psychiatric examiner that he could hear his attorney's thoughts. On this day, he apparently could not. On this day, Isaiah felt he needed to read all the information that was being gathered as part of the mitigation report, felt he was not being told what people were saying about him. His lawyers argued otherwise to Judge Hayden, detailing very regular contacts with Isaiah. "I do disagree with Mr. Kalebu that he has not been kept informed," Schwartz told the judge. "But I think, oftentimes, when we do inform him of things, I don't believe that he actually processes that in a normal fashion."

Isaiah had at this point been in the King County Jail for six months and had attempted suicide several times. At first, the jail prescribed him lithium, following the treatment recommendations from his time at Western State in 2008, treatment recommendations that Isaiah had never complied with for very long. In the King County Jail, Isaiah continued to resist medication, hoarding his lithium pills in a makeshift cloth sack tied to his scrotum rather than swallowing them. Eventually, the jail psychiatrist, Dr. Brian Waiblinger, came to the opinion that Isaiah wasn't bipolar at all.

This opinion was not shared by the majority of psychiatrists who would ultimately come to examine Isaiah, but Dr. Waiblinger felt he wasn't seeing any signs of mania or depression in Isaiah, even absent lithium. Instead, Dr. Waiblinger saw Isaiah as severely narcissistic, impulsive, and a great challenge to engage. A lawyer for the jail likewise described Isaiah as "a very difficult patient to treat" because of his intelligence and manipulative manner. Directly quoting Dr. Waiblinger, this lawyer would tell Judge Hayden, "Mr. Kalebu has really bad affective instability. This is also known as lability, where your mood changes a lot." Dr. Waiblinger noted that affective instability can often be mistaken for bipolar disorder. Of course, this would mean the reverse could be true as well.

In line with this diagnosis of "really bad affective instability," Dr. Waiblinger stopped trying to give Isaiah lithium. Instead, for "relational problems," Dr. Waiblinger prescribed him buspirone, an antianxiety medication.

None of this came up at the closed hearing at which Isaiah was attempting, again, to fire Schwartz. It would come up much later in the proceedings. And Schwartz, for his part, didn't offer any specific diagnosis for Isaiah, though he did tell Judge Hayden that Isaiah's mental disturbance was a "major reason for the delays" that Isaiah was presently complaining about. Schwartz also told Judge Hayden, "This case has significant overtones of, perhaps, a mental health defense."

"May I speak, please?" Isaiah asked.

"You may in a moment," Judge Hayden said.

When that moment came, Isaiah complained, again, that he and Mr. Schwartz were "not on the same page" about the effort to have him examined by Dr. Lymberis. "I had requested that I did not want this continued any further," Isaiah said. "I did not want the expert. I did not want to proceed in that direction."

Judge Hayden explained to Isaiah that if no mitigating materials were presented to the King County prosecutor, the prosecutor might well go ahead and seek the death penalty.

"I'm okay with that," Isaiah said.

To this part of Isaiah, on this day, delays were apparently worse than death. An examination by a psychiatrist was apparently worse than death. A mental health defense was apparently worse than death.

Judge Hayden said he was not prepared to let Isaiah fire his lawyers or make a decision contrary to their advice. "Whenever any society decides that they may exact the death penalty on someone, it becomes a societal issue, becomes a justice issue," he told Isaiah. "We can't do it and not be careful about it."

Isaiah said, "I don't have confidence in the attorney."

"Well, I do," Judge Hayden said.

An end to the argument reached, some paperwork was handed around the courtroom in order to officially allow more time for preparation of the mitigation report. "I'm not signing shit," Isaiah said. Nevertheless, the examination with Dr. Lymberis went ahead a month later. She sat with

Isaiah for a total of nine hours over two days. It was the longest any psychiatrist had ever spent with Isaiah one-on-one.

When Dr. Lymberis met with him, his hands and feet were shackled, and one of his attorneys and a jail guard were present. "He sat across from me," she wrote, "was courteous and well-mannered throughout. He engaged with full eye contact. Initially, his affect was somewhat constrained, though appropriate. He was alert, oriented, and on the whole, outwardly cooperative. He is intelligent and articulate, with no obvious speech or language problems."

Dr. Lymberis diagnosed Isaiah as bipolar, "with a history of both manic and depressive episodes with recurrent chronic suicidality and several serious attempts." She also saw him having a "mixed character disorder with Borderline and Narcissistic features." She noted as well a history of head injuries, "from accidents and beatings," although she also noted there was no evidence of Isaiah's having any neurological impairment and that the jail neurology wing had recently checked and found nothing wrong with him.

In her report, Dr. Lymberis detailed Isaiah's "history of persistent childhood and adolescent adversity," his depressed mother and her suicide attempts, his parents' chronic, severe marital conflict, the chronic family violence and jail time for both parents, his repeated moves throughout childhood and through his teenage years, his separation from his father in childhood, his separation from his family in adolescence. She noted that during her meetings with Isaiah, he told her his marijuana use hadn't affected his thinking. Rather, he said, it "gave me a different perspective." He wouldn't talk to Dr. Lymberis about sex or about the events that led to his being taken to Harborview in 2008, but he did deny having any delusions and told her he'd been resisting medication because he didn't need medication. "He tried to maintain a willful, controlled stance," she wrote. He described one of his coping strategies this way: "I choose not to remember. There is no point. Save brain capacity." But he added, "They say you remember in your subconscious."

As their time together continued, Isaiah's control began to come apart. "It was at the end of meeting with him when his thinking became more disorganized," Dr. Lymberis wrote. "Overtly delusional, tangential, with loose associations, paranoia, and grandiosity." He said he'd worked for the government chasing sex offenders and specified to Dr. Lymberis that he'd been focusing on "sex crimes against minors." He said his aunt, Rachel Kalebu, knew about a U.S. plot to infect Africans with HIV, that it had all been covered up, and that the U.S. government was now monitoring him because of this. His statements and his thinking became rigid, his ideas only jaggedly connected. "I talked shit about the government," he told Dr. Lymberis. "I said we should have a revolution. America, all it needs is a spark and it'll go off. Shoot at the government makes people violent. There are more people than police. I read the Unabomber's manifesto. America is a violent country. They are arrogant. We are now the bad guys, we are torturing people. I say tortured people should be released and that is what happened. I predicted Fort Hood. I'm for what suits me best. Everything is for sale. Experience is the best teacher. You should not trust anyone." He continued, "Grand inquisition and trauma. The government is used to control minds . . . They used mind control on me. I fought it successfully but I don't want to talk about it."

Dr. Lymberis described this as "a demonstration of his psychotic, disorganized, fragmented and defective function. He is using very primitive psychological defenses to keep himself from total decompensation. His sense of self is very damaged. His grandiosity serves to keep him from total disintegration. His judgment and reality testing are impaired. He has no insight into his illness and is consciously trying to appear sane." In fact, she wrote, "he had told his attorney that his goal during his meetings with me was to be proven sane."

Soon afterward, Dr. Lymberis's report was delivered to the King County prosecutor, Dan Satterberg. Citing input from Jennifer Hopper, who had privately told the prosecutor she was opposed to the death penalty, and from Norbert and Dolly Butz, who privately told the prosecutor to use his best judgment, and also citing Isaiah's "documented history of mental illness," the prosecutor decided not to seek Isaiah's death.

32

An interesting situation now developed. In *State of Washington v. Isaiah Kalebu*, the state had come to see Isaiah as mentally ill enough that he should not be put to death. However, it continued to see him as competent enough to stand trial. This was because Isaiah's history of mental illness did not rise, as the King County prosecutor put it, "to the level of a defense against the criminal charges."

Isaiah might have suffered from a serious mental disorder, and he might still be suffering from a serious mental disorder, but in the prosecutor's mind Isaiah was also capable of understanding reality and making choices, which meant Isaiah could be held accountable for his actions. Isaiah's attorneys saw things differently, and soon they were in front of Judge Hayden to discuss this.

Isaiah had first been brought to the King County Jail in the late summer of 2009. It was now the spring of the following year, and Isaiah's other defense attorney, Ramona Brandes, was telling Judge Hayden that Isaiah was in a dire state of decompensation. The date: May 12, 2010. Brandes told the judge that Isaiah hadn't been eating for twelve days and that he'd been observed curled up in a corner of his cell for twenty-four hours straight. She noted that although Isaiah didn't believe he had any problems, at least four different mental health professionals had so far diagnosed him as bipolar. "He does seem to cycle in and out of demonstrating major symptoms in approximately a two-to-four-week cycle," Brandes told the court. She said that earlier in the previous month she'd noticed

Isaiah had "a very aggressive demeanor," as well as "some very demanding behaviors" and "poor grooming." When she saw him a few weeks later, he "presented with a very flat affect. He exhibited signs of grandiosity in reference to himself as an emperor. He displayed paranoia and indicated that guards were encouraging suicide in the jail. He also had just had a suicide attempt three days earlier and was in a neck brace at the time." With Isaiah in court with her, Brandes pointed to "items in his hair" and "residue on his face." She said she was "gravely concerned."

Under questioning from Judge Hayden, Isaiah said he hadn't wanted to come to court on this morning. He was feeling "not good" about being there, and he confirmed he hadn't been eating. "They're poisoning my food," he said. "And my water." He said that he didn't know how he felt about the possibility of going back to Western State but that his lawyer had told him he had to go. Judge Hayden didn't request, and no one offered, an update on exactly what medications Isaiah was being prescribed. But the judge did ask Isaiah if he'd been taking his medication.

"No," Isaiah said.

"Why?" Judge Hayden asked.

"I don't know."

"All right. I'll sign an order for evaluation at Western State."

Isaiah arrived back at Western State six days later. He remembered being there two years previous, during the hospitalization when he'd been diagnosed as bipolar, prescribed lithium and Zyprexa, and sent back to Judge Gain with his competency "restored." He also appeared to remember the names of some of the Western State staff members, though it was later pointed out, in court, that he could have just been reading their name tags. He denied hearing voices or having hallucinations. He "reported a history of physical abuse by his father, and stated that his mother was an alcoholic." He seemed to have an appropriate affect, and he told doctors his bad mood was connected to his present incarceration, which was now in its tenth month. He requested to be placed on a coed ward. The request was denied. He discussed the details of his case in a way that made clear he understood both the charges against him and his legal options, and, as usual, he insisted on his sanity. "I know I'm not crazy, but I am willing to do my time here," Isaiah told a nurse. "I was sent here because I tried to hang myself in jail." That was not exactly it. Isaiah was sent to Western State because his attorneys believed he was decompensating and perhaps not competent to stand trial.

That same afternoon, a nurse wrote, "Patient approached me as I was serving lunch, asking to clean tables for extra food. I let him know that I did my own cleanups at mealtimes. 'Then just give me something extra.' I explained to him why I couldn't, and he walked away. He returned in a few minutes pointing to a tray on the counter, asking for it. He was told no once again. 'Come on, you can bend or break any rule you want.' Behaviors reported to charge nurse."

This lunchtime interaction was later used by Western State doctors as evidence that Isaiah believed normal rules didn't apply to him, and while it could be the case that Isaiah believed this, there is another possible explanation for the interaction: hunger. Isaiah hadn't been eating for twelve days before he was ordered down to Western State. There is no evidence in the Western State report that doctors there were aware of this, and the hospital will not discuss specific cases because of medical privacy concerns.

Judge Hayden had authorized this stay at Western State to last up to fifteen days. On Isaiah's fourth day at Western State, he was returned to the King County Jail with a finding that he had no mental illness whatsoever. "Mr. Kalebu showed no active or acute symptoms of either psychosis, depression, or mania despite being on no psychiatric medications," stated the seven-page report from Western State. It acknowledged that two years prior two other doctors at Western State had diagnosed Isaiah as

"Bipolar NOS," meaning bipolar not otherwise specified. But, the report went on, "without any psychiatric medication treatment currently or in the interim," Isaiah was no longer displaying any symptoms that would warrant that diagnosis. His "most significant clinical issue," according to Western State, was "his character pathology." That character pathology, in the opinion of the state doctors: antisocial personality disorder. This was supported by the idea that Isaiah believed normal rules didn't apply to him, and it included, the Western State doctors said, "lack of remorse for the effects of his actions upon others."

Isaiah now arrived back at the King County Jail, deemed competent to stand trial and, essentially, viewed by Western State as a sociopath. While this was seen as a pathological character deficiency, Isaiah did not have, in Western State's opinion, any "major mental illness" that should prevent his participation in legal proceedings. To underscore this point, Western State said that if Isaiah were to be found innocent of the crimes against Teresa and Jennifer, there would, legally speaking, be no reason to have him undergo a mental health evaluation upon release, because there was no mental illness for which to evaluate him. He could simply be returned to society to wander among the other innocent sociopaths.

Isaiah refused to come to court to discuss these findings. "Convey to Mr. Kalebu," Judge Hayden said, "my sentiments that refusal to attend court proceedings will not become a pattern in this case." In another statement he ordered to be conveyed to Isaiah, the judge added, "If forced to, I can require the jail to bring him down without his consent."

"Understood, Your Honor," said Schwartz.

"I expect him to be here at the next hearing."

Isaiah was there for the next hearing, and events continued to demonstrate the considerable challenges in handling a dynamic mental disorder within the static realm of the legal system. While Western State had seen a calm and focused Isaiah over a span of four days, right off the bat Judge

Hayden wanted to know, "Is there any evidence that between the time he was evaluated and today he has decompensated in any fashion?" The judge, it seems, was entertaining the possibility that Isaiah, as his defense attorney had observed, was someone who cycled in and out of symptoms.

"Nothing that we feel free to present to the court, Your Honor," Schwartz said.

Isaiah was quiet at this hearing. But, Judge Hayden noted, "he seems aware of his surroundings, at least from his image." When Isaiah was asked if he wanted to say anything about the Western State report, he shook his head no.

Judge Hayden ruled him competent to stand trial.

As in the outside world, within the criminal justice system Isaiah was experiencing a fragmented approach in the way people were dealing with him. Western State believed one thing about his mental state. His defense attorneys appeared to sense another thing but were legally constrained by their responsibilities to their client. Judge Hayden, because of legal, strategic, and administrative factors mostly beyond his control, was not being updated on Isaiah's current medications. In addition, Judge Hayden was not a psychiatrist, as he would repeatedly point out. As a consequence, within the criminal justice system the interests of Isaiah's mental health and the interests of the law kept cycling in and out of alignment at the same time that Isaiah was cycling in and out of his various dispositions. Asked whether all of this might contribute to a defendant's disturbance, Judge Hayden later said to me, "The system on the crazies is crazy? Well, I'm not gonna disagree with that too much."

It continued. A month passed, and Isaiah was back in court over a concern about the jail's interfering with his communications with his lawyers. The concern was quickly remedied but not to Isaiah's satisfaction. "I'm a political prisoner," he said. "This is bullshit. You guys are holding me against my will. I'm the king of America and not—this is ridiculous. No, I'm the king of America. You're holding me against my will. No, this is bullshit."

The next month, at the request of his defense attorneys, Isaiah was examined by Dr. David Dixon, a forensic psychologist, to try to determine his state of mind at the time of the attacks. Isaiah had insisted he did not want to pursue a mental health defense, sometimes known as an "insanity defense," and Dr. Dixon didn't get very far in his effort. He met with Isaiah in the King County Jail in the late summer of 2010, at a time when Isaiah was on suicide watch, dressed in a white ultra-security uniform, his hands and feet shackled, his facial hair grown out. He wasn't being allowed a mattress in his cell, only a blanket, and was frequently being dressed in a "suicide smock," a flop of fabric with no strands or clasps that could be used for self-harm. After tying a noose with a rope made from toilet paper, Isaiah had been denied toilet paper. "Currently all of his medication has been discontinued," Dr. Dixon wrote.

When asked how he was feeling about the evaluation, Isaiah said to Dr. Dixon, "It's nice to have somebody to talk to." When asked how he'd been feeling for the past three days, Isaiah said, "Bad. I like being alone, but I keep hearing that I should hang myself. They keep laughing at me and telling me I'm no good." He would not talk about his state of mind at the time of the attacks.

Dr. Dixon did get another description of Isaiah's childhood. "Sometimes good, sometimes bad," Isaiah told him. "It was good when my parents weren't fighting, and when we spent family time together. It was bad when my parents were fighting and the police were called. They were in lots of fights." In his report, Dr. Dixon wrote, "The defendant denied any history of physical or sexual abuse. When asked about mental or emotional abuse, he stated, 'I don't know what that is.' When it was explained, he replied, 'Yeah, I got that all the time. I heard that every day. You're no good. You're worthless. You're garbage.'"

Isaiah was then asked what three wishes he would want. It was the same question his younger siblings had been asked seven years earlier by the Family Court social worker. Isaiah told Dr. Dixon, "Not being in jail," "perfect health," and "smart enough to know what the best thing to wish for would be." Dr. Dixon deemed him "marginally cooperative with the evaluation" and "a seriously disturbed man" who described hearing voices and having visions of maggots crawling through his ears, eyes, and nose. He was "poorly attached to others, with chronic and severe mental illness." In Dr. Dixon's opinion, he was not competent to stand trial.

33

T he report from Dr. Dixon was "quite in contrast" to Western State's report, a prosecutor noted at the next hearing before Judge Hayden. "We would ask for a second opinion." All parties agreed this was a good idea, and as a result Isaiah was sent back down to Western State with another fifteen-day stay authorized. It was his fourth court-ordered trip to the facility in two years, and he arrived not long after his twenty-fifth birthday. He came back, eight days later, with the same finding as before. "Mr. Kalebu presents with no diagnosable symptoms of a major mental illness, nor any sign of cognitive impairment," the same doctors who had last evaluated him wrote. This time, however, they added that they thought Isaiah was malingering, meaning faking, a serious mental disorder.

He had told the doctors, on arrival at Western State, that he felt confused and disoriented. Immediately after, he was greeting staff by name again and saying, "I'm back!" He then played cards with other patients with no difficulty. The day before he was to be sent back to jail, at his "competency interview," Isaiah said over and over that he couldn't remember the charges against him. When they were explained, he said, "You mean I'm charged with misdemeanor jaywalking, right?" Later, a Western State doctor would testify that Isaiah could have been mocking them with these responses. Still, to demonstrate that it wasn't a believable response regardless of motivation, the doctors noted in their report that Isaiah "showed no signs of hearing impairment" and that, when asked, he could recall all kinds of details from his stay at the facility. He also discussed a number of other things. "He has a wide vocabulary," one doctor who evaluated him said later in court. "He mentioned the amount of time that Nelson Mandela had been in a cell. He quoted Nietzsche. He quoted Oscar Wilde. He was much more well-spoken, and came across as having a much wider fund of knowledge than most defendants we interview, and probably many of the staff."

In their report on this visit, the Western State doctors wrote, "Mr. Kalebu has the capacity to understand his legal situation and to communicate effectively with counsel in his own defense *when he so chooses*." They italicized those last four words for emphasis. Whatever was afflicting Isaiah, they believed, it had not taken away his intelligence or his capacity to self-direct.

For the first hearing upon his return from Western State, Isaiah refused to come to court. Judge Hayden threatened, again, to sign a "drag order." For the next hearing, Isaiah was brought down, pursuant to Judge Hayden's "drag order," in a restraint chair on wheels. The judge told Isaiah he didn't want to have to do it again, "but I will." Isaiah said nothing. There had now been enough conflicting psychiatric opinions that a competency hearing was set, at which almost all the mental health professionals who'd seen Isaiah would appear. It began on December 7, 2010. By that time, Isaiah had been in jail for about sixteen months.

The competency hearing stretched over three court days and ended in January 2011. It didn't shed a lot of light. Isaiah tried to fire his attorneys at the outset and declared he wanted to represent himself, which could have resulted in his cross-examining the doctors who had once examined him. Judge Hayden didn't allow it.

On the stand, Dr. William Donald Richie, one of the doctors who evaluated Isaiah at Western State in 2008, said he never got the impression that Isaiah was faking a mental disturbance. Dr. Richie's co-evaluator,

Dr. Gregory Kramer, agreed, saying that in 2008 Isaiah had been doing "exactly the opposite" of faking a mental disturbance. "He was very adamant that he did not have a mental illness," Dr. Kramer said. "He resisted all attempts to acknowledge it." Moreover, it was hard to imagine what motivation Isaiah would have had for fabricating the mania that his mother, his sister, the police, and doctors at Harborview had all observed in the weeks before Dr. Richie and Dr. Kramer evaluated him.

As the long path to this competency hearing demonstrated, Isaiah's resistance to acknowledging any psychological challenges had only escalated after his 2008 trip to Western State. When Judge Gain required Isaiah to take medication and to see a community mental health worker, Isaiah disobeyed the judge's orders. In 2009, after Isaiah's aunt talked about his bipolar disorder in court, and after Judge O'Malley encouraged him to take medication for his "bipolarism," Isaiah scared his aunt so badly that she filed for a restraining order against him. The next day, Isaiah's aunt and J. J. Jones, who'd suggested Isaiah be kicked out of the house because of his instability, were dead. When Isaiah then sought out his father, and his father told him he needed to be restrained so he could get help, Isaiah, angry, told him, "You don't know who will be next." A few days later, the attacks in South Park.

The question at the competency hearing became, how did Isaiah get from adamant, furious denial of any mental disorder to behavior that even the defense's Dr. Dixon, upon reexamining Isaiah, agreed could be an attempt at faking mental illness? A theory emerged.

Being a smart and controlling man, this theory went, Isaiah might have come to see that being found incompetent could delay, or even prevent, a trial—which of course would be an experience very much out of Isaiah's control. At the same time, being a person with an enduring perception of himself as not mentally ill, he might have thought something similar to what he'd told a nurse at Western State: "I know I'm not crazy, but I am willing to do my time here." He might have thought, *I know I'm not crazy, but I'll just act crazy, and this will fool the doctors and delay my trial. I'm smart enough to pull it off.*

It would have been a grandiose and delusional idea, but Isaiah had been determined by several psychiatric professionals to have issues with grandiosity and delusional thinking. He'd once told Dr. Waiblinger, the jail psychiatrist, that he was smarter than everyone in the jail, including all of its staff. Perhaps he believed the same was true at Western State, where even one of the doctors who'd examined him had admitted Isaiah probably possessed a wider base of knowledge than some of the people who worked at the hospital.

This would explain the strange circumstance in which Isaiah was calmly quoting Nietzsche and Oscar Wilde to his Western State doctors while at the same time trying to show them he was unable to assist his attorneys. The Western State doctors saw that behavior as evidence Isaiah was malingering, pure and simple. In the jail, where Isaiah liked to read *The New Yorker,* officials had called similarly strange behavior "performance art," and Isaiah himself had actually used the term "performance art" as well, employing it to refer to certain suicide attempts that had no chance of succeeding, attempts that were sometimes accompanied by poetic suicide notes.

Isaiah, apparently, saw it all as a smart strategy, but it is more than a little off to believe one can trick and manipulate psychiatric doctors, or jail officials, this easily. "There's a combination," Dr. Dixon, the evaluator chosen by Isaiah's own lawyers, said on the stand. "I think he has bipolar, and he also can malinger at times. But he's not malingering the predominant primary bipolar affective disorder." Dr. Dixon described Isaiah's faking, when it arose, as being "somewhat of a manipulative quality to try to get what he wants at the time."

It was a complicated assessment: a manipulative, demented faker inside a disturbed but uncommonly intelligent mind, all of this contained within a body being held by a system not normally disposed to examining a defendant's statements for something other than literal content.

Judge Hayden roughly adopted this line of thinking. Though he continued to repeat that he was not a psychiatrist, in the end he had been forced to play one in this case. "The defendant does indeed have a proper diagnosis of bipolar," Judge Hayden said at the end of the competency hearings, describing Isaiah as an intelligent person who also "feigns symptoms when they are in his interest." At other times, the judge noted, "he acts appropriately when it's in his interest." In other words, Judge Hayden said, "his behavior's been incentive-motivated rather than motivated by his mental illness." The conclusion: still competent to stand trial.

After this ruling, Isaiah withdrew his request to represent himself. He was back to pretty much where he'd been in 2008: diagnosed as bipolar, awaiting trial, deemed competent, refusing to take medication. One key difference: he was now in jail, and so outbursts connected to any pretrial decompensation could be contained, even if he was not being effectively treated. They arrived quickly.

Four days later, a "status hearing" was held and quickly terminated when Isaiah tipped over a chair at the defense table and started to walk away. Jail officers had to restrain him, and Judge Hayden ordered Isaiah out of the courtroom, declaring he had "voluntarily absented himself." At the next hearing, less than a month later, Isaiah tried to fire his lawyers again. He complained, again, that things were taking too long. Schwartz tried to explain the situation to the judge. "It seems to be Mr. Kalebu's complaint that it's his belief that he's not competent to stand trial—"

If true, this would be a new belief. Isaiah interrupted his lawyer: "My complaint is that you motherfuckers are wasting my time here and trying to play this fucking game."

He went on, saying people weren't doing their jobs right. Judge Hayden tried to interrupt him: "Mr. Kalebu."

"I'm not done yet. I'm not done talking."

"No. You are done talking, Mr. Kalebu."

"You should shut the fuck up and listen if you want to hear me fucking say why I'm firing my goddamn attorneys."

"He won't interrupt."

"You're interrupting me."

It went on like this, Isaiah unwilling to relinquish control of the room, unwilling to acknowledge his own role in his current predicament, searching for a procedural upper hand. "How can I work on this fucking case?" he asked. "How do I keep legal materials when you take everything I have? I don't even get fucking shit. I'm wearing a fucking smock . . . I can't eat. These motherfuckers poison my food every day . . . I'm not being medicated. And you motherfuckers expect me to have stable fucking good behavior in court when I can't even maintain? How the fuck is that supposed to be?"

Judge Hayden saw the opening and took it: "Are you asking for medication?"

Isaiah didn't directly answer. Judge Hayden asked three more times. After the third time, Isaiah said, "I'm asking to be treated for my mental illness."

34

Whether Isaiah was admitting a mental illness because he truly believed he had one, or because he believed it would be strategically advantageous at this particular moment, is unknown. "I think in his heart of hearts he knew he had an issue," Judge Hayden later told me. "But he was not willing to turn control of it over to someone else."

At the time, the standoff raised the question of whether Judge Hayden could force Isaiah to take medication. One problem was that the judge had just deemed Isaiah competent to stand trial. Judge Hayden could theoretically decide that Isaiah was decompensating and send him back down to Western State for "competency restoration" via medication. But there was also a problem with that. Western State had just said it didn't think Isaiah needed any medications to be competent, so doctors there weren't likely to prescribe him anything. Another, related problem: Isaiah didn't have a current prescription for anything except buspirone, the antianxiety medication given to him after the jail psychiatrist decided he didn't need lithium.

"Do I think he would be better off with medication?" Judge Hayden said at the hearing. "I sure do. Would I be happy if he would take his medication voluntarily? Absolutely. But the mechanism they give us trial judges is not to try to medicate our defendants to put them in the best emotional and mental state possible, but simply to make a determination whether they meet the threshold level of competence."

To Isaiah, Judge Hayden said, "Mr. Kalebu, I'm trying to help within the boundaries that I have. I can't simply order on a prescription pad what you need to take."

Again, they had reached the law's limits. Still, Judge Hayden summoned the jail's lawyer to court to explain, in greater detail, the jail's view of Isaiah's present mental health needs. He had to sign another drag order to get Isaiah to this hearing, and Isaiah arrived again in the restraint chair, with a suicide smock on. "He also has a netting around his head and face that is normally used when an inmate is spitting or expelling or biting," Schwartz said.

Judge Hayden began by reminding everyone that competency is "a minimal standard." He said he stood by his competency ruling but explained, "My concern is that I have a bipolar defendant, at least in my judgment, a defendant who may be decompensating as I sit here, who clearly has issues, notwithstanding the fact that I believe he is competent, and notwithstanding the fact that Western State believes he is competent."

The jail's lawyer, Nancy Balin, told him it was "strongly" the jail's opinion that Isaiah was not bipolar.

"Give me some fucking clothes," Isaiah interjected. "I am sick of this shit. I am cold."

Balin moved closer to Judge Hayden's bench so that he could hear her over Isaiah's outbursts, and then she explained how the jail had moved from prescribing Isaiah lithium, which he had refused to take in either pill or injection form, to prescribing him buspirone, which he apparently also wasn't taking.

"I ain't taking that shit," Isaiah interjected. "They're trying to poison me."

"If you keep interrupting," Judge Hayden told him, "I will have a hard time doing anything that can be of any help to you, including getting you into regular clothes or not."

Isaiah kept interrupting. He said he was being treated like a dog. "I deserve way better than this," he said. "I've accomplished so much shit in my life. I am a fucking emperor, and you guys treat me like this. I'm a million times better than you guys. You are fucking taking advantage of the situation."

Balin said it was Isaiah who was attempting to take advantage of the situation, that this was all part of Isaiah's "master plan," which according to the jail psychiatrist, Dr. Brian Waiblinger, was to benefit from poor communication between the jail and the court and to try to make his behavior look like a failure of his medication, whatever that medication might have been. To what specific end, Balin didn't say. "He's a very, very smart individual," Balin told Judge Hayden. "The other side of his intelligence and his cognitive abilities is that he is extremely manipulative and everything he is doing is according to a plan. What he just said in court is exactly what Dr. Waiblinger says he says all the time. What Mr. Kalebu just said that I hear is, 'I am ready to be done with this bullshit.' What Dr. Waiblinger clearly believes from two and a half years now of treating Mr. Kalebu, give or take, I don't remember when he came in"—it actually had been about one and a half years that Isaiah had been sitting in the King County Jail, rarely medicated and awaiting trial, but perhaps it seemed longer to all—"is that he knows exactly what he is doing and he is of a mind to get out of here, and he will figure out how to do it. He is done with this bullshit. That is what he tells Dr. Waiblinger and his staff every single day, along with other things like, 'You are dead to me'"—which is exactly what Isaiah had told his mother in 2008, after he was released from Harborview and his mother told him to take medication—"and, 'When I get out . . . ,' terms like, 'You will be seeing me.' He is scaring some of the staff because he does have a plan and it is very clear."

Judge Hayden tried to square the jail's current diagnosis for Isaiah with Isaiah's history. "If he was indeed bipolar in 2008," Judge Hayden said, "my understanding is that he doesn't become non-bipolar in 2010." The judge acknowledged that perhaps some symptoms had subsided but said he'd never heard of anyone being "cured" of a bipolar disorder. He asked, "Am I wrong?"

"I am not a psychiatrist," Balin replied, declining to answer.

Judge Hayden asked, "So, is Dr. Waiblinger saying to me, through you, that there were no medications that they can give him that would correct the behavior that we have seen repeatedly in this courtroom?"

"I would say he would say no," Balin said. She described Isaiah's courtroom behavior as being a consequence of "choice and purposefulness," not a consequence of "his mental state or lack thereof, mental health or lack thereof."

Isaiah interjected, "Why don't I have a mattress if I'm not going to kill myself?"

They were at another impasse.

Isaiah's lawyers were not in a position to ask the court to force their client to take lithium if he didn't want to take lithium. The jail didn't think Isaiah needed lithium anyway. Judge Hayden, as he'd said so many times already, was—like Balin—not a psychiatrist. "I am not going to prescribe drugs," the judge said, making the point again. One of the prosecutors said, "We don't disagree with the court's analysis of the situation."

In this sense, too, Isaiah was back to where he had been before. He would not be forced to take any medication he didn't want to take, because the system either didn't see the need or didn't have the means to make it happen. For Isaiah, this might have been a victory of sorts, a small amount of retained control, a route to remain unknown by those he didn't think should, or could, know him, a way to lash out at a supposedly concerned apparatus that hadn't cared to know him until now, a path to being his idea of a man.

Schwartz, the defense attorney, described it all as "a dog chasing its tail" and called the jail's decision that Isaiah was not bipolar "farcical," because the jail had, for a time, demonstrated that it agreed Isaiah was bipolar by prescribing him lithium.

They were all—judge, jail officials, attorneys, Isaiah—now standing in the center of a grand psychological thicket, with no way out. One possible way of avoiding such outcomes had been suggested by Dr. Dixon, who at one point during the competency hearing had cause to point out something basic: correct diagnoses take time. "The strongest variable we have," Dr. Dixon said on the stand, "is to continue to see someone over time, to see if their presentation is consistent." This had never happened for Isaiah before he entered the criminal justice system, and once he entered the criminal justice system, there was little incentive or ability to make it happen. The person who'd spent the most one-on-one time with Isaiah was Dr. Lymberis, and the grand total for that encounter was nine hours over two days.

In addition, as a doctor from Western State pointed out during Isaiah's competency hearing, the criminal justice system was not much bothered by Isaiah's many different diagnoses, or even by Western State's own differing diagnoses, because its only charge was to figure out whether or not Isaiah was competent to stand trial. "It's really not a matter of getting the diagnosis right," said Dr. Margaret Dean, one of the Western State doctors who determined Isaiah had no diagnosable mental illness. "It's a matter of looking at the relevant capacities." He was competent to stand trial, Dr. Dean had determined. Judge Hayden had agreed. And now, whatever his proper diagnosis, Isaiah's time was up.

He was sent back to jail, forced medication off the table, and Judge Hayden announced that he was pondering having him watch the trial from a remote location because of his outbursts. Isaiah was now just over halfway between his twenty-fifth birthday and his twenty-sixth.

A month and a half later, during a hearing about the logistics of summoning a jury, Isaiah interrupted. "I'm done," he said. "Take me back." When

Judge Hayden said he would like Isaiah to be present for his trial if possible, Isaiah spoke of a grand conspiracy against him and told everyone to fuck off, individually. "Fuck you, fuck you, fuck you." It went on. In the transcript of this hearing, Isaiah is recorded using thirty-four "fucks." Someone tried to calm him down. "Can't calm me down," he said. "Fuck this shit." He was taken back to jail, and the hearing continued without him. A month later, Isaiah was once again wearing his suicide smock, once again tried unsuccessfully to fire his attorneys, and once again loosed an impressive streak of swearing, some twenty-six "fucks" recorded. "Fuck this," Isaiah said. "Get me out of this goddamn chair . . . You'll fucking pay." He told the judge, "You are fired." Judge Hayden said, "Send him back now to the jail. He will watch the remainder of these proceedings—through deliberations and verdict—from a remote location. I won't have this in front of the jury."

Judge Hayden then addressed Isaiah directly: "Mr. Kalebu, I will not be seeing you again for some period of time."

"Fuck that," Isaiah said. Then, to Brandes, "Come see me. I got to talk to you."

"I can't come see you today," Brandes said. "I have other cases."

"Come tomorrow."

"I can't come tomorrow."

"Fuck you."

Isaiah had previously expressed a fondness for Brandes over Schwartz, had said her presence was reassuring to him. "Get me Ramona," Isaiah had told Western State doctors when he was asked which of his attorneys he wanted to be present for his interviews at the facility. "I like her a lot." At Western State, Isaiah also told doctors he preferred to interact with women because he couldn't "open up" to men and that he preferred female monitors to male monitors because "I can manipulate them better."

But when a woman was displeasing him, or when his attempts at manipulation were failing, Isaiah responded with rage and lashed out by whatever means he found available. At Western State, when a female staffer wasn't assigned to monitor him as he'd requested, he'd attempted to hang himself from a door handle that was specifically designed to make such suicide attempts impossible. Earlier in the pretrial proceedings, he'd once spit at Brandes in court when he was upset with her. Now he was upset with Brandes again and, from the chair he was strapped to, cursed her as he was being removed from court. The date: April 25, 2011. That spring afternoon, the judge and the lawyers set about the task of excusing all those potential jurors who had written in with hardships of hypertension, MRSA, and more.

The Trial

———————

35

Shrinking the jury pool down to manageable size took the entire month of May, and as the process moved forward, it continued to offer a unique tour of the social architecture of the city, as well as a running lesson in good humor and civics from Judge Hayden. A hardship request from a Drug Enforcement Administration employee was rejected as "weak." A King County prosecutor's hardship request, which complained of an extraordinarily busy trial schedule "due to large budget cuts," was granted. A man employed as the mascot for the Seattle Mariners, whose job was to run around Safeco Field at home games wearing a moose outfit, was excused.

"Come on," Schwartz said.

Brandes, his cocounsel, argued the other point of view. "I would miss him," she said, "if I were at a game and that moose did not show up."

She won, with Judge Hayden upholding his earlier decision. "Let the moose be the moose," he said.

A number of others in the pool were excused for reporting detailed knowledge of the case from media accounts and for offering opinions that Isaiah was guilty, or mentally ill, or both. One unusual situation was that of a man who told the court that on his first day of jury service, while waiting in the long line to get into the courthouse, he'd figured out on his own that the trial was connected to the South Park attacks. "So I started reading about it on my handheld," he said. The man also posted photographs of the long courthouse line to Twitter and Facebook. From his online reading, the man learned that Norbert Leo Butz was Teresa's brother and that Norbert had starred in *Catch Me If You Can,* which the man had seen in Seattle shortly after the attacks. The man was excused.

A woman employed by Boeing told the court she wanted to continue in the jury pool but her boss desired otherwise. Judge Hayden sided with the woman. Later, another Boeing employee, an engineer working on the 737 program, reported the same problem. "It is my recollection," one of the prosecutors said, "that we were not immediately excusing employees of large international corporations who do lots of business here in King County Superior Court without further information." Judge Hayden kept that Boeing employee, too. A FedEx pilot was excused for having an opinion about Isaiah's guilt. So was a man who knew someone who lived near the red house, another man who needed to be at AA meetings, and a woman who explained, in her hardship request, that she worked at a bicycle shop frequented by Judge Hayden. "Is she saying she doesn't like me?" Judge Hayden asked. The woman was excused.

As the pool continued to shrink, one man announced, "I've been invited on a business trip that I feel may really further my career."

It turned out his career was working in a strip club to pay his student loans, and Judge Hayden asked, "What kind of business trip advances the career of a person who practices that profession?"

"White river rafting," he said. "I'm the only manager invited, and they already bought my ticket."

"White river rafting is related to strippers?"

"It's a team-building exercise."

He was excused.

A man who worked as a bartender later announced that he regularly served another potential juror. "What happens in the bar stays in the bar," Judge Hayden said. "You know that." Neither of them was excused on this account.

A financial hardship request came in from Judge Janet Garrow of King County District Court. Judge Hayden was unimpressed. "Let me suggest," he said, "that if, indeed, a judge has hardship for going onto jury duty, then the solution is not for me to let the judge go but for somebody to revisit the issue of a judge's duties and how we pay judges." He called it "outrageous" that an elected judge would even suggest that jury service is too much of a hardship. "Fortunately," he said, "the press isn't here today to hear this, or I suspect it would be all over the evening papers." In fact, there were no evening papers left in Seattle at that point. Judge Garrow was kept in the pool.

A hairdresser, however, was excused for financial hardship. A woman who was needed to take care of an art collection was excused. A cyclist on "kind of an all-or-nothing team" was excused for a ride in Wyoming because, as he put it, "if I don't show up, nobody rides." ("Try touring Colorado," Judge Hayden said as they chatted, briefly, about elevation gains. The judge is an avid cyclist himself and for a time was also a motorcycle enthusiast, touring around Washington State on an old Russian Ural with a sidecar for his wife and their dogs.) The chief financial officer for Amazon was then excused, not for financial hardship reasons, but for business reasons. "We spent about five minutes listening about all of his meetings," one of the prosecutors said. A fisherman headed to Alaska was excused. A detective who needed to attend a wedding was excused. A custodian for the King County Courthouse, after being recognized by the judge and the attorneys, was offered the chance to argue for a return to work, but the custodian said he was allowed time off for jury service and was willing to stay.

Over the course of the month, a significant number of potential jurors were excused for knowing survivors of sexual assault or being survivors of sexual assault themselves and feeling this would interfere with the requirements of the job. "I was raped by a family member," said one woman. "My heart's racing right now," said another. "It immediately kicks up a lot of emotion." Still another woman spoke of being assaulted by a stranger in public, at night, when she was a teenager. She said she'd had a healthy recovery and wanted to serve on the jury. "It was a very long time ago," she said. "I've been very vocal about it as part of my recovery."

Brandes asked her, "Were you able to immediately report it, or was there a delay?"

"I didn't report it," the woman said. "I felt like it was something that was my fault, that I let it happen."

"Well, it wasn't," Brandes said.

"I know," the woman said.

She was kept in the pool.

One in five American women, and one in seventy-one American men, have been raped, according to a recent study cited by the Centers for Disease Control and Prevention. When Judge Garrow came back for an in-person discussion of her hardship request, it turned out she also knew someone who was a survivor of rape. "It was a friend who I met who had been raped during college," she said. "It's a terrible crime. It affects people for the duration of their lives. So, certainly, I am always sympathetic towards people who have incurred that sort of violence towards them." She was excused.

It was so common to know someone who had been sexually assaulted that the experience reached into the pool of people who ended up being selected as jurors. "My sister was attacked," one person selected as a juror told the court. "He was a neighbor." It was a long time ago, she said, and she and her sister hadn't discussed it in years.

On May 25, 2011, with the jury pool now a fraction of its original size and opening arguments getting closer, Isaiah's defense attorneys made one last attempt to have him found incompetent to stand trial. They'd hired another expert, Dr. Paul Spizman, at this point the seventh psychiatric professional on the case, to conduct another evaluation of Isaiah. "When asked if he could tell me what occurred that night," Dr. Spizman wrote, "he declined." An insanity defense remained off the table.

Dr. Spizman, like others, found Isaiah to be reluctant to admit any mental health problems at all. At the same time, like others, he found Isaiah to be faking some signs of mental distress—"by his own acknowledgement," Dr. Spizman noted. This seemed to confirm the theory at the competency hearing.

In his report, Dr. Spizman also bridged the findings of a number of previous evaluators, diagnosing Isaiah as bipolar with psychotic features and as having an unspecified personality disorder "with antisocial and narcissistic traits." He declared Isaiah incompetent to stand trial and tried to peel the onion this way: "Mr. Kalebu appears to exaggerate symptoms due to his paranoia and personality attributes. As far as can be determined, it seems that his paranoia prevents him from trusting or working effectively with others. Therefore, he is reluctant to provide adequate information, such as working with his attorneys. Then, given his personality traits (e.g., narcissism) it appears he attempts to take control of the situation by exaggerating his symptoms. His antisocial aspects may also create motivation to move against any system that is trying to exert control over him."

Isaiah was in court for this hearing, and Brandes noted "a distinct odor coming from the defendant," as well as him being "not clean-shaven." She recounted what she perceived as his renewed deterioration in recent months and also brought up the day when "Mr. Kalebu spit at me in court. I can consider that incident very much like I would as if an infant had spit at me. I don't believe it was within his volition."

Judge Hayden didn't move from his earlier opinion. "I do not view him as being incompetent," the judge said. "I view him as being goal-oriented, decisive, and volitional. He does act up in court. It's my view he acts up when he decides he wants to. He acts out his own perceived way of pursuing his own goals. His decision-making in that regard is often faulty, in my judgment, and he acts in a way that's counterproductive to his best interests, but he does not perceive it that way."

"Hey," Isaiah said. "Do I get to talk?"

He presented the now-familiar complaints but did not offer to begin taking medication. Still, he said, "You guys don't want to help me, you just want to fuckin' put me on TV and say I'm a big ass monster."

There was something to this. Local television stations had been airing tape of Isaiah's being wheeled to court in a restraint chair—"surrounded by officers," one TV reporter noted—and cursing in the courtroom. "Another profanity-laced outburst from Isaiah Kalebu," went one trial update from KING 5 News, Seattle's NBC affiliate. Another update, from the local ABC affiliate, began, "A psychiatrist calls the South Park murder suspect *a fake* for pretending to be mentally ill." The complexity of the situation tended not to make it into the evening news reports, though one determined television reporter at the local CBS affiliate did try to get to the bottom of things by approaching Isaiah as he was being moved through the courthouse hallways and asking him, point-blank, if he'd committed the crime. As recounted on the station's Web site, Isaiah replied, "Are you (expletive) retarded? Really, are you that (expletive) retarded?"

As the hearing on Dr. Spizman's findings wound down, Isaiah asked to talk to yet another doctor. The request was denied, the hearing ended, and Isaiah was taken back to the empty jury room on the ninth floor from which he would watch the trial remotely. Out of Isaiah's interruptive presence, jury selection moved toward its conclusion, while Isaiah's lawyers moved toward the opening of the trial, no witnesses to call, a client unwilling to explore any mental health defense, and so a strategy of, simply, "general denial."

The final days of voir dire saw 110 potential jurors gathered together, going through a series of in-court conversations with all four lawyers and the judge, talk-show-style.

"The Oprah method," Schwartz said. "Don't bother looking under your chairs."

Judge Hayden kicked things off by asking how many of the remaining 110 had been victims of violent crime. Eighteen people raised their hands, and five more raised their hands when the category was broadened to victims of violence in which no crime was charged. Judge Hayden then asked who'd had a pleasant experience with a police officer. Thirty-one people, including JoAnn Wuitschick, the human resources worker for the University of Washington, raised hands. When the judge asked who'd had an unpleasant experience with a police officer, five people raised hands.

The judge asked whether there were any questions he or the lawyers hadn't yet asked but should have. A woman raised her hand and said, "How about two of them: 'Do you know anybody in the law field?' I'm dating the assistant attorney general. Two, because this case was about two lesbians: 'Are you gay?' I am."

This was noted but not a problem.

A number of jurors now began voicing concerns about whether they'd be able to "stomach," as one put it, this trial. Second thoughts appeared to be settling in. The woman who was a survivor of rape, and previously said she wanted to serve on the jury, now changed her mind. "It would be re-traumatizing," she said. She was excused. A prosecutor then presented a hypothetical scenario in which Judge Hayden said to the pool, "Okay, I want volunteers. Who wants to do this?" A number of hands shot up, including two women who ended up on the final jury. "Very interested," said one of them. "It's our constitutional duty," said another person, who didn't end up on the jury.

Brandes, when it was her turn to ask questions of the pool, elicited opinions as to why some people engage in deviant actions or exhibit deviant sexual appetites. "There are no wrong answers to this," Brandes said.

"Well," said the woman who worked with pulmonary researchers and who ended up on the jury, "about the same as most everyone else has said: Would be either possibly mental, economic, the way an individual was raised. I think there are probably a number of root causes that would be hard to pinpoint."

Brandes then wondered whether any jurors would have trouble with a trial that didn't offer any explanation as to a defendant's motivation. She would have known at this point, but of course would not have shared during jury selection, that she had a client who didn't want his mental state used as a defense. "Is that something you're going to have: 'I wish I knew, where did this come from?'"

"I sometimes think it just happened," a potential juror who didn't make it into the box replied. "Facts are facts. They're actually facts."

This outlook was kin to the simple, core questions that would be considered during the trial. Did these crimes happen or not? And did Isaiah Kalebu commit these crimes or not? The jury would not hear about, or be instructed to consider, Isaiah's mental state. The jury would not decide on Isaiah's punishment, either. It would only decide on his guilt or innocence, based on facts established during testimony. Still, a number of potential jurors were becoming uncomfortable with what they might not know about how this process would play out. Fearing the death penalty might be involved, several told Judge Hayden they couldn't be part of a trial that could lead to someone's execution. They were all excused.

A flawed human system was nearing its worthy aim: a fair public trial for the accused, now days away.

36

On Wednesday, June 1, 2011, Judge Hayden swore in sixteen citizens. Twelve of them were actual jurors. Four were alternates. None knew who was who. It was now coming up on two years since the South Park attacks.

The following Monday, the trial began.

Isaiah watched remotely from the empty jury room on the floor above. Teresa's family sat in the front benches of Judge Hayden's eighth-floor courtroom, next to Jennifer and her family, and they embraced and supported one another. They had followed the pretrial proceedings loosely, mainly focused on the question of whether the trial was still happening or not. Now it was, and Carley Zepeda settled in, too, determined to watch every single day of testimony. "It was just something that I had to do," she said. "I felt like Teresa would have done it for me." She had a new tattoo on the inside of her forearm in honor of her friend, an exploding firecracker stamped with the letter *T*.

Not everyone could come. Norbert Leo Butz was on Broadway performing in *Catch Me If You Can*. Others came and went, like Isaiah's mother, who arrived to watch when she could and when her presence was required for testimony. Deborah came as well, wanted badly to hug Jennifer, but didn't, couldn't. The witnesses from South Park testified: the woman who put her newborn daughter to bed, heard screams, stood on the edge of her bathtub, and called 911; the young people who ran down the street—Israel Rodriguez, Diana Ramirez, and Sara Miranda-Nino.

Each day, Detective Duffy drove Jennifer to the courthouse. "I just wanted to offer that," Detective Duffy said. "So she didn't have to worry about parking, or how to get there, or what floor." Another friend of Jennifer's, a producer at a local television station, acted as a liaison between Jennifer and the media, making it known that Jennifer couldn't speak to reporters and, for now, didn't want her name used in public. "It was something I could do," the friend, Erica Hill-Rodriguez, said. Police officers testified: Thomas Berg, the first responder; Melissa Wengard and Nilo Dela Cruz, the first officers into the red house, the ones who walked the walls to determine the scene was clear; Brian Downing, from the canine unit. Carlos Valdivia and Les Davis, the paramedics who treated Jennifer at the scene, testified too. As it happened, Davis had just had shoulder surgery, so Detective Duty drove him to court.

One morning, Tim Butz was called to testify about the last time he saw his sister. It was during a trip Teresa and Jennifer took to Chicago just a few days before Teresa was killed. On the witness stand, Tim was shown a picture, State's Exhibit 10, and a prosecutor asked him to identify it. "That's my sister, Teresa," Tim said. He then spoke about the "chance meeting" they'd had in Chicago. Teresa was there for a Cards-Cubs game and to visit Rachel. Jennifer was there for work. When it turned out Tim was in town, too, he and Teresa met for coffee. He'd been planning to visit Seattle the following week with his wife and two kids, so they talked about that, and when they were done talking he said, "See you next Monday." Outside the café, they hugged good-bye. "She grabbed me really tightly," Tim told me later. "I was like, 'Jeez, Terese.'"

That afternoon, Jennifer was called to the stand. Like others, she had mainly followed the pretrial maneuvering to find out whether the trial would actually be going forward or not. Now she, too, felt something required of her. "My job was to tell the truth, and testify, and make sure that this man had just punishment for his crime," Jennifer told me. "It was that simple to me: this is what I have to do."

37

The prosecutor wanted to know about window coverings. He asked Jennifer, which windows in the house on South Rose Street, the house where you woke up to him standing over you with a knife that night—which windows had curtains that blocked out the rest of the world and which did not?

Jennifer answered the prosecutor's questions, pointing to a map of the small South Park home she used to share with Teresa. When the two of them lived there, it was red, a bit run-down, much loved, filled with their lives together. Now it was a two-dimensional schematic, State's Exhibit 2, set on an easel next to the witness stand. She narrated with a red laser pointer for the prosecutor and the jury: These windows had curtains that couldn't be seen through. These windows had just a sheer fabric.

Would your silhouettes have been visible through that sheer fabric at night?

Probably. Jennifer didn't know for sure. When she and Teresa lived in the house, she noted, "I didn't spend a lot of time staring in my own windows."

Everyone in the courtroom laughed a small laugh, a laugh of nervous relief, because here was a woman testifying about her own rape, and the rape and murder of her partner, and yet she was smiling at the current line of questioning, at the weird perceptual cul-de-sac to which it led. She appeared to understand why people might need to hear these answers, though. What happened to her and Teresa in that house in the early morning hours of July 19, 2009, is difficult to comprehend. Even when one knows the history of the man accused of these crimes, it is difficult to comprehend, and Jennifer did not know his history as she sat on the witness stand. Nor did the jurors, who by design were encountering his actions for the first time.

The question about window coverings, then, offered a possible beginning, a way to ease into the reality of what occurred, a way to imagine how he might have picked them. At least then there'd be some sort of arc to the story. Maybe the man had stalked them, looked in their windows, decided they would be his victims. Diana Ramirez had already told the court the man looked familiar. "His eyes," Ramirez said. She thought she might have seen him roaming the neighborhood on a bicycle. The prosecutor also pointed out that the red house had only a partial fence around its backyard, the yard where Teresa and Jennifer liked to sit on warm evenings, staring at the sky above the South Park Community Center and the trees in the large surrounding park. It would have been easy for the man to approach their home, unseen, through this park at night.

Maybe he'd noticed the women around the neighborhood during the day, both attractive, both shorter than he was, working in their front yard, or attending a local festival, or heading to and from Loretta's. It had been unusually hot that July. Teresa, recalling hotter summers in St. Louis, had thought it ridiculous to install air-conditioning in Seattle, the court was told. Maybe the man saw that these women, like others in the neighborhood, were keeping windows open at night.

It could not now be suggested because of the defense strategy, and because legal routes to discussion in open court were lacking, but there were other possibilities, too.

Perhaps he was the man who had been turned away from Nickelsville, the homeless encampment named after the mayor, earlier that evening. Perhaps he was the reason the grass was found matted down beneath a tree behind their house, the reason a small branch of that tree had been snapped, as if to screen someone from view. Or maybe he saw them from a bus he was riding, perhaps one of the lines that ran from neighborhoods he used to inhabit, through South Park, and onward into downtown Seattle. Maybe he was circling the paths of his past and stumbled upon them.

He was homeless. Maybe he felt hungry, out of control, furious, saw himself as abandoned and alone with demons to fight lest he lose. Maybe he wandered this neighborhood beneath the neighborhood where he had been abused, beneath the neighborhood where his parents had fought and been arrested, beneath the bedroom he destroyed after he learned of his mother's rape at knifepoint, and as he was wandering smelled food being grilled and heard the name Teresa in the hot, still night. Maybe he thought of his former defense attorney, Theresa Griffin, the last woman to tell him she could no longer defend his actions.

Or, maybe he saw two women together, and his mind, a blurred memory drawing, saw two other women who could no longer defend him, his mother and his aunt. Maybe, past and present sliding together, he saw the twins who had tormented him in elementary school. Or maybe he was just twisted by twenty-three years of steady twisting, darkly desirous, decompensating, vulnerable, searching for a way to feel in total control. Maybe he just wanted to be with his father.

And then, maybe he saw their love for each other, noticed it in silhouette or on a sidewalk, a love that was exploding that summer, making the women inseparable, a love that had grown into plans for their commitment ceremony that September. It was a love containing promises he had not known. Maybe he realized he could turn that love against them, mercilessly, use it to control them in their own home, each subdued by the threat that he would kill the other.

They were two, and he was one. But maybe he saw that in a sense they were one. He was six feet tall, two hundred pounds, muscled. He would have two knives with him. Maybe he thought that if it did become a fight, the numbers would be on his side.

Jennifer understood, sitting up there on the witness stand, why people might need to imagine her window coverings. But this was not what she had come to talk about. The mechanics, both psychological and practical, of how the attacks might have come to pass were now well beside the point.

So she sat before the packed and sweltering eighth-floor courtroom at the King County Courthouse on June 8, 2011, nearly two years after she lost Teresa, wearing jeans and a short-sleeved black blouse, hands clasped over knees, a jury of strangers taking notes, a crowd of family and friends and strangers observing, a bunch of media recording, to say what was true: This happened to me. You must listen. This happened to us. You must hear who was lost. You must hear what he did. You must hear how Teresa fought him. You must hear what I loved about her. You must know what he took from us. This happened.

She was thirty-eight then, and she held the room with a transfixing emotional frankness. She cried at times. She set her jaw and pressed on when it got exhausting, the reliving of an ordeal that probably lasted around ninety minutes but took close to six hours over two days to retell in court. She showed regret and terror and humiliation and grief and fury. She showed that she appreciated how awful, really absurdly awful, this all was, and she welcomed opportunities to laugh—at herself, at odd things Teresa had done when she was alive, at an inelegant, unintentionally impolite question from the prosecuting attorney about a trip she'd made to Weight Watchers with Teresa on their last morning together, as part of their plan to get in better shape before their commitment ceremony.

The prosecuting attorney asked something like, how'd it go at Weight Watchers? Without missing a beat, without shame, Jennifer framed her body with her hands, moved them up and down, and said, "Well . . ."

As if to say, Look at me. Go ahead, look at all of me. It's okay. And laugh at the awkwardness of this, as everyone in the courtroom is doing right now, if that's what you all need to do. It's okay. Really. Look at me.

And thank you for being here to look, because later in this trial the prosecutor will step up to the witness stand and pull my straight black hair back from my neck so that I can more easily point out, for all of you who are looking, the four slashing scars that run from below my left ear toward my throat, the scars from when the man cut and stabbed me with his knife. I am not scared. I have nothing to hide here. Not anymore. Not for something as important as this, the opportunity to prevent him from doing it again.

She spoke of the perfect ordinariness of their last days together. How, the Friday before the attack, she stayed late working at her office in downtown Seattle and got an impatient call from Teresa: "Are you coming home?" She went home and saw Teresa sitting on a red couch in their little red house in South Park, the house that back when they first met by happenstance during that downtown Seattle workday in 2007, Teresa had brought up before almost anything else. How there was lots of weeding to do. How it wasn't the nicest "but she loved it."

On this Friday, Teresa was sitting on the red couch, and, Jennifer recalled, "she had a pen and paper." Teresa was excited. She had gone through all their finances. They had the money they needed for the commitment ceremony.

They decided to go to Loretta's, the place with the converted Airstream and a Ping-Pong table out back. The second booth in from the door was theirs. It always seemed to be free for them. Teresa ordered a bourbon and water, Jennifer a margarita. They ate the tavern steak and a salad. They felt great.

"We had one of the deepest conversations that we'd had in a long time," Jennifer said on the stand. "She'd always had this dream of—I think she always wanted to work for herself. And she had this dream of owning a café-slash-movie theater. She wanted to call it the Reel Café. We were talking about it, what it would mean, what it would take . . . We came to this decision that we would work at our corporate jobs for as long as it took to make that happen, and then she would do that."

They talked about children. Teresa, who was thirty-nine that summer, who had never been the one they thought would carry the child, announced, "Maybe I'll have the baby."

The prosecuting attorney asked, "All of this happens at Loretta's?"

Jennifer laughed. The crowd in the courtroom laughed. It did seem remarkable.

"Yeah," she said. "We were there for a few hours . . . It was our place."

They drove home through South Park, through faint cones of streetlamp light and long stretches of darkness. They stopped at a gas station along the way, and Teresa bought some Bud Light. She wasn't a regular smoker, but she was craving a cigarette. She knew Jennifer hated the smell, so she asked, "Is that okay?" Jennifer replied, "Do what you need to do." They sat in the backyard of the red house, staring at the trees, the community center, the sky above. "It was really hot that night," Jennifer recalled on the stand. "Probably like in the eighties or nineties." They drank. Teresa, it turned out, had come away from the store with three or four cigarettes. She smoked them all.

"It was just one of those nights," Jennifer said. "I remember thinking, 'In this moment, my life may not be perfect, but I am so happy.'"

The next day was Saturday, July 18, 2009. Weight Watchers in the morning. Then a fun thing a friend had gotten them into: a double-decker bus tour of microbreweries in the South Park area. Teresa played bartender on the bus. A friend took pictures of them together. "I remember the sun was shining," Jennifer said. "It was really hot. And I remember a few times I glanced at Teresa, and she had her face up. She loved the sun. She was in heaven."

There was a late-afternoon trip to a dressmaker who was working on a custom wedding gown for Jennifer, who is not a $70 wedding dress kind of woman. The dressmaker wrapped her in a muslin cutout of the pattern.

"I felt so beautiful," she said. They were invited to a friend's party up north of Seattle that night, a sleepover kind of thing so that people wouldn't have to worry about driving home. But they were both feeling tired. They decided to go back to South Park instead.

They bought steaks and potatoes—"stuff that she loved"—and while Teresa grilled the steaks outside in the backyard, Jennifer made the rest of the meal inside. There was a phone call from Teresa's mom. "This beautiful, amazingly connected call with her mom, who she loved so amazingly much," Jennifer recalled. It sounded as if Dolly, who they knew had some reservations about their commitment ceremony, would indeed be coming. "While they may not have agreed with our choice," Jennifer said on the stand of some members of the Butz family, "there was no question that they loved Teresa, and there was no question that they loved me."

Dinner. Then a movie that had been lying around the house for a while, a musical that made them both cry. It was around midnight. Teresa checked the locks multiple times, like always; she brushed her teeth multiple times while flossing in between, like always; she took the left side of the bed, like always, right next to her water and her lip balm. Jennifer took the right side of the bed, like always. They said good night.

"I kind of leaned in to her and said, 'I love you so much,'" Jennifer said.

"She said, 'I know you do.' And that was it. We went to sleep."

Jennifer doesn't know how long they slept.

"I woke up to a start," she told the court. "There was a man that I could see was naked, standing over the bed with a knife in his right hand . . . And the knife immediately went to my throat."

She gasped. She thought, "This is a dream."

"And then," she told the court, "it's just processing that there's a person here and something's going to happen."

She didn't know whether Teresa was awake with her, but she didn't want to take her eyes off the man in order to find out.

"He said, 'Be quiet, be quiet.' Because I made that noise or whatever. And he said, 'I don't want to hurt you. I just want pussy.'"

Teresa was already awake, and Jennifer remembers her saying, "Sir, I'm on my period."

The man's response: "I don't care."

Neither of them knew who he was. He told them to take their clothes off.

"So she took her pants off, and her shirt as well, and he got on top of her," Jennifer told the court. "He started raping her."

The man held on to the knife the whole time, kept it ready. Whether it came from the kitchen of the red house or elsewhere was never definitively established, but prosecutors brought the alleged knife to court as evidence. It was more than a foot long from tip to handle.

"I was as still as humanly possible," Jennifer said. "I feel like I tried to put my arm as close to her as possible so she would know that I was there. I was terrified. I thought he'd kill us with the knife. I'd already had it to my throat. Already it was clear, you know—the energy was, if you don't do what he says, he'll kill her . . . It wasn't just our own lives that we were worried about."

After a time, Jennifer said on the stand, "He got off of her, and he told me to take my clothes off, which I did. And then he told her, 'Lick her pussy.' And she got in the position, but she didn't do it. She pretended. I was really grateful for that. But I remember I could just feel her near me. And I watched him walk by the dresser near the window, and he just, one by one, shut all three windows."

In the courtroom, it felt like windows were closing. Everyone was still, as if hoping that this would keep him from hurting them.

He raped Jennifer next.

"I remember I laid very still, or very flat. I remember thinking, 'Just get through it and he'll go. He'll go. Don't do anything crazy.'"

She recounted how he smelled ("clean"), what his build was like ("muscular"), his race ("black"), how much hair he had on his body ("very little"), the volume of his voice ("soft"), the speed of his speech ("medium"), and the manner in which he spoke ("Other than using the word 'pussy,' which kind of seemed lower brow, to be honest, the rest of his speech was very intelligent").

She remembered feeling Teresa reach for her arm, remembered Teresa saying, "I'm so sorry."

"Then," Jennifer told the court, "he told me to get on my knees on the bed."

The prosecuting attorney asked, "Why?"

"Because he wanted to. Well, he did. He put his penis in my anus."

Already, Teresa had been praying out loud through the ordeal: "Our Father, please help us. Our Father in heaven . . ." Jennifer now began praying, too: "Please, God, let us live."

Then, "He stopped and he stepped away. And he told Teresa to get down on the floor on her knees in front of him . . . I heard him say 'swallow,' and I heard what sounded like gagging noises from her."

Jennifer visualized waiting, getting through this, the man leaving, then calling someone to come get them. At some point, he was done forcing Teresa to perform oral sex, and the two women both "scuttled up" on the bed, backs against the headboard, knees pressed to chests, arms around knees. Teresa told him their purses were in the kitchen, that they didn't have much cash but he could have whatever he wanted. They didn't know, but their purses had already been rifled through and left on the kitchen floor.

"He said, 'I'm not going to hurt you. Don't worry, I'm not going to hurt you.' Then he said, and I remember, 'Don't get too excited. That was just round one.'"

He stood there, leaning against the dresser in their bedroom, naked, knife in hand, staring. Jennifer noticed his expression.

"He wasn't smiling. He wasn't scowling. He was just staring."

For Jennifer, this waiting for more pain was worse than experiencing the pain in the moment.

The prosecuting attorney asked, "How many rounds, to use his term, were there?"

"Three."

Her first day of testimony ended. The next morning, June 9, 2011, Jennifer was back on the witness stand. In a building filled with horrors enacted by one human upon another, this courtroom was about to go well beyond the norm, beyond what most people are brave enough to imagine, let alone recount. It is not necessary to recount all of Jennifer's testimony. It got very gruesome. But in order to understand their bravery, it is necessary to hear, as much as possible, what was endured.

Teresa's mother, Dolly Butz, sat listening to the testimony on one of the wooden benches, just as she had every day of the trial so far, other members of the Butz family tight on either side of her, a small woman, just like her daughter, who was only five feet two. One thought: If this woman can absorb, at the level of detail required for proof before a jury, the particulars of what happened to her daughter—can view the bloody crime-scene photographs, can listen to the 911 call from Sara Miranda-Nino leaning over Teresa and screaming "Ma'am, wake up! Please wake up, ma'am!" (while, to the 911 operator: "Please hurry, please hurry"), can hear the testimony about DNA evidence and what orifices it was recovered from—then no one else in this courtroom can dare turn away. Dolly's presence, too, created an imperative: This happened. You must listen.

Isaiah sat in the sealed jury room on the ninth floor, "voluntarily absented" from the trial, left to watch the proceedings on closed-circuit television while strapped into his restraint chair. Up to this point in the testimony phase of proceedings, he hadn't been fighting his confinement in the upstairs room, but this morning, of all mornings, Isaiah had changed from his green suicide smock into a dress shirt and slacks and requested that he be allowed to sit in the eighth-floor courtroom with his accuser. After his lawyers went up and talked to him, he retracted the request.

Jennifer began her second day of testimony with the awful silence of the man standing there that night, leaning against the dresser, staring, promising more, propelled by forces she had no idea of, a stranger she could not grasp. "So much had already happened," she said. "I was trying to imagine what else . . ." And, "I didn't feel like Teresa and I could communicate. I didn't feel like I could tell her, 'I love you' . . . I almost thought it would be worse, and I don't know why, if he knew I loved her too much."

The man said to the two women, "All right, get ready for round two."

The horror of what happened next made the court reporter's eyes well up, made the bailiff cry. The jury handed around a box of tissues. The prosecutor took long pauses to collect himself. The family and friends in the courtroom cried (though, truth be told, they had been crying throughout). The *Seattle Times* reporter seated next to me cried. I cried. The camerawoman who was shooting video for all the television stations in town cried and later hugged Jennifer as she left the courtroom for the midmorning break.

Perhaps it is enough to restate how one of the two prosecuting attorneys summarized the attacks in opening arguments at the beginning of the trial. Isaiah, this prosecutor said, "raped them every way imaginable. Vaginally, anally, orally. He wasn't wearing a condom, and he ejaculated several times."

Perhaps it is enough to know that Dr. Lymberis called the attacks "dynamically oriented." Perhaps it is enough to say that through his manipulations and torture Isaiah saw what he had not been able to share: a love strong enough to require self-restraint and self-sacrifice. Perhaps it is enough to hear some of the conversations in that room in the red house, as Jennifer recounted them on the stand.

The man asked the couple for lube before one of his rapes of Teresa.

When the women replied that they didn't have any, he said, "Too bad for her."

The man asked, at one point, "So are you guys lesbians or are you bisexual?"

Jennifer's mind spun. Which would be worse? Which answer would make him more likely to stop?

"I remember what I said was, 'Well, we've been together a long time, so I guess that makes us lesbians.'"

Jennifer felt that she deserved to ask him a question at this point, so she asked, "Have you seen us before?"

He shook his head no.

Teresa asked, "What if we'd been an old man?"

He just shrugged.

Jennifer made up a story that someone was coming to pick them up at 5:00 a.m. to take them to a wedding in Portland. She asked him if they were going to make the wedding. He said yes. She said, "Please don't hurt us. We're good people."

He said, "Yeah, you seem like you're good people. I wish we could have been friends."

Teresa replied, "Yeah, I wish we could."

"Which," Jennifer said on the stand, "is exactly what she would do . . . Even in that moment, she wanted to make some sort of connection. She said, 'Maybe we still can.'"

He asked, "Do I seem like a good person to you?"

"She put the tips of her fingers on his chest—I will never ever forget this—and said, 'I am sure there is some good in here.'"

He said, "No more questions."

"I just did what I had to do," Jennifer said. "At one point, I felt the tip of the knife just kind of touch my arm. I said, 'Ouch!' and he actually said, 'Oh, I'm sorry.'"

She remembers thinking, "There's no way he'd say 'I'm sorry' and be a murderer. We're going to get through this. There's got to be some level of compassion there or something."

Teresa was reacting differently, and at one point made a play for the knife. He said, "Don't do that! Don't do that!"

Jennifer, who was being raped at that moment and was in a more vulnerable position, also said to Teresa, "Don't do that. Don't do that."

Teresa stopped trying to get the knife. The man said, "I know you're going to call the police. They all do. But I'm going to be long gone. I always am."

He was not, and has never been, linked to any other rapes. Maybe this statement was grandiosity. Maybe it was manipulative braggadocio, meant to intimidate. Maybe, when he said "they all do," he was recalling all the women in his family who'd called the authorities on him over the last few years when he'd violated their senses of safety. Maybe he was recalling how many times the police had been called on his father. Teresa and Jennifer had no knowledge of what all it might mean, no way to take it at anything but face value: "They all do."

"Maybe we won't," Jennifer told him.

"Well, you might not," he said.

Then he looked at Teresa: "But she will."

The attacks became more sadistic. Things began to happen that were beyond Jennifer's worst imagining. She felt as if she were going to be ripped in half. She thought, "He's not going to kill me with a knife, but he's going to kill me this way."

Then she heard Teresa say, "Why are you cutting me? Why are you cutting me?"

The man said to Teresa, "Shut up, or I'm going to kill your girlfriend."

He took the women into another room in the house, where he'd undressed before waking them. He turned on the light and pulled another, smaller knife out of a pair of jeans he'd left on a guest bed.

The story he had been telling them, the story Jennifer had been telling herself, the story that he just wanted sex and was not going to hurt them, now completely shattered. "I remember seeing him," Jennifer told the court, "and there was a moment where we just stood there and he kind of looked at us, and I feel like in that moment I knew, he's going to kill us. I just knew. I just felt it. There was something different in his gaze. There was this kind of looking. I didn't feel fear from him, I didn't feel anger from him, I just felt this nothing."

He made them go back into their bedroom. They pleaded with him, tried to think of what they could possibly say. They told him they were on the board of a nonprofit that helps homeless people, which was true. He didn't respond. They were back on the bed, on their backs, one of his knees on each of them, pinning them down, similar to the way his father allegedly pinned down his mother, a knife in each of his hands.

The next thing she heard was Teresa saying, "You got me. You got me. You got me." He had slashed her neck seven times.

"I remember thinking, 'No. No. No. No. No. No. No. We were supposed to get to leave. We were supposed to get to go. She can't be dying.'"

The man was slashing Jennifer's neck now, too.

"He just cut, cut, cut, cut, and I remember just feeling the blood come down, some of the blood just spurting up and out. And I remember thinking, 'This is it. There's no way I can have my throat slit and live. There's no way. There's just no way.'

"The next thing I remember him doing was switching his hand from a cutting motion to a stabbing motion."

Each of the women had their hands up, trying to push him off. Jennifer realized, though, that the more she struggled, the more blood gushed out of her neck.

"It's the weirdest thing. You don't hurt. Blood's spurting out of you, but you don't feel anything," she told the court.

She thought, "This is how I'm going to die."

It was, she said, "sort of a moment of peace."

She thought, "Maybe what Teresa tells me about heaven is true. Maybe it will be okay."

She stopped fighting and released.

"The next thing I felt was just this powerful surge of energy."

Teresa had pushed and kicked the man off the bed.

"I remember screaming, 'Get him!'"

He punched Teresa in the face. (An autopsy later showed her three bottom teeth broken and pushed back.) He stabbed her in the heart. Teresa grabbed the nightstand.

"I saw her holding that metal table, that little teeny tiny table. She kind of pushed him back with it."

No stories mattered anymore. No hopes. No promises. No mitigating factors. No human systems and their flaws. No excuses. It was now fight or flight in that room, kill or be killed. Teresa threw the table through the window. She pushed herself through the jagged glass, fell to the ground outside, leaving a hole in the window big enough for the white curtain to flap through. She got up, sprinted to the curb, ran into the street. Then, Jennifer said, "as quickly as she started running, she just fell straight back."

The man and Jennifer were still standing there in the bedroom, and they looked at each other.

He ran out of the room.

Jennifer ran to the front door.

"I remember I couldn't get the front door open because my hands were too bloody," Jennifer told the court. Eventually, she did get it open, and she ran to the neighbors across the street, ran past Teresa lying on her back on South Rose Street, because both of them needed help right now, because it seemed as if they didn't have much time. "Just ran as fast as I could," Jennifer told the court. She was naked. They were both naked. She reached the neighbors' front door.

"I bang on the door as hard as I can," she said. As she did, she noticed the skin open on one of her arms, muscle popping through. She didn't even remember being stabbed there. Her flat palms left perfect bloody prints on the door. The neighbors weren't home.

"So I just turn around and start screaming, 'Help us! Help us!'"

Indifferent silence. Unanswered cries. A murderer and rapist running away through the night. Cruelty unchecked.

And then human civilization, which did not stop this from happening, which did not even know this was happening, slowly returned, slowly wrapped itself back around the women, layer by insufficient layer.

Jennifer saw Israel Rodriguez running toward them. "He just ran," she told the court. She saw Sara Miranda-Nino leaning over Teresa. She saw Diana Ramirez take off a sweatshirt and hand it to her. "I just grabbed her sweatshirt and held it up to my neck," Jennifer said. She told a young man to call her mom on his cell phone and tell her mom she loved her. "And the next thing I remember at this point is an officer coming up to me and kind of abruptly telling me to stop screaming." It was Officer Berg, trying to secure the area so that the firemen and paramedics, waiting down the block, could rush in, blue smocked and white gloved, and try to help whomever they could. "I remember they came to me," Jennifer said, "and they didn't go to her, and I was like, 'Go to her! Go to her!'" Other firemen and medics would go to Teresa, but it would be too late.

The ambulance holding Jennifer would leave, lights and sirens, for Harborview. The canine unit would come to track the man's scent. An emergency room physician would swab Jennifer for evidence and, for a time, with her best interests in mind, withhold from her the information that Teresa had been killed. Officer Woo would do the same. The coroner would take custody of Teresa's body, and in the hospital Detective Duffy would put her hand on Jennifer's arm and tell her the truth, take her statement, tell her to start from the beginning. The crime lab would process the evidence: fingerprints on the dresser and the bathtub, a bloody footprint on a piece of paper, DNA in and on the bodies of Teresa and Jennifer. Four days of running down leads, and then Detective Duffy would call Jennifer at Sundecker's in St. Louis, overlooking the Mississippi River, underneath the Martin Luther King Bridge, tell her, "We have him."

King County prosecutors, public defenders, and a judge would be assigned to the case. Jurors would be selected. The component pieces of this effort to be civilized, even toward those accused of defying the demands of civilization, would fall into place.

And then Jennifer would testify, relive and recount it all, bear witness and bare her pain for the hope of justice.

Before all of this, though, the firemen and paramedics who tried to get Jennifer to sit down on South Rose Street, to stop her screaming so they could help. She would not sit down and stop her screaming. Not after what happened. Not after all that silence. Not anymore.

A part of her knew Teresa's fate. Still, she shouted into the night. Even if Teresa couldn't hear her anymore, maybe someone would hear: "I love you, Teresa! Fight! Fight! Fight! Fight! Fight!"

38

The prosecutor reached the end of his questions. Brandes, Isaiah's public defender, rose to cross-examine Jennifer. She began by checking and reconfirming certain details, mostly about the knives, what they looked like. Then she explored the attempts Jennifer and Teresa had made to, in Brandes's wording, "humanize" themselves to the man who was attacking them. This done, Brandes attempted to humanize their attacker, her client.

"You've described some very hard actions that you had to suffer through, and some callousness from this man," Brandes said. "But there were times when he wasn't entirely callous."

"I don't believe that," Jennifer said.

"Well, how about when he let you give Teresa the water?"

"So she can better use her mouth on him? I don't see that as not being callous."

"And there were times when he petted or stroked you?"

"How is it not callous to stroke a rape victim who doesn't want to be stroked? That's not kindness. That was probably the worst part for me."

"Well, I am certainly not suggesting it was a kindness to you."

Brandes moved on.

The rest of her questions focused mainly on which had happened first: the slashing and stabbing with the knife or the physical resistance. Jennifer explained, again, that the cutting with the knife came first. Then, when they began to resist, he took them into the other bedroom to get a second knife.

"This is when he says, 'Get up'?" Brandes asked.

"Yes."

"Takes you to another room, gets the knife, everything moves really quickly."

"Yes."

"And that's when he cut your throat?"

"Yes."

"I don't have any other questions."

"Members of the jury," Judge Hayden said, "I have some things to handle with counsel for the afternoon in this matter and, therefore, I'm going to give you a break for the afternoon. I don't think any of you will be too upset by having the afternoon off. So, you're free to go home. Tomorrow's Friday, right? We're not back in session until Monday. So you've got some time to decompress."

After the judge released the jury for the afternoon, JoAnn Wuitschick went for a walk along a beach in North Seattle, a beach that, though she did not know it, sits directly below a hill that held one of the apartments in which Isaiah spent his early years. She figured it was probably against the rules to write about what she was experiencing in her journal, so these walks along the Salish Sea had become her outlet. "Just walked," she said. "Thought, 'Wow.' That's all I could think. And just cried. In my head, I was just telling her, 'Keep your head high, honey. You're going to be fine.' She just seemed like, to her core, a strong person, an amazing woman."

At home at night, in her fourth-floor condo, JoAnn had begun, for the first time, locking the sliding glass door to her balcony. She was living alone then and knew her fear was irrational, one of the quiet ripples from the crime. "I mean, nobody could get up to my balcony unless they rappelled down from the roof," JoAnn said. Still, she began standing empty wine bottles flush against her front door, too, so that if someone opened it at night she'd be awakened.

That Sunday evening, as the jurors and lawyers were getting ready to head back to court, Norbert Leo Butz was in New York, seated in an unusual spot for him, the audience of a theater. The Tony Award for best actor in a musical was announced, and it went to him, for his portrayal of the dogged FBI agent in *Catch Me If You Can*. As he accepted it, he suggested the trial was with him, too. "This is for my father, who I based this character on," Norbert said, "and for my sister. I love you, Teresa. We remember you every night."

That Monday morning, the juror who'd once talked about having a cart and working as a repairman called in to say he'd been up all night, sick, and couldn't appear. He was excused from jury service. The jury box was now down to fifteen people.

More witnesses for the prosecution were called that week. Doctors, the medical examiner, a state crime lab employee. On Tuesday, while watching the trial remotely from the floor above, Isaiah swallowed a small pencil. He was taken to Harborview, then brought back so proceedings could continue. During the trial's third week, when Detective Duffy and other witnesses for the prosecution were testifying, Isaiah was again taken to Harborview and returned. This time reasons were not specified.

On the Monday of the fourth week of testimony, Isaiah's mother took the stand, as did the bus driver who spotted Isaiah near Magnuson Park and Officer Leon Towne, who'd arrested Isaiah. Then, that afternoon, with the prosecution ready to rest, Isaiah's lawyers informed the court of something that seemed to surprise them, too: Isaiah wished to testify in his own defense.

"If he wants to do this," Schwartz said, "he's calling himself to the witness stand. His counsel have no questions for him."

The defense team had long ago announced that it intended to call no witnesses and instead just pursue the strategy of "general denial," which, Schwartz had reminded jurors during voir dire, is a perfectly legitimate defense at a criminal trial, where the burden of proof beyond a reasonable doubt lies entirely on the prosecution.

Outside the presence of the jury, elaborate preparations were now made to provide Isaiah with his right to testify. The courtroom was reconfigured so that Isaiah could sit not on the witness stand but at a table across the room from the jury. This would shield from jurors the fact that he would be sitting in a restraint chair, his hands covered by white mittens meant to immobilize them, a Taser-like device, called a Band-It, strapped to his forearm so that jail guards could remotely shock him into submission if he became uncontrollable.

Isaiah arrived for his testimony wearing a canary-yellow dress shirt and slacks and was sworn in on a Bible, as he'd requested. He'd also requested that he be allowed to wear a black judge's robe. That request had been denied. So had his lawyer's last-minute request for another competency evaluation. In denying that request, Judge Hayden said, "I abide by my view that much of his behavior is volitional in nature and his own strategy, however unusual that strategy may be."

The jury was brought in. The state rested. And now, for the first time, the jury saw the defendant in the case. The palms of JoAnn Wuitschick's hands began to sweat. "My mouth dropped open," said Debra Young, another juror.

Judge Hayden had already ruled that Isaiah had to testify in a question-

and-answer format, not a monologue. So, even though Schwartz had said Isaiah's attorneys had no questions for him, Brandes now asked Isaiah what he wanted to be asked. She gave the address of the red house on South Rose Street and asked him, "Mr. Kalebu, do you know anything about the events that occurred in the early morning hours of July 19, 2009?"

"I was there," Isaiah replied. "And I was told by my God, and the God of Abraham, Isaac, and Jacob, to attack my enemies. I did so. I followed the instructions by God."

Brandes now asked another question, though it was unclear whether it was a question Isaiah wanted asked: "Mr. Kalebu, have you ever been diagnosed as having a mental illness?"

"Yeah," he said. "I have been diagnosed several times."

A prosecutor objected. Brandes said the information was within bounds. The jury was sent out so the lawyers could argue further.

"He can testify as to his state of mind," Judge Hayden said. "But I don't think he can diagnose himself with anything."

Technically speaking, however, Isaiah hadn't actually diagnosed himself with anything. He'd just stated what was true: He'd been diagnosed by others.

After more discussion, Judge Hayden clarified that Isaiah could offer his own opinion of his mental health but not a diagnosis, which would require expert testimony. In other words, Isaiah would be allowed to say the one thing he'd so often refused to say. As Judge Hayden put it, "I will allow him to tell the jury he thinks he's mentally ill."

"Let me see if he wishes to proceed," Brandes replied.

They were at a familiar impasse, though it was not an impasse that would be familiar to anyone seeing Isaiah for the first time at this trial. Without revealing anything, Brandes signaled for the jury to be brought back in.

Isaiah's last statement was stricken from the record. Jurors would be allowed to consider his admission that he was at the scene of the crime but not his discussion of his past mental health diagnoses. Now Brandes had an opportunity to ask Isaiah for his own opinion of his mental health, if he indeed wanted her to ask the question.

Apparently, he did not.

"No further questions," Brandes said.

Isaiah was now boxed in, once again, by his resistance to accepting his disturbance. At the table where he was seated, something appeared to be happening. Debra Young saw Brandes push away from her client in her rolling desk chair. The prosecutor asked that the jurors be sent out again, and they were.

"I heard Velcro," Brandes said once the jurors were gone. Isaiah had been trying to take off the restraint mittens, had succeeded in getting his hand out of one. "He was trying to remove the Band-It," said a jail officer. "It is secure now."

Next moves were discussed, as was the heat in the courtroom. "A lot of people in here," Judge Hayden said. His bailiff said she'd inquired about getting it cooled down.

It was agreed Isaiah would leave now and return to watching the trial remotely from an upper floor. Brandes then argued that based on what had occurred, the jury should be given the option to find Isaiah not guilty by reason of insanity. It was far too late in the proceedings to begin pursuing an insanity defense, Judge Hayden ruled. The law did not allow such things. In any case, it was a defense Isaiah had not wanted to pursue. The jury was brought back in, the judge went through the jury instructions with them, and then closing arguments began.

39

"Unspeakable acts were committed against two unsuspecting women who wouldn't have hurt anybody," the prosecutor said. He urged the jurors to convict Isaiah on all counts. Schwartz, when it was his turn, rose and said, "These are undoubtedly two very, very brave women, with courage someone like myself cannot measure." Then he tried to poke a few holes in the prosecution's case, casting the DNA evidence, for example, as riddled with uncertainties. (A prosecutor, in rebuttal, noted that DNA evidence had only a "one in 13 quintillion" chance of being wrong. "That's 18 zeroes," he said.) Schwartz also warned the jury that reaching this decision was the most important thing they'd ever do in their lives—"other than raising a child."

It was now time for deliberations to begin, but first the alternate jurors were revealed and excused. JoAnn Wuitschick, it turned out, was one. She was hugely disappointed. "Because I take great notes," she said. Also, she wanted the closure of moving toward a verdict with the rest of them.

The jury room was behind a thick wooden door in the back of Judge Hayden's courtroom, and it was tiny. "Crappy chairs, small quarters," Debra Young said. "The bathroom was right there, so it's like you go into the bathroom and I felt obligated to turn on the water so people couldn't hear me peeing." As the twelve jurors piled in, Isaiah's testimony was still fresh in several minds and was provoking divergent reactions, similar to the way his words and actions had provoked divergent reactions among so many already. "I felt like he was faking," said Jamie Dellaringa, the Costco employee. "I felt like he already planned exactly what to say to make himself sound crazy." Debra Young felt something different. "Something wasn't right," she said. "It was weird. What he said was weird. Something wasn't right with him."

Still, as had been the case for many years, the law was not concerned with exactly what was right or wrong with Isaiah. "We were asked whether he did something or not," said Dan Butler, another juror. "We weren't asked why."

They didn't do much that first afternoon, because it was nearing the end of the day. The next morning, a Thursday, they began with a basic question: Was Isaiah there that night or not? It took almost the whole day to answer, in part because one man on the jury held out for quite some time. As he did, he spoke of how he himself had once been misidentified, suspected of being a terrorist at an airport. What finally brought everyone around was the accumulation of evidence they had with them in the jury room and the difficulty in arguing with it: the knives, the fingerprints, the crime-scene photographs, their juror's notebooks filled with what they'd written down during testimony. At one point, Jamie Dellaringa pulled Isaiah's pants out of an evidence bag, turned them inside out, and noticed there was blood on the inside of them. When Isaiah put his pants back on that night, she came to believe, he'd had Jennifer and Teresa's blood all over him.

By the end of the day, they'd all come to the same conclusion. Isaiah was there. "If there was any hope of getting the guy off for not guilty, that would have been the only way to do it," Dan Butler said. "Once that was determined, there was no question." He was there, and if he was, they all agreed, then he was the one who committed the crimes.

Though determining why was not part of their task, it was hard not to wonder. Michelle Abercrombie theorized it was a consequence of Isaiah's need for control. The crime itself, she saw, was all about control, and she believed that he became more violent as the reactions of Jennifer and Teresa to what Isaiah was doing began to get too far out of his control. "He had to be in control," she said.

The next morning, the question of premeditation came up. It was the second day of deliberations, a Friday. "That was the hardest one for a lot of us," said Jamie Dellaringa. "Did he mean it? Was it his plan?"

"I don't know what his intention was going in the house," said Michelle Abercrombie. "It could have just been burglary, because he was watching them sleep." She imagined him standing there after rifling through their purses and tossing them on the kitchen floor. Perhaps his first interest had simply been money, and then, looking around, he'd noticed a large kitchen knife. "If he had gone in there with the intent to murder them, I think he would have just murdered them," she said.

At 11:18 that morning, the jurors sent a written question to Judge Hayden, asking him to clarify how long it takes to form premeditation. He told them to read their jury instructions. The instructions said, "Premeditated means thought over before hand . . . The law requires some time, however long or short, in which a design to kill is deliberately formed." Like others, Jamie Dellaringa had assumed premeditation would be something that involved months, or weeks, or maybe days of planning. "But it's not," she said. In the understanding she and others on the jury developed, it's that a person thinks about doing something, and then that thing is done. "He stabbed both of them once," she said. "They didn't die. And then he did it again and again and again and again. At that point, he knows what he's doing and he is planning. He's trying to kill them. He is thinking about it." It took them only a few more hours, with a lunch break included, to unanimously reach their final decision.

On the afternoon of Friday, July 1, 2011, nearly four weeks after the trial began, eighteen days before the second anniversary of Teresa's death, and two days after deliberations started, the jury announced its verdict in *State of Washington v. Isaiah Kalebu:* Guilty on all counts. Guilty of aggravated, premeditated murder in the first degree, for the killing of Teresa Butz, which the jury found was committed "in the course of, in furtherance of, or in immediate flight from" the first-degree rape of Teresa Butz. Guilty of felony murder, for the killing of Teresa Butz. Guilty of first-degree attempted murder, for the premeditated attempted murder of Jennifer Hopper. Guilty of rape in the first degree, for the rape of Jennifer Hopper. Guilty of burglary in the first degree, for crawling through an open window in the couple's bathroom in the early morning hours of July 19, 2009.

All of these crimes, the jury found, were committed with a deadly weapon and with sexual motivation or deliberate cruelty.

"Everybody was tired and exhausted and kind of emotionally traumatized," Dan Butler said. He was also relieved: "My role was done."

Jennifer was in the courtroom as the verdict was delivered, and she cried, as did many of the jurors and much of the crowd that had gathered. "It's been a long road together," Judge Hayden told the jury. "I saw a lot of anguish. But you made it through the process, and I want to thank you. Deeply. Thank you for having gone through it with us when most folks, when presented with the opportunity to do this, would have said, 'I can't do it.'"

He offered certificates of jury service, which he acknowledged, to laughs from them and the rest of the room, "don't mean much." He offered the jurors counseling, which some later took him up on. All jurors declined, through the bailiff, the opportunity to talk with members of the media. They just wanted to go home.

40

The hearing to hand down Isaiah's sentence came a month and a half later, on August 12, 2011. Eleven days earlier, Isaiah's twenty-sixth birthday. "This is a case of extreme, deliberate cruelty," the prosecutor said at the outset. "Certainly one that cries out for an exceptional sentence."

Before the sentence, though, the "victim impact statements." Norbert senior had flown in from St. Louis to address the court. So had Teresa's older brother Jim. "Your Honor," Norbert senior began, "people in the courtroom, I—in my wildest dreams, I thought I would never have an experience like this, and I've had a lot of experiences in my life. But Teresa was the ninth gift from God out of eleven of our children, and to know her was to love her. I don't mean to make a saint out of her because she had issues, as we all do in life, but she was a good student, an avid soccer player, and a catcher in grade school, high school, and in college, and she was just . . ." He talked about her childhood, her tough disposition, the place she made for herself in that large family. "She was really a blessing by God, and it's one that Isaiah took from us, and he didn't have a right to do that, but he did it, and we're living with that," Norbert senior said. "He took her life, but he couldn't take her spirit and her soul. She still lives with us daily. We have a tree planted in our backyard; it's called Teresa's tree, and I watch it grow every day, and that's a blessing."

He spoke of how Teresa was always drawn to the underdog. He spoke of his own struggles with thoughts of revenge. "You can't imagine," he said. "And I still don't forgive him; I don't excuse what he did." He thanked "the community, Detective Duffy, the police force, the court system, the jurors that had to sit through this diabolical situation."

Jim Butz spoke next. "It's a strange providence that's brought this whole group of human beings into a single room," he said, "and there's a lot of stories represented here." Some of the jurors had shown up to watch. Carley and Carmen were there. Jennifer and her family were there. The media, on this day, observed from the empty jury box. Jim Butz spoke of Teresa's "zealous sense of justice," and he spoke directly to Isaiah, saying, "I don't know you, and you don't know me, and we're just two human beings, and I don't know your backstory." He told Isaiah he felt no right to judge another person. "I don't," Jim Butz said. "I swear, I know that's true. And I'm dead serious, I've prayed for you every single day since this happened."

"Thank you very much," Isaiah said.

"And I hope to see you in heaven. I'm serious."

"I'll be there."

"And that's all I'd like to say."

"God bless," said Isaiah.

Next to speak was Jennifer. She began facing Judge Hayden, her back to Isaiah. "I have thought a lot about what I would say today, and I tried on numerous occasions to write something down," she said. "And the trouble that I have is that, one, I feel like I've said pretty much everything I had to say when I sat up there and told the story of what happened to us that night. But I knew that I couldn't let today pass without doing a couple of things, and one was to show my gratitude, which I could not show that day, to you"—and here she was addressing Judge Hayden—"for being fair and listening and hearing me and everyone that day. And to everyone here, the media who left me alone, my friends, the jurors, everyone, for protecting me and surrounding me with love when I needed it the most."

Then she turned to face Isaiah. "But I also knew that I couldn't let today go by without again addressing you." She spoke of how the things Teresa taught her, by example and word, had helped her to heal and get through. "I realized," Jennifer said, "that there may be nothing I can say to you, because I did beg you for my life, and she begged you for her life. And I tried to show you our humanity, and any shred of goodness that I was hoping you could see, and it didn't matter that day, so I can't understand how it would matter today. But I do say to you that I do wish you peace, and I do not hate you, and I'm so sorry for whatever it is in your life that brought you to this." She spoke of being glad that he wouldn't be able to hurt anyone again. She said, "I wish I could say to you that I've not been broken. I actually wrote the words down on a piece of paper, that, 'Yes, you took so much from me, but I am not broken.' But pieces of me are and will always be. But I will fight every day of my life to be as whole as I can. That I promise you, and I promise everyone here. But I wish you no harm. I never wanted you put to death. I don't seek revenge, I don't want anything bad to happen to you in prison, nothing. I wish you peace every last day of your life. That's all I have to say."

"Who will present on behalf of the defense?" Judge Hayden asked.

"Mr. Kalebu chooses not to exercise his right to allocute, Your Honor," said Brandes. "There's not a lot that—as a defense team—that we can say. It's been a difficult case, I think, for all parties. The court, your staff, the prosecutor, the defense team, the jurors, those who suffered through the events that happened that night, and all I can say is this: That we are in awe of the grace of Ms. Hopper and of the Butz family. We are saddened by the internal demons and delusions that Mr. Kalebu has struggled with, not just during the two years that we've known him, but for the few years leading up to this incident. We appreciate the voice that Ms. Hopper has given to women who have suffered from sexual violence and to people who have committed, loving relationships, no matter what they are. We know what the sentence of this court will be. We'll file our appeal and have the appellate court review that for any errors that may have occurred, and we wish that everyone go in peace."

Judge Hayden then spoke of having been at a wedding the previous evening, "a marriage that should have been celebrated by Jennifer and Teresa, a marriage that, perhaps in the future, within her lifetime, will be possible within this state . . . I think within your lifetime, your next ceremony, whoever it's with, may indeed be a marriage ceremony, and I would say to everyone gathered here that that would be a much more joyous occasion for everyone, where the tears could flow for good."

Isaiah now interrupted the judge. His speech was back to a manic speed, so fast the words blurred together and the court reporter couldn't keep up, writing, "All you people hoping we have gay marriage, do you realize that if we have gay marriage it's going to make [indecipherable] really. See what's going to happen is first we have gay marriage, then the polygamists are going to piggyback on that . . ."

"Mr. Kalebu," Judge Hayden said, "you've had your chance to speak."

"So we have gay marriage, and then we have polygamy. We have polygamy. All the Muslims who are polygamists are going to bring their five wives and 25 kids over here, and then, boom, it's a charade of a country, just like that."

In my notes, I wrote, "it's a Sharia country, just like that," but who knows what Isaiah actually said. It was hard to follow because it came out so fast. Afterward, Brandes said the outburst didn't change her sense of the motivation for the crimes. "They were not motivated by antigay animus," Brandes said. "We have specific reason to know that." She did not elaborate.

Judge Hayden let Isaiah spin out, which didn't take long, and then he asked, "Are you finished?" Isaiah said nothing.

The judge delivered his sentence. Because the mandatory minimum for Isaiah's crimes was life in prison without the possibility of parole, Judge Hayden conceded that the other parts of his punishment would be largely symbolic. "But," he said, "in our system of justice symbols are important. What we do is important, and what we say is important. Jennifer Hopper and the family of Teresa Butz and, indeed, even members of the jury deserve to know that this defendant's brutality and the horror of that evening warrants the maximum penalty that I can impose under the law." He used Isaiah's life expectancy—seventy-three years—to calculate the exceptional sentence, which came out to life without the possibility of parole, plus what amounted to two more life sentences beyond that. Isaiah also lost his right to vote and own a gun.

"Does that conclude this matter, Counsel?" Judge Hayden asked.

"Yes, Your Honor," the prosecutor said.

"We'll be at recess."

Four days later, at a brief restitution hearing, Isaiah was ordered to pay a little over $40,000 for expenses incurred by the Butz family as a result of Teresa's death. If he did work while in prison, it would be taken out of his paycheck. "I don't want to go to prison!" Isaiah interjected at one point.

This was noted, but it made no difference.

A short time after the restitution hearing concluded, Isaiah was loaded into a special van with tinted windows and a steel cage inside. With him secured inside this cage, a driver took Isaiah up and over the crest of the Cascade Mountains, down the other side, across the dry flatlands of eastern Washington, across the wide Columbia River, and into Walla Walla, the city where Isaiah had briefly been in college not too many years earlier and where his old friend Kayla Manteghi had seen him and thought he'd seemed the same. The campus for that college is a ten-minute drive from the Washington State Penitentiary, which is located, through a dark bit of civic planning, at 1313 North Thirteenth Avenue.

41

Three years later, on a spring evening in Seattle, Jennifer is at home decompressing, wearing a lightweight red hoodie and black slacks in an apartment many floors up from the street, an apartment with a secured front entry. She's just spent the day speaking at a Seattle Police Department employee retreat on the topic of resilience, telling officers, supervisors, and 911 operators how she moved forward from the attacks and the trial. At one point during her talk, she referred to her attacker as "Mr. Kalebu," and an officer raised his hand. He wanted to know how she could give him any honor, even a small honorific like "Mr.," after what he'd done. How could she find any forgiveness?

It didn't come all at once.

She recalls a picture. Maybe in the newspaper. Maybe on television. "I don't really remember," Jennifer said. "I just remember the image." It was an image of Isaiah's mother at the arraignment right after his arrest for the South Park attacks. She was leaning against a glass partition that separated courtroom visitors from participants, watching her son in handcuffs. "He was somebody's child," Jennifer said.

"As soon as I pictured him that young," she continued, "and that vulnerable, it's like I could see his humanity, and that led me to being able to be in the space of forgiveness."

The space has specific meaning for her. "I heard somebody describe forgiveness as restoring what there was before," Jennifer said. "And that forgiveness didn't mean that it was okay, or that there's no responsibility, or that, like, 'I forgive you, it's okay that you did that to me.' It's more like you're restoring the relationship to what it was before. And with him, the relationship that we would have had before is that we would have been strangers. And I would wish him what I would wish any stranger, which is pretty much that I hope they have a good life." She would refer to any male stranger as "Mr.," just out of decency, she explained to the officer who'd raised his hand at her talk.

"Someone also described to me," she continued, "that when you forgive, you no longer allow what that person did to diminish you." Her forgiveness, she makes clear, "has nothing to do with him. It has everything to do with me. He can no longer diminish me, inside of forgiveness."

She doesn't think about him a lot these days. "I really don't," she said. "And that gives me freedom. That's massive freedom, considering what happened. And yeah, there were people who said to me, 'Man, I hope he gets his own when he gets to prison.' To me, that for sure doesn't bring Teresa back. For sure, it doesn't make me feel whole, and it just has me participating in the same kind of way that created the violence that had him hurt me. I'm not interested in that. I actually do hope he has whatever peace he can have in prison. I said it at the sentencing, and I mean it, and I probably mean it in an even deeper way now than I did then. Then, it was still the beginning."

The sense of forgiveness continues to grow, as does her sense of what it does, and does not, encompass. Once, not long after the trial ended, she went to speak at a women's prison, and an inmate asked her if she would accept an apology from Isaiah. She remembers telling the woman that she didn't feel Isaiah was capable of doing that. "But," she said, "if someone from the prison said, 'Hey, he's had this kind of transformation, and it would make a difference,' I would. But it would be for him and not for me."

Jennifer believes Isaiah is mentally ill. She also believes he knows right from wrong. She also knows this: "We didn't do anything to him. It's a crime of, like—we were accessible somehow. Like, with an open window. I still don't believe that he stalked us out or anything. Who knows. But even then, we happened to be someplace that he saw us. And he said he'd go, and he didn't . . . Very smart guy."

She does still wonder if there was any antigay motivation to his violence. She wishes Brandes, his attorney, could say why she's so certain antigay animus had nothing to do with Isaiah's crimes. "Also," Jennifer said, "it doesn't matter. I remember at the trial, when he started that line of 'God told me to do it . . .' I was like, 'Ask him why!'" She was whispering now. "'Ask him why!' In the back, I was like, 'Ask him why!'"

She stopped whispering and continued, "Because there was a part of me that wanted him to say, 'Because they were sinning,' or something like that, and then suddenly"—she snapped her fingers—"we were turning it into something else. But, really, who cares? He got beyond life. So what are we gonna do, tack on ten more years because it was a hate crime? At this point, it was a violent crime. It was a violent crime against women. You can almost call that a hate crime sometimes. Rape just reads to me as a hate crime. There's this, like, 'You're a woman, so by the very fact that you're a woman I can overpower you and make you do what I want you to do.' Which—there is some hatred there, that's for sure. So I don't know if it really would have been distinct."

Some part of her would still like to know why he chose them.

"But then again, who cares?" she said. "There's really nothing I would have changed about how we lived our lives."

42

After the fall of 2011, when Isaiah arrived at the state penitentiary in Walla Walla, years passed with no one visiting him.

He remained in touch with the outside world, however. Isaiah's mother told me she'd written to him early in his prison term and that he'd written ten or twelve letters back to her. She said he'd also called her on the phone. "I did say to Isaiah, a few times, I said, 'I'm so sorry, Isaiah, that you're in there. I wish you weren't in there,'" his mother told me. "And he said, 'You should be sorry.'" That stopped her short.

"I don't understand why he says that to me," she said. "I think he's blaming me for something, but I'm not quite sure what it is. Whether it's because I allowed him to go live with his aunt and he's blaming me—I don't know what it is . . ."

She continues to believe her son is schizophrenic. "I'm not sure what bipolar is," she said. "But the stuff I saw through Isaiah was the exact same things I saw through my mother, my cousins, my brother, relatives of mine."

Seeking some form of interview, I wrote half a dozen letters to Isaiah between the summer of 2013 and the end of 2014. I told him I was working on this book. I asked for his side of things, proposed a visit, asked him to write to me at a P.O. box that I rented for the possibility of a letter from him, asked him to call the number of a cheap cell phone I bought for the potential of a call from him. I sent him a small amount of money for his prison postage and phone accounts, enough that there would be no obstacle to his reaching out if he desired.

As I waited for some response, Deborah told me she'd heard, through her mother, that Isaiah had been up and down. "He's getting worse," Deborah said in one of our earlier conversations. "He needs to be in a facility where they can medicate his ass." She said Isaiah had been talking, in phone calls home, about government plots and FBI work. The state prison system won't release records related to Isaiah's mental health because of medical privacy concerns, but the records that can be released suggest a continued reluctance about medication. In December 2011, just a couple of months after he arrived at Walla Walla, a prison guard spotted a pill on Isaiah's cell desk. The explanation: "Saving it for later."

Prison records also suggest Isaiah spent considerable time in the section of the Walla Walla penitentiary used for housing mentally ill offenders. Those same records chronicle Isaiah's infractions, for things like having a "filthy" cell and refusing to clean it (to which he pleaded "not entirely guilty") and trading the halal meal he requested for another inmate's kosher meal (to which he pleaded "guilty"). He initially refused to do prison work or get involved in prison education programs, with a report from November 2013 reading, "Offender spends all his time in his cell watching television, only coming out to eat."

His mother sent him that television, and this particular report recommended Isaiah lose his TV privileges for ten days as punishment for a cell that was, again, "filthy." Isaiah tried to contest the punishment at a prison hearing, blaming the prison vents for always blowing dirt and debris in, thwarting his cleaning efforts. He was punished nonetheless. By the end of 2014, his infractions numbered about a dozen and appeared to ebb and flow in unpredictable cycles. What that might mean, if anything, is unclear.

"He has never been treated," Dr. Lymberis said of the situation, angry, exclaiming, "He has never been treated. He continues not to be treated. It's not a new thing. This case illustrates our societal problem."

It has been estimated that between 20 and 30 percent of Washington State's prison population is mentally ill, which is about average for this country, and the Washington State Legislature not long ago appropriated millions of dollars to build a new facility at Walla Walla to keep up with the state's rising number of inmates.

A little over three years after he arrived at Walla Walla, on the morning of October 6, 2014, Isaiah did something that led to a change in his surroundings. According to state penitentiary records, Isaiah "came up to the pill line, handed Nurse Scott a piece of paper, and asked for a band aid." When the nurse asked Isaiah what the paper was about, he told Nurse Scott to turn it over. On the back was a handwritten note that included lines like "You are beautiful," "Seeing you is the best part of my day," and "I wish there was a way I could spend more time with you." In response, "Nurse Scott informed the inmate he couldn't be doing stuff like that and handed him a band aid. Inmate said ok and walked away."

Isaiah's note was "uncomfortable and threatening" to the nurse, the records say, and as a consequence he was cited for, and found guilty of, sexual harassment. He spent time in "isolation," the prison's term for solitary confinement. "They put him in the hole," said his mother, who wishes her son could be confined to a mental hospital rather than a prison. Records show that Isaiah's mother called Walla Walla several times during this period expressing concern, wondering when her son would be released from solitary, hoping prison officials were remembering to give him his mental health medication. "Explained she can be told very little info due to privacy laws," a note in the records states, "but assured her son is safe and well."

Then, in December 2014, because his sexual harassment infraction made him ineligible to remain in the mental health units in Walla Walla,

Isaiah was transferred back across the Cascade Mountains to the Clallam Bay Corrections Center. It's a smaller, newer facility that sits on the northern edge of the Olympic Peninsula, in a wooded area near the Strait of Juan de Fuca. Across the strait is Canada's Vancouver Island and, to the northeast, San Juan Island, where the body of Isaiah's schizophrenic maternal grandmother reportedly washed up when he was an infant. Clallam Bay has the ability to hold "maximum security" prisoners, but Isaiah's status when he arrived there was somewhat lower: "close custody."

Isaiah never responded to any of my letters. But shortly after his transfer to Clallam Bay, I learned that prisoners in Washington State have access to e-mail. I sent him a message, and a week later, on February 12, 2015, a reply from Isaiah arrived in my in-box:

> Eli I refuse to speak with you until I have digested what you have written about me good and bad. After I that I may consider speaking with you, maybe. I suggest you send me a comprehensive sample of your work emphasizing your covrage of my alleged "crimes," arrest, incarceration in county jail and mental institutions, trial and subsequent confinement within D.O.C. Also include anything you have written about my so-called "victims."
>
> I have heard you have won a Pulitzer Prize writing about my "crimes" and "victims" Congratulations please include information about the Pulitzer Prize such as eligibility requirements, amount of competition, awards assoicatied with said prize including information about your award ceremony, and a transcript of you acceptance speach if there was one.
>
> Well Eli since you're writing a book about me it's a safe bet that this e-mail will find it's way into that book. A direct firsthand quotation from Kalebu, must be like water in the desert huh.

I wrote back to Isaiah. I expressed polite gratitude for his reply, and I sent links to materials I thought might satisfy his request. He responded that he couldn't open any links, "as I do not have access to the internet only this limited excuse for e-mail." He suggested I send paper copies of the materials, "through snail-mail" and also "through a lawyer for confidentiality purposes." I did as he suggested, but as of this writing, five months after he last communicated with me, I have received no further word from Isaiah.

He remains in touch with his mother and Deborah, however. In June 2015, his mother told me she'd had a phone conversation with him and that, while not admitting any guilt for the crimes against Jennifer and Teresa, Isaiah had expressed to her some sorrow for what occurred, calling Jennifer "nice" and saying, "I wish nothing had happened to her or Teresa." Around the same time, Deborah told me she'd just become comfortable hearing Isaiah's voice over the phone again, more than three years after he was sent to prison, and that in conversation he'd expressed to her some sadness at Rachel Kalebu's death. "He cries about it," Deborah told me. "He's hurt about it. He talks about how much he misses her. He's like 'I hate that Mamma Rachel's died.' I know my brother's in pain."

Perhaps these are things he would say only to his mother and Deborah. Like others, the last interaction I had with Isaiah conveyed the impression of a man in a demanding, unrepentant, and unreflective place, diagnosis a mystery, underlying issues unknown, sentence unending.

The River

43

For four years, the neighborhood of South Park went without its drawbridge over the Duwamish. At first, the old bridge just sat there, abandoned, condemned for safety reasons, alternate routes required to get to Loretta's or the community center baseball diamond. Voters in King County had rejected raising taxes for a replacement, and when President Obama and Congress released billions in federal stimulus funds to help stem the Great Recession and promote infrastructure improvements, the South Park Bridge project was initially passed over. Instead, funds went first to downtown Seattle, to fix highway approaches near Amazon's growing world headquarters and a biotech hub constructed on land bought and sold by Microsoft's cofounder Paul Allen. It had always gone this way.

Eventually, funding did come, $34 million from a later round of stimulus that, when combined with other sources of money, was enough to replace the weary span. The old drawbridge was torn down, some of its worn gears saved so they could be incorporated, decoratively, into the new one. Coffer dams were built in the Duwamish muck so that new, firmer footings could be sunk, and atop these new footings a brand-new bridge, much like the old one but sturdier, began to take shape. Its steel girders were welded together in Montana and then trucked to the Duwamish River valley, where they were lifted into place by cranes floating on barges. Steel deck gratings came from Pittsburgh, the rail for the pedestrian walkway from Tacoma. The concrete supporting the new watchtowers—and holding up the new approaches, and creating the new footings—was sent from a factory just downstream.

To raise its run-down decks, the old bridge had relied upon two mammoth mechanisms stored inside cavernous chambers beneath its approaches. These flawed mechanisms had been held in place by gravity, gears loaded with staggering weight and grinding back, forth, open, closed, across fixed paths arranged like toothed railway tracks. Everything had to stay in alignment, or nothing worked, and over time, due to inattention and the bridge's own vulnerabilities, everything had not stayed in alignment. For the new bridge, weight was taken off the gears and instead focused on a rolling trunnion, a spinning steel core capable of rotating back, forth, open, closed, while not being ground down by its burden. This different way is not invulnerable. But it can be rattled, by earthquakes or other disturbances, and still function.

In the summer of 2014, the new South Park drawbridge opened. A deep crowd filled the west approach, people wearing Sikh turbans and Seahawks hats and bicycle helmets and saris. Near the front, a towering African American man in shades and a construction hard hat with the American flag painted on it. He was standing close to a woman who'd run the beer garden at the old bridge's funeral, which was a grand affair featuring a black casket bearing the phrase "died of neglect" and a parade of last drives across the condemned structure. Speeches marking the new bridge's arrival mixed Spanish and English and came from a U.S. senator, a congressman, the mayor, and the county executive who, years earlier, painted a pledge on the side of the old County Line Bar and Grill—now closed and demolished—promising to do everything in his power to rebuild the connection to the other bank of the Duwamish. Tribal elders offered prayers, and at the appointed moment fireworks shot from the tops of the open spans, which then descended, restoring the neighborhood's best link to the rest of the river valley and, through it, the city beyond. Within a short time, a woman with elaborate thigh tattoos was roller-skating across in a car lane as lesbian couples walked their kids along the bridge sidewalks.

In the neighborhood, better sewage and drainage pipes were scheduled to be installed, a measure intended to cut down on the basement flooding. A brand-new city dump facility kept odors more contained. From downtown, new pledges to reduce the upstream pollution that flows into the Duwamish, and from the Environmental Protection Agency, after a record number of public comments, a commitment to spend $342 million, over almost two decades, in an effort to rid the Superfund stretch of 90 percent of its pollutants. The money will come from responsible parties—Boeing, King County, the City of Seattle, the port—but it will be wasted if upstream pollution is not halted, and the EPA admits that even in the best-case scenario the river may never be safe to eat from again without caution.

Overall, though, the direction appears as it should be, or at least as promised by an imperfect system that, particularly when it is in euphoric overdrive, tends to lack insight into its destructive potentials, its predictable cycles of manic highs and desperate lows, the fact that someone is always going to lose.

Israel Rodriguez was not at the opening ceremony for the bridge. He had graduated from Chief Sealth International High School, named, at a time of less concern for correct pronunciation, after Chief Si'ahl. A $5,000 scholarship helped him attend community college until the money ran out, and then he moved to Kent, a working-class city south of Seattle, and began a job at the Oh Boy! Oberto sausage factory. "I'm trying to go back to college," he told me in the spring of 2014. "Now I got kids, though, so." No one ever told Israel about the result of the trial at which he testified, and he never asked, though he had wondered and was interested to learn. He feels good about what he did that night and remains in occasional touch with Diana Ramirez and Sara Miranda-Nino. The house they all ran toward—the house that, afterward, was found to contain the address sign Teresa stole off her childhood home in St. Louis, as well as a framed picture of the *Delta Queen* steamboat—still sits there on South Rose Street. It's now painted a new color.

Detective David Duty is retired from policing, but Detective Dana Duffy continues to work cases, continues to add to her cubicle's wall of the dead. She's out of the basement apartment now and sharing a town house with a new boyfriend, a fellow law enforcement officer whom she got to know after the South Park investigation was complete. "We met at a trooper-shot-in-the-head scene," Detective Duffy said. She won an award for her work on the South Park attacks, "this really beautiful, kind of, glass award," she said. It read, "Detective Duffy, South Park Homicide." "Or something— I don't remember, because I immediately took my award and gave it to Jen. If anybody deserves it, it's her." The two of them still see each other from time to time, though Detective Duffy lets Jennifer pick the times. "I'm still the detective who had to go through all that gory shit with her," Detective Duffy said. "So I just know that we have our special place, and I do what I do, and she's out there."

Judge Gain is still at the Regional Justice Center in Kent, still seeing a huge number of defendants each day, still of the opinion that there is "no benefit" to his commenting directly on his dealings with Isaiah. At the same time, in his last letter to me, Judge Gain wrote, "I wish you luck in your endeavor. Hopefully, it will focus attention on the prevention of tragedy in the future." In 2014, Judge O'Malley retired after twelve years on the bench, his hopes of bringing a mental health court to Tacoma unrealized, the scarce resources that frustrated him still scarce. "Unless society is willing to make the commitment to examine this and take corrective action—and that means spending some money—what's gonna change?" he asked. "What's gonna change? And that is tragic."

Judge Hayden retired in 2013, at the age of sixty-five, and counts the trial of Isaiah Kalebu among his most memorable in twenty-one years on the bench. The King County Courthouse where he worked for so long is now being restored, when possible, to its pre-"modern" grandeur, a function of its historic landmark status. But Judge Hayden lives a hundred miles away and spends his retired days thinking about other things while out in his woodworking shed, or riding his bike, or heading for ski slopes. He still hopes Jennifer finds someone to marry, especially considering that gay marriage became legal in Washington State in the fall of 2012, just over three years after Teresa and Jennifer had planned to have their illegal wedding and it instead turned into a memorial. "She, quite literally, was the best witness I've seen on the stand in my career," Judge Hayden said. Ramona Brandes, Isaiah's public defender, said exactly the same thing. After the trial, both she and Michael Schwartz, Isaiah's other public defender, continued their work representing people who can't afford attorneys (though Schwartz, in 2015, was appointed as a superior court judge in the county that holds Tacoma). In a statement Schwartz and Brandes filed with the trial court before Isaiah's sentencing, they'd warned that "systemic flaws in the state's method of dealing with the mentally ill still present a looming threat."

Theresa Griffin has also continued her public defense work. She's one of the people who heard news of what had happened in South Park that summer of 2009 and got an uneasy feeling connected to Isaiah, her former client. "I just kind of knew," she said.

Jennifer is not married, but she's had a couple of serious relationships since the attacks. One night, a woman she was dating, a volleyball coach, took her to a game north of Seattle, and the two of them ended up in a sideline conversation with a man who turned out to be Officer Ernest

DeBella, the second responder to the calls from South Park that night in 2009. When Officer DeBella realized who Jennifer was, he seemed to have difficulty talking to her, had to excuse himself. Before that, though, he told Jennifer he wished he'd been in the neighborhood earlier that night. Maybe he could have seen Isaiah running away from the scene of the crime and caught him right then.

Norbert Leo Butz is still acting and singing, sober many years now. He calls Teresa his "spiritual sponsor," drew on her courage to get himself to the point where he could admit to his family that he had a problem with alcohol and drugs, that he wanted to stop but couldn't. "Once you can say that and mean it, you're on the way to getting clean," he said. "That was the gift she gave me. Next to my wife and kids, it's the most precious thing anyone has ever given me."

In the summer of 2013, he put on a well-received cabaret show called *Girls, Girls, Girls,* a tribute to the women in his life, including Teresa. That same summer, not long before the fourth anniversary of Teresa's death, Jennifer flew from Seattle to New York to see Norbert's show and, at the end of it, got up onstage with him to sing "Proud Mary," a song set on steamboats and the Mississippi River. The two of them had performed the song before, in the spring of that year in St. Louis, at a benefit concert arranged by Teresa's lifelong friends Rachel and Jean. Money from the St. Louis show went to a nonprofit all of them have created to help survivors of sexual violence through music therapy.

The idea arose from what they all instinctively did after Teresa's death. They sang at her funeral, at her memorial in Seattle, with each other. They explained it to themselves and others with a quotation from the poet Heinrich Heine: "Where words leave off, music begins." At a friend's house, and then at a professional studio, they recorded an album over four days and sold it where they could, generating seed money for what they call the Angel Band Project. On the album they made, Norbert Leo Butz and Jennifer both cover Patty Griffin songs.

———

In April 2014, at Seattle's Neptune Theatre, just off "the Ave" where Jennifer's mom once sold beaded necklaces, the Angel Band held a second fundraising concert. Norbert, Jennifer, and Jean were all there. The singer Brandi Carlile was there, too, having launched something called the Fight the Fear Campaign after reading about the South Park attacks. Her campaign is "inspired by the life and loss of Teresa Butz," and it's meant to help young women learn how to prevent sexual assault. At the Neptune concert, Carlile performed a duet with Jennifer and, in front of the large audience, told her, "On my best day, you could sing me under the table." Susan Bardsley, Jennifer's old vocal coach from high school, later came onstage to sing in a background choir for one of the final songs. Norbert senior was there in the audience. So were Jennifer's mom and Carley Zepeda and JoAnn Wuitschick, who no longer keeps a trip wire of empty wine bottles in front of her condo door at night.

Back in St. Louis, Teresa's old boat mate John Schuler. He eventually followed her out of the closet and now lives with his longtime boyfriend. "Teresa and I always kind of had this relationship where she forged forward, and I was always kind of behind," John said. "I worked on that boat a year and a half, two years, before I acted on my—before I had my first gay affair. Which, I can tell you, the guy sitting down on that couch downstairs is the same person."

Teresa's tree, the one Norbert senior spoke of in court before Isaiah's sentencing, is a weeping cherry tree that still grows in the backyard of the Butz family home. "It's kind of like Teresa's personality," Dolly said. "Going in every direction, but looking beautiful, too." Norbert senior is no longer there to keep daily watch over the tree, however. He passed away in May 2015 at the age of eighty, surrounded by family, and was buried in a military cemetery on the banks of the Mississippi River. Dolly still keeps an eye on the tree, and on Teresa's grave. It sits on a gently sloping hill at a cemetery not far from the insurance office that Norbert senior used to go to, well into his retirement years, to make himself useful to his sons Steve and Mike, who now run the business. In the winter, Teresa's older brother Tim has seen Clydesdales run by in a field below the cemetery, part of the stable of horses Anheuser-Busch keeps nearby for commercials. In the spring and summer, he hears the crack of the bat from neighboring ball fields. Her gravestone is simple, flat against the earth, shaded by a tree. "Teresa Ann Butz, Oct. 19, 1969–July 19, 2009."

Jennifer now lives with her mother, Marcia, their cohabitation begun after Vance, the man who helped get Marcia off methadone cold turkey and who attended every day of the trial, passed away from bone cancer not long after the verdict was handed down. "We get along really well," Marcia said, "and I feel like it's an opportunity for me to give to her. To do what I didn't do back then . . . I don't think I was there enough—present—for Jen at some times." Those times seem distant and foreign to Marcia now, but still, she said, "I wish it never happened . . . I forgive myself, but I still think, 'Oh my God, you did that?'" Now their life together works. "I think I'm pretty easy to live with," Marcia said. "I try to help her and try to make her life a little bit easier, and she does the same for me. I think we have a good rhythm going, and we each have our space, and I know when to give her space, and vice versa. It's fun." In this life as roommates, Jennifer finds herself drawing inspiration from her mother, who at this point has had far more sober years than addicted years, more purposeful years than drifting years. "Put this in the book," Jennifer said to me one evening at the condo they share. "I'm tremendously proud of her. And it is entirely possible that I would not have known that something else was possible, on the other side of what happened to me, if I hadn't seen her be dark in her life."

Jennifer's grandmother passed away in March 2013 at the age of ninety-seven. A year later, on the first anniversary of her death, a ruling arrived from the Washington State Court of Appeals regarding a request Isaiah Kalebu had made for a new trial. His appeal was paid for by the state because he was indigent and facing a life sentence, and he had argued, through his publicly funded attorney, that his rights had been trampled in Judge Hayden's courtroom. Isaiah's request for a new trial was denied; he appealed to the Washington State Supreme Court, and five months later that court declined his petition for review. The high court's decision came on August 5, 2014, a few days after Isaiah's twenty-ninth birthday. Two months later, in the pill line, he passed the note that got him sent to solitary and then to Clallam Bay.

JoAnn Wuitschick, like other jurors, sometimes finds herself wondering what Isaiah's day to day is like in prison. Is he getting his medication? Has he had any more suicide attempts? "He's there for the rest of his life," she said. "And then what?" She thinks, "What a waste. What a waste."

Deborah, though she hasn't felt ready to try to visit, continues to wonder all kinds of things about her brother. She thinks of Jennifer often, too. "I can only imagine what she goes through on the daily," Deborah said. She feels certain there need to be reforms in how people like her brother are handled and, though she doesn't wish her family's pain on anyone else, finds herself wishing others could feel what she feels, believes they would agree with her then, would know, like her, that something must change. "No one's gonna feel that way until they actually feel it," Deborah said to me. "Go through it. And that's why I deal with you. No one understands."

Deborah told me she has followed, with frustration and sadness, news of violence committed by other disturbed individuals who seem to have slipped through the cracks. JoAnn Wuitschick has, too, in particular a stabbing in downtown Seattle in 2013 in which a disturbed man from California used a knife to attack a couple heading home from a Seattle Sounders game. He first cut the wife and then, when her husband moved to protect her, stabbed her husband to death. The murdered man was an English professor at the local community college Jennifer attended after she moved back to Seattle from New York. The following year, a young man with a history of serious psychological disturbance and access to a gun shot three students at a Seattle college, killing one of them. For his first court appearance, he wore a green suicide smock and had Brandes as his public defender.

Deborah also spoke about the pain Isaiah's father carried with him from the brutality he'd witnessed as a young man in Uganda. "That would affect anybody," Deborah said. "But at the same time, I believe in breaking cycles, and healing, and getting over it, and not using it as an excuse to hinder the rest of your life, where you take it out on your children and then on your children's children. I think there's a point where you say, 'Okay, I'm gonna use my situation to make me better.' Or help someone else that's been through it. I don't believe in people who use issues as an excuse. It may sound harsh to others, but to me—like, the situation with my brother. It hurts the hell out of me. I didn't just lose Isaiah. Meaning, the victims weren't the only ones killed." (This was an inexact way of stating it, because both victims were not in fact killed, only Teresa. But it echoed something Jennifer often said, without noticing, during our interviews, referring to that night as the night "when he killed us.") Deborah continued, tallying up the losses: "I lost Isaiah. Mama Rachel's gone. JJ's gone. . . . And, honestly, I don't know if I'm here half the time. But I have to keep going, because I have my children to live for, I have my mother to be strong for, I have my little brother and sister to be strong for. They're in college, and I want them to succeed and not worry about this." She told me she hadn't been sleeping well since the trial ended. At the time she said this, it had been almost two years since the trial ended.

Isaiah's mother told me she, too, couldn't sleep after Isaiah was sentenced. She stayed inside her house for three months straight, had to take all of Isaiah's pictures down. "And then I cry all the time," she said. "It still affects me to this day. If I see a young man that looks half like Isaiah, I think it's him, and I just start crying. It's just ridiculous."

Like Theresa Griffin, Deborah had a bad feeling when she heard what had happened in South Park that summer of 2009—a feeling connected to Isaiah. She wishes her brother would talk to her more about that crime. She also wishes he'd talk more about the arson that killed her aunt Rachel and J. J. Jones, which is still technically an open case in Tacoma. She told me, "I wanna know: What the fuck happened?" In her day to day, Deborah draws inspiration from what she watched Jennifer say and do in court. "I said then, 'If she can do this, and she can be strong enough to share it—and was actually in the moment, and seen all this, and seen her love die—I can do it,'" Deborah said. "'I can do this little bit, and be strong for my mom and my family and everybody else.' She is why I do what I do all day. 'Cause that was so sad. And to know that somebody that I've known since birth may have been the one—is being said to be the one who did this—I felt just as much at fault." Deborah has wondered if she played too rough with Isaiah, or teased him too much, or had any inadvertent hand in how he developed. "I want to say, 'Sorry, sorry,' over and over again, and apologize," Deborah said. "But I can't bring back nothing for her. I can't erase those memories. And that's why I can't sleep at night . . ."

She has worried that her mother might think her a traitor for sharing all of this publicly. "But maybe that's the problem," Deborah said. "If everybody's keeping it private, there's no change. It's gonna keep happening. But I want it to stop." And then, "Always know, Eli, I love my brother Isaiah Kalebu as much as the first time I ever seen him. I love him, I love him, I love him. And Mom loves him."

———

Perhaps someone inside the prison system has now developed a firm sense of what's disturbing Isaiah. It seems likely, however, that what Dr. Margaret Dean, the psychiatrist from Western State Hospital, said in the winter of 2010 remains grimly relevant. "It's really not a matter of getting the diagnosis right," she told Judge Hayden during one of Isaiah's competency hearings. "It's a matter of looking at the relevant capacities." Now that Isaiah, in part based on this outlook, has been deemed competent enough to be tried and sentenced to life without the possibility of parole, the Washington State prison system can run ahead with one of his old diagnoses, or come up with a new one, and it can try to medicate him if that's thought necessary. But like the rest of the justice system, the prison system does not have the capacity, or the mission, to do much in terms of extended therapeutic interventions. It's really not a matter of sitting and working with the man to get him into a better state of mind.

As Dr. Dean also noted on the stand, it is true that even in the most therapeutic of environments there can be challenges in getting to diagnoses that feel correct. She spoke of how she was trained by Dr. Allen Frances, who helped create the fourth edition of the *Diagnostic and Statistical Manual of Mental Disorders,* designed to be the most complete inventory possible of all recognized (and billable) mental disturbances, and she told the court this training made her "a bit of a stickler" for by-the-book diagnoses, though at the same time she acknowledged the book's shortcomings, including a certain amount of arbitrariness. Her mentor, Dr. Frances, has gone further with his own sense of the book's shortcomings, evolving over time into a loud critic of the *DSM.* A year after Dr. Dean's testimony, in a letter to the *New York Times,* he lamented a situation that had "gotten out of hand," producing a sprawling diagnostic regime corrupted by pharmaceutical companies focused on marketing to the worried well. "Meanwhile," Dr. Frances wrote, "we are neglecting the severely ill who can be accurately diagnosed and effectively treated. State budgets for mental health have been slashed, radically reducing access to care for people who most need medicine and are likely to benefit from it." This situation—an abundance of drugs and diagnoses for the worried well, a shortage for the desperate and destitute—was described by Dr. Frances as an "absurd misallocation of resources."

The Washington State Department of Corrections doesn't calculate costs per day for individual prisoners. Some prisoners are more expensive. Some prisoners are less expensive. It all depends on an individual prisoner's needs and behavior. But the department will say that the average daily cost for someone being held at the state penitentiary in Walla Walla is $114. At the newer Clallam Bay Corrections Center, where Isaiah is now, the average daily cost per prisoner is $110.

Records suggest Isaiah has been a more-expensive-than-average prisoner. But take just the average prisoner costs and multiply them by the years involved. Isaiah is serving life without the possibility of parole. He was sent to the Walla Walla state penitentiary at the age of twenty-six. He was sent on to Clallam Bay at age twenty-nine. If he remains at Clallam Bay until age seventy-three, which is his life expectancy according to Judge Hayden's calculations, then Isaiah's prison incarceration alone will cost the State of Washington more than $1,850,000. That's assuming he only costs the average amount, and that's not counting the costs already incurred by King County for keeping Isaiah in jail for nearly two years while awaiting his rape and murder trial. The county estimates those costs at $114,519. It's also not counting the costs of Isaiah's pretrial evaluations at Western State Hospital, which cannot be disclosed because of privacy laws, or the costs of his multiple trips to Harborview while in custody.

The public also paid to prosecute Isaiah (nearly $550,000), and to defend him (more than $702,000), and to allow him a lawyer to appeal his guilty verdict (more than $16,700). The true cost of Isaiah's crimes is not calculable, of course, but the grand total set to land on the public bill: well over $3 million.

————————

If Isaiah's crimes could have been prevented through early psychiatric intervention, it could well have saved the public money. This is why advocates continue to argue that it's shortsighted and self-defeating for political leaders to continually cut, and perpetually underfund, public mental health programs in this country while much more easily approving funds for things like new prisons. Simply having had a few counseling sessions during his parents' divorce proceedings, as was recommended by the Family Court social worker, might have changed the course of events for Isaiah. Those sessions would not have cost $3 million. In fact, Isaiah could have seen a counselor every day, from the first sign of concern in his childhood to the day he was sent away for life, for far less than $3 million.

Or, because we are not yet able to predict which of our children will become violent as adults, and may never be, that $3 million could have been used to provide seven struggling young people, including Isaiah, with once-a-week counseling over the same period. This is a core idea behind the so-called social safety net. Catch those in need, not knowing which of them, without help, will become much more destructive in the future and much more expensive to the rest of society.

The law can also be a catchment for those sliding toward violence, and during those chaotic summer months that left the adult Isaiah wandering homeless—"accompanied only by his dog and his delusions," as his public defenders put it, "until he encountered Teresa Butz and Jennifer Hopper"—the existence of one particular type of law might have helped. The best example of this type of law is in New York State, which in 1999 passed Kendra's Law in response to a murder committed by a disturbed man who had a long history of violence and was off his medications. It was named after the man's victim, Kendra Webdale.

This law says that if an adult has been diagnosed with a mental illness, and that adult is likely to create unsafe situations without supervision, *and* that adult has a history of noncompliance with treatment that has been connected to previous hospitalizations or violence—all descriptions that arguably applied to Isaiah in the summer of 2009—then this adult can be ordered by a court into outpatient commitment. Which, in New York, is essentially community treatment with close supervision, plus immediate consequences for treatment noncompliance (among those consequences, potentially, involuntary commitment).

Uniquely, the New York law also commits the state to funding better community treatment, so that people can be prevented from deteriorating in the first place, when possible, and then, when necessary, effectively handled through outpatient commitment. This system has been described as a sort of mutual involuntary commitment—the state committed to better mental health care, the individual committed to better mental health—and it has proven, so far, to be a money saver for New York taxpayers. Bouncing people around to various parts of the system, and then eventually incarcerating them, is, it turns out, more expensive.

Brian Stettin, policy director at the Treatment Advocacy Center, said that by the time Rachel Kalebu filed for a restraining order against her nephew in the summer of 2009, there would have been a "slam dunk" case for triggering Kendra's Law. That is, provided Washington State had such a comprehensive law on the books, which it did not. Stettin added that Isaiah's case has disturbingly familiar elements. "It's Andrew Goldstein, the guy who pushed Kendra Webdale onto the subway tracks," he said. "It's what we hear again and again. It's somebody who's a ticking time bomb."

Cracks like the ones Isaiah slipped through exist all over the United States, where the norm is underfunded mental health systems and a crazy quilt of local policies applying to people in Isaiah's situation. Measures as expansive and well supported as Kendra's Law remain a rarity, in large part because of institutional inertia and lack of resources. There also remains, among some advocates and policymakers, an understandable resistance to the government's having too much power to force psychological treatment based on predicted future behavior (rather than on obvious, in-the-present-moment behavior that creates an incontrovertible "danger to self or others"). Yet had Washington State been better able to respond to Isaiah's pressing needs—for counseling as a young man, for intervention as an adult—the cost-conscious public might have had the opportunity it regularly tells pollsters it's seeking, the opportunity for government to spend less. More important, three families, and the wide circles of humanity they intersected with, might have been spared tremendous anguish.

Instead, in Washington State money for mental health care continues to be difficult to come by and, when it is found, insufficient to the need. At the same time, legislators in the state capital of Olympia have demonstrated that large sums can be allocated, even in a shaky economy, when other things are at stake. In the winter of 2013, when the Boeing Company threatened to move production of a new airliner out of Washington State, lawmakers scrambled to call a special session and quickly offered the company $8.7 billion in tax breaks and subsidies to stay. It was the largest subsidy ever granted to a private company by any state. By the next winter, a report from Mental Health America was ranking Washington near the bottom of all states in terms of access to mental health care.

In 2015, under continued pressure from mental health care advocates, the legislature began to make some repairs. Lawmakers passed Joel's Law, named after Joel Reuter, a young, bipolar software engineer who was killed by Seattle police in 2013 after he shot at officers, thinking they were malevolent zombies. Joel's parents, who feel their son should have been detained by mental health officials before the shooting, had lobbied for the new law. It allows family members to appeal to a judge for a second opinion if a disturbed loved one has been evaluated, deemed not a threat to self or others, and released.

Had Joel's Law existed in March 2008—when Isaiah was brought to Harborview by the police at his mother's urging, evaluated, and then released because he wasn't deemed a threat—Isaiah's mother and her family could have appealed that release, provided they had the resources to do so. Similarly, had Joel's Law existed in the summer of 2009, when Isaiah's aunt, Rachel Kalebu, called mental health officials to her home but those officials declined to detain Isaiah, she could have appealed that decision.

Washington's legislature also amended its involuntary commitment law in 2015, adding some language modeled on Kendra's Law and creating new routes to outpatient commitment (or assisted outpatient treatment, as it's more politely known). This new language, had it existed in the summer of 2009, could also have been used to try to halt Isaiah's slide. Still, even the prime sponsor of this particular change to the state's law has pointed out that in order for it to be effective, significant funding for outpatient treatment and prevention services must be provided, as was done in New York. It remains unclear whether sufficient funding has, in fact, been provided; lawmakers did not fund Washington's assisted outpatient treatment program at recommended levels, and the state's wraparound care programs for people in serious psychological distress are not as robust as New York's. When Washington lawmakers passed Joel's Law, they also declined to fund it at a level certain to meet the potential need. Mental health advocates in Washington State remain concerned about its still-frayed system for dealing with people in serious psychological distress, as well as its perpetually underfunded court system.

Similar concerns can be found all over the country, often connected to crimes that echo Isaiah's. In Virginia, in the winter of 2013, an intelligent young man who had been decompensating for some time, would not take his medication, and was fascinated with knives found himself turned away from an attempt at involuntary commitment. The reason: a lack of beds at state-funded facilities. At home, he stabbed his father and killed himself. His father, the Virginia state senator Creigh Deeds, still bears scars on his face from the attack and at the National Press Club in Washington, D.C., in March 2014, spoke about the activism and regret his son's death inspired. "I was face-to-face with deficiencies of a system that I and other legislators created," he said. "I could either be lost in my grief, or I could act. I chose to act." He admits, though, that the changes he's been able to push through the Virginia legislature remain "modest."

More than a decade ago, President Bush's New Freedom Commission on Mental Health put the annual indirect cost of mental illness to the U.S. economy at $79 billion. Most of that was from lost productivity due to demands on family members, or incarceration, or early death. Since then, the costs associated with our lack of investment in mental health, both direct and indirect, have continued to mount. At the same time, cuts to the nation's mental health care programs have spiked, with $4.35 billion cut from state mental health budgets alone between 2009 and 2012. The consequences are apparent. A study released in the spring of 2014 found there are now ten times as many mentally ill inmates in this country's jails (over 350,000) as there are in state-funded psychiatric hospitals (35,000). It would be hard to argue that American taxpayers have come out ahead in this bargain.

Exactly how many lives have been saved by the New York bargain, which includes Kendra's Law and the increased spending on outpatient services that comes with it? This is the problem with motivating people to support preventive measures, at either the state or the federal level. By definition, one cannot prove what has specifically been prevented from happening, because it didn't happen. At the same time, looking backward, one can see the combined downstream effects of a lack of preventive measures and imagine a different world.

At dusk on the Duwamish, downriver from the South Park drawbridge, the lights of the city come up in the distance. They glow from a beckoning space beyond the barges, beyond the cement silos, beyond the dry docks where the ferries that cruise the San Juan Islands are built and repaired, beyond a ship holding a school bus and other material bound for Alaska, beyond a processing plant bearing the slogan "Where the fruit of the sea meets the salt of the earth." The river water is brackish, though it shouldn't be tasted to find out. In the right season, its surface breaks with the jumping of migrating salmon, and all year round harbor seals and river otters pop their heads and backs into the air, briefly, before swimming onward, propelled, too, by instinct. Ospreys land on nests set atop poles erected by conservationists to lure them back, and herons step around an area of riverbank that Boeing is proactively rehabilitating, on the long-sighted theory that significant money spent early will actually save the company money when it comes to future remediation costs. At another Boeing property, on a grimy railing above a dirty dock, a billboard from the company filled with images of lush vegetation and splashed with the promise "Future home of wildlife habitat."

A group of people who call themselves the Duwamish River Cleanup Coalition offer kayak tours along this stretch of the river in the summer, an attempt at building political awareness among those in the city who might prefer to ignore a problem that seems complex, expensive, beyond repair, too long in the making, too far from the comfort zone. Leading one recent tour, the great-great-great-great-grandson of Chief Si'ahl, Ken Workman, paddling the one oxbow bend in the river that remains untouched by the straightening. He tells of a drive to eat from the river, even though it is polluted, in order to know his ancestors. Around him, on old pilings, optimistic sorts have hung gourd-shaped nests meant to lure back purple martins that used to roost in the area, birds that were originally drawn by hollowed-out gourds discarded by the Duwamish people. The purple martins are returning to these new offerings.

In the city beyond, behind new skyscrapers and condo towers, an old, neon-lit globe that used to spin atop the offices of a newspaper called the *Seattle Post-Intelligencer*. Back in 2008, before the newspaper stopped printing a few months into the financial crisis, the *Post-Intelligencer* ran the headline "State Pays in Blood for Flawed Mental Health System." The paper's globe only occasionally spins now, and the neon lights up unevenly, if at all, a function of disrepair and lost purpose. It may be destined for the same museum that holds the rolltop desk Judge Hayden's great-grandfather-in-law saved from the Great Seattle Fire of 1889.

In this city in the distance, one of the most liberal and educated populations in the nation. In this city, as well: the homeless, the deranged, the untreated, the impoverished. The educated people of Seattle would regard it as insane to tell their polluted river to clean itself. They would not ask it to pay for the accident of its birth in a beautiful location that ended up not supporting its health. Still, in their state capital, their city's abundant tax revenues continue to be used in a manner that disproportionately hurts their city's homeless, deranged, untreated, and impoverished citizens, a shortsighted strategy that creates the certainty of more pain that seems to arrive with sudden brutality from an unknowable beyond, but does not.

Maybe someday people will be able to stick cheap probes into vulnerable rivers like the Duwamish, or even scan the river's surface from above, determine the exact chemical composition of the damage and its exact future course, then drop in some reasonably priced, specially designed additive to clean it all up, no immediate adverse consequences, no long-term side effects, nothing more than a matter of helpful chemical reactions fighting unhelpful chemical reactions. Perhaps. Yet without waiting for the fulfillment of science fiction, we know how to prevent a river as far gone and dangerous as this one. It is simple in concept, if difficult in human practice. Prevent harm, as much as possible, in the first place. When harm cannot be avoided, respond in time, and work to minimize its impact. Weathered signs at the marinas along the riverbank say it: "No Wake." An impossibility to one already in the water. Also, a necessary reminder. Without trying, we are all witnesses to a crime in progress.

AUTHOR'S NOTE

This work could not exist without the openness and generosity of the people most affected by the crimes it describes: Jennifer Hopper and her family, the family of Teresa Butz, and the family of Isaiah Kalebu.

It is a work of nonfiction, created using the tools of journalism—primarily interviews, public records, and documents provided to me by individuals hoping to shed purposeful light on this tragedy. In total, I interviewed more than fifty people with insight into the events the book recounts. Whenever possible—and in the majority of cases—those interviews were audio recorded. I also drew on home video, old news footage, letters, e-mails, and photographs. Among the public records used to build this work are audio and video recordings from court proceedings, police car video, police reports, prison records, psychiatric evaluations, and financial records pertaining to the cost of Isaiah Kalebu's trial. Obtaining some of those financial records required a court order.

In all, thousands of pages of publicly available documents were used, but some sets of documents are worth special mention. The full transcript of Isaiah Kalebu's trial, which covered everything from his first case-setting hearing in August 2009 to his sentencing in August 2011, allowed me to reconstruct those in-court moments that I missed. This was essential because, while I attended many days of his jury trial as a reporter, including the days when all key witnesses testified, I could not attend most of the pretrial hearings due to the demands of other stories.

When it comes to the psychiatric records used, it should be clear that a particular debt is owed to the report of Dr. Maria Lymberis, whose clarity and rigor in exploring Isaiah Kalebu's life stand apart from all other attempts at understanding his challenges and the possible origins of his behavior. I was also helped by phone interviews with Dr. Lymberis. In one of our conversations, she mentioned that she felt she'd worked well beyond what she was compensated for in this case but didn't mind. "I consider that my civic contribution," Dr. Lymberis said. "We have to do this. It's very important. Once I accepted the case, I could not abandon it."

In the preceding pages, when words are attributed to various individuals through the use of quotation marks, they are either what that person wrote in a document I obtained, what that person was recorded saying to me in an interview, or what that person was recorded as saying by a source I consider reliable (for example, an audio- or videotape or a trial transcript). In the relatively few cases in which I have modified a person's quotation for the sake of clarity, I have taken care to preserve its original meaning. Any errors are mine.

ACKNOWLEDGMENTS

For believing and guiding, Bill Clegg, John Siciliano, Emily Hartley, and Ben George. For essential feedback before the beginning, Dan Simon. For interview transcribing, Joseph Staten. For early and late reads and more, Angela Garbes, Brendan Patrick, Christian Patrick, David Schmader, Amnon Shoenfeld, Rebecca Brown, Judge Ronald Kessler, and Judge William Downing. For help in finding an excellent fact checker, Sydney Brownstone and Maddie Oatman. For excellent fact checking, Rebecca Cohen. For geological assistance, Professor David Montgomery. For the use of their cabin, the Otto-Stenhouse clan. For support and a powerful front porch, the Fields family in Montana. For their love and enduring encouragement, my family. For making the place where some of this work began, and for giving me room to return while finishing it, everyone at *The Stranger*, including the high command: Tim Keck, Dan Savage, Christopher Frizzelle, and Kathleen Richards. For beyond words and back, Dr. Donald Ross. And for his love, patience, and first to last readings, forever, with my deep love and gratitude, Colin Fields.